Urban Tourism in China

China has witnessed a dramatic development of tourism in urban context in the past thirty years, especially with its success in hosting the Beijing Olympic Games in 2008 and the Shanghai World Exposition in 2010. Urban areas as tourism destinations are receiving increasingly more popularity than traditional destinations such as national parks, natural reserves, and historical relics.

Deriving largely from a special issue on "Urban Tourism Development and City Destination Marketing" (*Journal of China Tourism Research*), *Urban Tourism in China* presents the readers with a collection of nine independent research reports examining issues such as consumer behaviour in urban destinations, the social impact of tourism, destination image, leisure, regional collaboration, and heritage tourism in ancient towns. The investigations covered urban areas of different scales and diversified nature from major metropolises such as Beijing and Guangzhou, to ancient towns like Lijiang and Pingyao. Readers who have interests in tourism research, business development, and in-depth understanding of urban life in China may find the book informative and interesting.

This book was published as a special issue of the *Journal of China Tourism Research*.

Mimi Li, PhD., is Assistant Professor in the School of Hotel and Tourism Management at The Hong Kong Polytechnic University. Her research interests include tourism planning, destination marketing, consumer behaviour in hospitality and tourism, and China tourism.

Bihu (Tiger) Wu, PhD., is Professor and Director of the Centre for Recreation and Tourism Research at Peking University. His research interests include tourism geography, city tourism and resort planning, destination marketing, tourism policy, and tourism education.

Urban Tourism in China

Edited by
Mimi Li and Wu Bihu

Routledge
Taylor & Francis Group

LONDON AND NEW YORK

First published 2013
by Routledge
2 Park Square, Milton Park, Abingdon, Oxon, OX14 4RN

Simultaneously published in the USA and Canada
by Routledge
711 Third Avenue, New York, NY 10017

Routledge is an imprint of the Taylor & Francis Group, an informa business

© 2013 Taylor & Francis

This book is a reproduction of the *Journal of China Tourism Research*, vol. 7, issue 2. The Publisher requests to those authors who may be citing this book to state, also, the bibliographical details of the special issue on which the book was based.

British Library Cataloguing in Publication Data
A catalogue record for this book is available from the British Library

ISBN13: 978-0-415-62382-7

Typeset in Times New Roman
by Taylor & Francis

Publisher's Note
The publisher would like to make readers aware that the chapters in this book may be referred to as articles as they are identical to the articles published in the special issue. The publisher accepts responsibility for any inconsistencies that may have arisen in the course of preparing this volume for print.

Printed and bound in Great Britain by the MPG Books Group

Contents

Introduction: Urban Tourism in China

Mimi Li and Bihu Wu

Cities have been among the most significant of all tourist destinations since urbanization began (Edwards, Griffin, & Hayllar, 2008). City areas are distinctive and complex places characterized by four commonly accepted qualities: a high density of physical structures, people, and functions; social and cultural heterogeneity; economic multifunctionalism; and a physical centrality within regional and interurban networks (Pearce, 2001). Present-day tourism occupies substantial amounts of space within urban destinations via tourist-historic urban cores, museums of all kinds, urban waterfronts, theme parks, and specialized precincts (Edwards, et al., 2008).

A city may have different roles as a gateway, a tourist source, or a destination. The appeal of cities lies in the variety of things to do and see in a reasonably compact, interesting and attractive environment (Karski, 1990). Significant numbers of tourists visit urban areas for a primary purpose other than to go on vacation: the large populations in cities naturally attract visiting friends and relatives; the easy accessibility and large stock of accommodation and other support facilities appeal to the business and meeting, incentive travel, convention, and exhibition (MICE) markets; the well-educated and senior travelers may appreciate the heritage and historical sites on offer in cities; and young people are attracted by the excitement or urban environment, along with entertainment, nightlife, and sporting events (Edwards, et al., 2008). Given that visitors are normally drawn to a city by the completeness of its urban ambience, the demand for urban tourism is multidimensional and frequently multipurpose in nature (Ehrlich & Dreier, 1999).

Until the 1980s, studies on urban tourism were fragmented and not recognized as contributions to a distinct field (Edwards, et al., 2008). An upsurge in interest in urban tourism was sparked by Ashworth's work, in which he stated that "the failure to consider tourism as a specifically urban activity imposes a serious constraint that cannot fail to impede the development of tourism as a subject of serious study" (Ashworth, 1989: 33). In his pioneer work, Ashworth (1989) outlined four extant approaches to analyzing urban tourism: 1) the facility approach, which focuses on the spatial analysis of the location of tourism attractions, facilities, infrastructure, and zones; 2) the ecological approach, which focuses on the structure and morphology of urban areas and features the identification of functional zones or districts, such as central business districts (CBDs); 3) the user approach, in which a marketing perspective is adopted to focus on tourists; and 4) the policy approach, which is concerned with a range of policy issues, including infrastructure provision and destination marketing (Ashworth, 1989).

A significant amount of research has been published since Ashworth's groundbreaking work. The literature covers topics such as heritage conservation (e.g., Chang, Milne, Fallon, & Pohlmann, 1996), urban planning and governance (e.g., Albalate & Bel, 2009), the regeneration of inner cities and waterfronts (e.g., Gospodini, 2001), the sustainability of urban tourism (e.g., Savage, Huang, & Chang, 2004), and urban tourist behavior (e.g., Suh & Gartner, 2004). Studies in these areas have largely focused on two types of cities: de-industrialized cities such as those found in many parts of the U.S. and the U.K. (e.g., Bramwell, 1997; Judd, 1995) and heritage cities, most of which are in Europe (e.g., Caffyn & Lutz, 1999; Chang, et al., 1996). Later in a study that sought to address the research gap in urban tourism, Edwards, Griffin, and Hayllar (2008) developed a research agenda for urban tourism using Delphi studies and focus groups in academia and the tourism industry. Their study identified the top issues that were most highly valued by both groups, including the tourist experience and behavioral issues, the impact of tourism on urban areas, destination development and management, and spatial relationship issues.

Despite academic efforts in this area, the complexity of urban tourism has undoubtedly delayed the research carried out, and the tourism and urban studies literatures scarcely overlap. One of the major research gaps is that, with few exceptions, the existing literature has been limited to studies on Western cities. With histories of hundreds of years, the Western cities analyzed in these studies generally have a well-established urban configuration and fabric, but have suffered at some stage from economic decline, environmental decay, community dereliction, growing unemployment, and/or a deteriorating image, especially after World War II. Many of these studies have shown that tourism serves to foster new economic opportunities that result in a restructuring of post-industrialization cities and revitalize heritage cities. However, the prior literature has ignored Asian cities, in which the booming tourism industry of recent decades has represented a developmental opportunity rather than a route to revitalization.

Urban Tourism in China

In the sightseeing era of tourism development in China over the past three decades, most tourist attractions such as national parks, natural reserves, spas and beaches, historical relics, and minority people villages have existed far from the downtown areas of cities. However, researchers and tourism operators have recently found that business tourism, such as MICE, and entertainment activities are becoming increasingly popular in urban areas, especially with the successful hosting of the Beijing Olympic Games and the Shanghai World Exposition. City or urban tourism has demonstrated its importance as a major contributor to the prosperity of local tourism. Rapid economic development brings more disposable income to urban residents as urbanization swiftly spreads throughout the country. All of these changes mean that cities become a source of both short excursion trips and long-haul travel in addition to attracting visitors from both international and domestic markets.

This trend necessitates urban tourism research in China. A brief review of the literature on China's urban tourism revealed close to 800 publications, the majority of which have been published in Chinese journals. These investigations were conducted from a wide variety of perspectives including tourism, geography, economics, environment and resources, and social science. The literature covers topics such as the spatial structure of metropolitan tourism (e.g., Bian, 2003, 2009; Wu, 2001), the image of urban tourism destinations (e.g., Gu, 2000; Xu & Gu, 2005), the competitive advantages of urban tourism destinations (e.g., Zhou & Bao, 2005), urban tourism theory (e.g., Liu & Fan, 2008), urban tourism planning and governance (e.g., Wu & Zhang, 2003; Zhu, Liu, & Bao, 2002), urban tourism resources and products (e.g., Wang, 2004), and the driving forces behind urban tourism development (e.g., Bao & Liu, 2002; Peng, 2000). While contributing enormously to the understanding of urban tourism development in China, empirical case studies are still dominant in this area of study, whereas studies grounded in solid theories are rare.

This Book

This book is largely based on *The Journal of China Tourism Research*'s special issue on "*Urban Tourism Development and City Destination Marketing*" (volume 7, number 2, 2011), for which we were guest editors. We distributed a call for papers from a very broad pool of potential submissions and encouraged contributions from different perspectives, including but not limited to the following subject areas: cities as international destinations, urban tourism policies and planning, business travel to/from cities, mega events in cities, shopping and recreational business districts, city destination marketing, the image and branding of tourist cities, heritage tourism and tourism-oriented redevelopment in cities, urban tourism interpretation, museum and arts tourism, shows and performances for tourists, theme parks, urban entertainment industries, and recreational belts around cities.

This book includes five articles from the special issue (volume 7, number 2, 2011) and four articles from previous issues of the journal. It is the editors' hope that by presenting a number of perspectives on urban tourism in China in a single volume, this special collection might help promote theoretical and methodological awareness of urban tourism research in China.

The contributions in this book address distinct issues relating to urban tourism in China. Drawing on new economic growth theory, Shan Li, Min Xiao, Kun Zhang, Jing Wu, and Zheng Wang investigated in Chapter Two the spatial interaction processes between Shanghai, southern Jiangsu province, and northern Zhejiang province with the concept of tourism spillover effect. They propose an improved measurement model capable of enhancing the understanding of regional tourism cooperation and competition.

Chapters Three and Four focus on the impact of city tourism on historical towns in Pingyao, Shanxi province and Lijiang, Yunnan province, respectively. Philip Xie and Kai Gu present a case study of spatial morphology in Pingyao, an ancient walled city. A longitudinal analysis of urban planning documents and fieldwork from 2005 to 2009 shows that the development of urban tourism played a critical role in shaping and transforming the city's morphology. The chapter concludes that in historical towns such as Pingyao, where tourism is a dominant source of economic growth, tourism should be integrated into urban planning to better balance heritage development and preservation. In Chapter Four, Xiaobo Su and Chunyuan Huang investigate the impact of tourism on public space in Lijiang. The public space in the ancient town has been commodificated and museumized as the result of rapid tourism development, which has altered the city's urban function. Possible roles that tourism could play in preserving Lijiang's urban texture and local culture are discussed.

One of the major characteristics of tourism in urban areas is that it is only one of many functions fulfilled by a city. Tourists share or compete with local residents for many spaces and services and the tourism industry competes with other industries for resources such as labor and land. This type of competition is particularly intense in Hong Kong, where land and other resources are scarce. Recognizing the importance of leisure and recreation to urban residents' wellbeing and the subsequent healthy and harmonious development of the city, in Chapter Five, Shan Yang, Honggen Xiao, and Chau Yeung Tse examine Hong Kong university students' perceptions of leisure by drawing on the results of in-depth interviews structured around open-ended questions pertinent to their participation and experiences. Four categories of activities and four types of benefits are identified, and the meaning of leisure and its association with quality of life and work are discussed in a non-Western context.

A very important yet often ignored stakeholder in urban tourism planning and policy making is the local community. Chapters Six and Seven address this issue by examining the social impact of urban tourism in two major cities in Northern China: Beijing and Harbin in Heilongjiang province. In Chapter Six, Chris Ryan and Huimin Gu analyze the results of interviews with 40 residents and over 40 business people to examine attitudes toward tourism as expressed by residents of Beijing Hutong. Four major impact groups are identified, including changes in the physical appearance of the Hutong, increased noise, increased congestion, and safety and public order issues. These impacts are attributed to an increase in the number of migrant entrepreneurs and the specific growth of the pedicab business. A Hutong destination life cycle, based on Butler's life cycle, is also proposed along the localization-globalization-glocalisation continuum through the addition of a further axis that represents the quality of life of local residents. In Chapter Seven, Yu Wang, Gang Li, and Xuemei Bai explore residents' perceptions on the impacts of tourism development in Harbin by analyzing the results of face-to-face interviews. Local residents' attitudes toward tourism development are found to be different across various interest groups.

The last three chapters address the tourists to urban destinations. In Chapter Eight, Shaojun Ji and Geoffrey Wall examine the image of Qingdao, Shandong province, as perceived by tourists and local residents through questionnaire survey. The perceptions of both groups are compared along two dimensions: cognitive and affective image. Shopping facilities are an indispensable part of urban tourism destinations and shopping is widely recognized in the extant literature as one of the major activities in which tourists frequently participate while traveling. In Chapter Nine, Qiuju Luo and Xiangyu Lu examine inbound business tourists' shopping behavior and the influencing factors in Guangzhou through analyzing the results of a survey and in-depth interviews. It is found that inbound business travelers' shopping behavior can be influenced by the overall image and retail environment of the destination, the tourists' association with and experience of the destination, and their personal tastes.

In Chapter Ten, Philip Pearce, Yongzhi Wu, and Aram Son develop a framework to assess and present visitors' responses to Chinese cities using five dominant themes from the literature on place evaluation. This framework provides a comprehensive view of cities using method-based triangulation that is further illustrated through the city of Xi'an, one of the oldest cities in China.

By sharing urban tourism studies we have actually brought forth very limited research activities and academic findings in the field of urban tourism development and city destination marketing. In April 2011, PATA, the largest tourism NGO in the world, celebrated its 60th anniversary in Beijing though it was established in the U.S. and being headquartered in Thailand. A special workshop was prepared for the celebration, with "China, the World's Opportunity" as the theme. We believe that China could be the next big tourism research opportunity. However, as we witnessed in editing the special issue and this book, there are still many obstacles to overcome, particularly in relation to the language barrier. The cross-cultural communication and comprehension challenges that exist between the English-speaking and Chinese-speaking worlds must be addressed.

Finally, we wish to acknowledge the diligent work and kind support of the referees who participated in the double-blind review process for these manuscripts. Without their commitment and expertise, this special collection would not have been possible.

References

Albalate, D., & Bel, G. (2009). Tourism and urban public transport: Holding demand pressure under supply constraints. *Tourism Management, in press.*

Ashworth, G. (1989). Urban tourism: An imbalance in attention. In C. C. (Ed.), *Progress in Tourism Recreation and Hospitality Management* (Vol. 1, pp. 33-54). London: Belhaven.

Bao, J., & Liu, X. (2002). An analys of the driving factors of urban inbound tourism in Guang-dong. *Tourism Tribune, 17*, 44-48.

Bian, X. (2003). Research on urban tourism spatial structure *Geography and Geo - Information Science, 19*(1), 106-108.

Bian, X. (2009). Analysis on the forming mechanism of metropolitan tourism core-periphery spatial structure: In view of coordinated development between urban tourism central and peripheral districts. *Areal Research and Development, 28*(4), 67-71.

Bramwell, B. (1997). Strategic planning before and after a mega-event. *Tourism Management, 18* (3), 167-176.

Caffyn, A., & Lutz, J. (1999). Developing the heritage tourism product in multi-ethnic cities. *Tourism Management, 20*, 213-221.

Chang, T., Milne, S., Fallon, D., & Pohlmann, C. (1996). Urban heritage tourism: The global-local nexus. *Annals of Tourism Research, 23*(2), 284-305.

Edwards, D., Griffin, T., & Hayllar, B. (2008). Urban tourism research: Developing an agenda. *Annals of Tourism Research, 35*(4), 1031-1052.

Ehrlich, B., & Dreier, P. (1999). The new boston discovers the old: Tourism and the struggle for a livable city. In D. Judd & S. Fainstein (Eds.), *The tourist City* (pp. 155-178). New Haven CT: Yale University Press.

Gospodini, A. (2001). Urban waterfront redevelopment in Greek cities: A framework for redesigning space. *Cities, 18*(5), 285-295.

Gu, M. (2000). On the positioning of Dalian's urban tourism image and overall planning. *Tourism Tribune, 5*, 63-67.

Judd, D. (1995). Promoting tourism in US cities. *Tourism Management, 16*(3), 175-187.

Karski, A. (1990). Urban tourism: A key to urban regeneration. *The Planner, 6*, 15-17.

Liu, Z., & Fan, X. (2008). Study on urban tourism: Multidimensional perspective and developing model. *Tourism Tribune, 6*, 33-36.

Pearce, D. (2001). An integrative framework for urban tourism research. *Annals of Tourism Research, 28*(4), 926-946.

Peng, H. (2000). Preliminary research on driving mechanism of urban tourism development. *Human Geography, 15*(1), 1-5.

Savage, V., Huang, S., & Chang, T. (2004). The Singapore river thematic zone: Sustainable tourism in an urban context. *The Geographical Journal, 170*(3), 212-225.

Suh, Y., & Gartner, W. (2004). Perceptions in international urban tourism: An analysis of travelers to Seoul, Korea. *Journal of Travel Research, 43*, 39-45.

Wang, X. (2004). World Expo and urban tourism: Creating mutual brilliance in the midst of mutual-action. *Tourism Tribune, 19*, 70-75.

Wu, B. (2001). A study on recreational belt around metropolis (ReBAM): Shanghai case. *Scientia Geographica Sinica, 21*(4), 354-359.

Wu, B., & Zhang, W. (2003). Review on the master plan of tourism development for Shandong Province, China. *Human Geography, 18*(4), 26-31.

Xu, F., & Gu, K. (2005). Study on Nanjing urban tourism image. *Geogra phy and Geo-Information Science, 21*(3), 93-96.

Zhou, C., & Bao, J. (2005). Urban tourism competitiveness analysis of Zhaoqing—Discussion of an analytical framework of urban tourism competitiveness. *Areal Research and Development, 24*(2), 78-83.

Zhu, H., Liu, Y., & Bao, J. (2002). The exploration of the old industrial cities' tourism planning: A case study of Huangshi city Hubei Province. *Economic Geography, 22*, 252-257.

Measuring Tourism Spillover Effects Among Cities: Improvement of the Gap Model and a Case Study of the Yangtze River Delta

城市间旅游溢出效应的测度：缺口模型改进及长江三角洲案例

SHAN LI

MIN XIAO

KUN ZHANG

JING WU

ZHENG WANG

In an open economic system, tourism spillover occurs widely between cities, making it a useful index for regional tourism cooperation or competition. This article improves the gap model on tourism spillover between two cities, suggested by S. Li and Wang (2009a), in three aspects: (a) an impact factor is added to the model; (b) more objective indicators are applied to the definitions of variables; and (c) more rational methods are used to estimate parameters. The case of the Yangtze River Delta is reexamined based on the improved model. The results show that the new gap model explains tourism spillover more effectively than the original one; it could also provide more help and advisement in developing regional tourism cooperation.

在一个开放的区域经济系统中，城市之间的旅游溢出效应广泛存在，并成为区域旅游合作与竞争的内在动力。本文对李山及王铮（*2009a*）提出的测度旅游溢出的缺口模型进行三方面改进：*1*）在模型结构上增加一个影响因子；*2*）在变量定义上使用更客观的指标；*3*）在参数估计上采用更合理的方法。运用改进后的新模型对长江三角洲城市群之间的旅游溢出进行计算，结果发现新模型具有更强的现象解释能力，能更合理地测度城市间的旅游溢出效应，从而更有效地指导区域旅游合作与旅游圈建设。

Shan Li is Associate Professor of the Key Lab of GIScience at East China Normal University, Shanghai, China (E-mail: sli@geo.ecnu.edu.cn).

Min Xiao is a graduate student of the Key Lab of GIScience at East China Normal University, Shanghai, China (E-mail: xiaomin_0619@hotmail.com).

Kun Zhang is Associate Professor of the Key Lab of GIScience at East China Normal University, Shanghai, China (E-mail: kzhang@geo.ecnu.edu.cn).

Jing Wu is Associate Professor of the Institute of Policy and Management at the Chinese Academy of Sciences, Beijing, China (E-mail: wujing666@hotmail.com).

Zheng Wang is Professor of Institute of Policy and Management at the Chinese Academy of Sciences, Beijing, China (E-mail: wangzheng@casipm.ac.cn).

Introduction

The new economic growth theory (Lucas, 1988; Romer, 1986) points out that spillover effects are indispensable for sustainable economic growth and significant for the common growth of a multiregional economy (Caniëls & Verspagen, 2001; Grossman & Helpman, 1991). Employing the "learn by doing" model, Arrow (1962) first used spillover effects as an externality, which arises when a person engages in an activity that influences the well-being of a bystander and yet neither pays nor receives any compensation for that effect (Mankiw, 2009), to explain the spillover effects on economic growth. Grossman and Helpman (1993) primarily pointed out that knowledge spillovers of one country or region bring economic development to nearby countries or regions in which a systematic concept of spillovers emerged as a positive content. Spillover effects, the same as externality, have both positive and negative aspects (Bretschger, 1999; Z. Wang, Gong, & Liu, 2003). Previous studies have shown that such effects also exist widely in the tourism industry (Lazzeretti & Capone, 2009; S. Li & Wang, 2009a), meaning that tourism resources and capital may not only benefit their owners but also bring advantages (positive spillovers) and disadvantages (negative spillovers) to their neighbors. The spillover effects of tourism are usually presented in terms of how the variation in one region's tourist numbers or income influences the variation of its neighbors (Gooroochurn & Hanley, 2005). Two cities within the same region are probably motivated to cooperate if a positive spillover effect exists between them; for a negative spillover, these two cities will tend to compete. Therefore, to understand the competition and cooperation trends of regional tourism, as well as to develop rationally a regional tourism destination circle, it is necessary to identify those factors affecting tourism spillover and to measure the spillover effects quantitatively.

In recent years, the spillover effects on the tourism industry have drawn more notice from academia, and two measuring methods have emerged. These are the simultaneous equations method (Gooroochurn & Hanley, 2005) and the gap method (S. Li & Wang, 2009a). By establishing two multivariate regression equations on tourism income for two tourism regions, the simultaneous equations method considers the expenditure of long-haul visitors as an explanatory variable of spillovers (because long-haul visitors normally visit more than one region in a single trip), and parameters are estimated using long-term tourism data (Gooroochurn & Hanley, 2005). In China, based on the improved Mundell-Fleming (MF) model (Z. Wang, Liu, & Liu, 2003), F. Li and Huang (2008) introduced this method to analyze GDP (Gross Domestic Product) spillovers to measure the intercity tourism spillovers in two tourism regions in China. The study, building multiple regression equations using tourism GDP of one city as an explanatory variable of spillovers to the other, can be recognized as the simultaneous equations in essence. Explaining the relative intensity of tourism spillovers between cities, the simultaneous equations, however, failed to take the potential influence from geographical distance, tourism products type, and tourism products quality, even though it has been suggested that those factors are related to the spillover effects. For instance, Chen and Bao's (1988) study on the spatial behavior of long-haul visitors revealed that positive spillover is more easily generated between regions with tourism products of similar quality. Bao (1994), Bao and Liang (1991), and Y. Wang (1993) suggested the existence of competition among homogeneous tourism products in adjacent areas, demonstrating that in fact similar tourism products generate a negative spillover effect more easily than do diversified products.

In 2004, Deng, Wang, and Li proposed the gap model, which is derived from the knowledge-spillover model proposed by Caniëls and Verspagen (2001) and which references the definition of the knowledge gap. The model's rationale is grounded in certain similarities between tourism products and knowledge products in both diversity and publicity. In the gap model, the impact factors of tourism spillover are summarized as four explanatory variables, namely, the tourism grade scale gap, the tourism type difference gap, the geographical distance gap, and the learning ability gap, among tourism cities. Using the gap model, S. Li and Wang (2009a) analyzed tourism spillover in the Yangtze River Delta. Although the results illustrated the general trend of regional tourism cooperation, there remained some deficiencies. For example, the results showed that the spillover generated by Shanghai city was lower than the regional average value, making it difficult to explain the regional consensus that Shanghai is the center of the Yangtze River Delta. In addition, the results indicated a negative spillover between Shanghai and Huangshan, making it hard to explain the ongoing tourism cooperation among Shanghai, Hangzhou, and Huangshan.

In this article, we aim to improve the gap model. The article is divided into three parts. First, we provide an improved model, including the definition of each parameter; second, we present a case study of the Yangtze River Delta and compare the calculation results with the original model; and finally, we discuss our conclusions.

Model Improvements

We improved the gap model proposed by S. Li and Wang (2009a) by making three changes. To the model structure, we added a new impact factor and adjusted the meaning of one parameter. We also used more objective data with respect to the data source. Finally, we adopted a new way to estimate parameters.

Model Structure

The gap model proposed by S. Li and Wang (2009a) is as follows:

$$S_j^{(i)} = \delta_j e^{-(\frac{1}{\delta_j^{(l)}}G_{ij}^{(l)})^2 + \delta_j^{(k)}G_{ij}^{(k)} - \beta r_{ij}} \qquad i \neq j \tag{1}$$

Our improved model is the following:

$$S_j^{(i)} = q_i \delta_j e^{-(\frac{1}{\delta_j^{(l)}}G_{ij}^{(l)})^2 + \delta_j^{(k)}G_{ij}^{(k)} - \beta r_{ij}} \qquad i \neq j \tag{2}$$

Table 1 lists the meanings of each variable and parameter.

As Table 1 shows, two improvements were made. First, we added a tourism scale q_i, because it is believed that a tourism destination of a larger scale (tourism revenue or visitors) may have a greater potential impact on its surrounding areas; it is also supposed that the spillover would be proportional to the tourism scale. Second, we simplified the meaning of $G_{ij}^{(l)}$ from "scale grade gap" to "grade gap." Because two regions with a similar tourism grade may have large differences in tourism scales, it is suitable to measure scale and grade separately.

Table 1. Description of Variables and/or Parameters in Equations (1) and (2).

Parameters	Meaning in Equation (1)	Meaning in Equation (2)
i, j	i denotes the region generating the spillover, and j is the region receiving the spillover	The same
$S_j^{(i)}$	Spillover generated by region i and received by region j	The same
q_i	—	Tourism scale of region i
$G_{ij}^{(l)}$	Tourism grade scale gap between regions i and j	Grade gap between regions i and j
$G_{ij}^{(k)}$	Tourism-type difference between regions i and j	The same
r_{ij}	Geographical distance between regions i and j	The same
$\delta_j, \delta_j^{(l)}, \delta_j^{(k)}$	Learning capabilities of region j	The same
β	Spatial interaction parameter	The same

For the exponential part, we set the first sign to negative, implying that the larger the difference in grade between two regions, the less likely they would share the same market; this would hinder the model in generating positive spillovers. We then set the second sign to positive, implying that the larger the tourism-type difference between two regions, the more likely they would benefit each other, thus encouraging the model to generate positive spillovers. The sign before r_{ij} was negative, demonstrating that as geographical distance increases, the positive spillover effects would decline.

The learning capacity variables $\delta_j^{(l)}, \delta_j^{(k)}, \delta_j$ have the following influences on the model. First, tourism regions with a better learning capacity would be likely to alleviate the dampening effect of the scale gap, as implemented by $\delta_j^{(l)}$ in Equation (2). Second, tourism regions with a better learning capacity would magnify the enhancement effect of the tourism type difference gap, as implemented by $\delta_j^{(k)}$. And third, the greater the learning capacity of tourism region j, the more spillover it would receive, as implemented by δ_j.

The improved model showed that the level of tourism spillover was negatively correlated with both the grade difference and the geographical distance among tourism cities. Moreover, the spillover was positively correlated with the tourism-type difference among tourism cities, the learning ability of the spillover-receiving city, and the tourism scale of the spillover-generating city.

Following the definition of S. Li and Wang (2009a), we defined the exponential part of Equation (2) as spillover index I_{ij}, namely:

$$I_{ij} = - (\frac{1}{\delta_j^{(l)}} G_{ij}^{(l)})^2 + \delta_j^{(k)} G_{ij}^{(k)} - \beta r_{ij} \tag{3}$$

We used the spillover index to judge the spillover effects of region i toward j, which could be positive or negative. If $I_{ij} > 0$, spillover effects would be regarded as positive; if $I_{ij} < 0$, they would be taken for negative. In particular, if $I_{ij} = 0$, the spillover that region j received from i would be considered as "background" spillover; at this point, $S_j^{(i)} = q_i \delta_j$ could be regarded as the "background" value of tourism spillover. Thus, the result of tourism spillover showed that region i had a multiplier effect on the background spillovers (δ_j) of region j. When the spillover index $I_{ij} > 0$, $S_j^{(i)} > q_i\delta_j$; this was a multiplication effect in which j received a positive spillover from i. When $I_{ij} < 0$, $S_j^{(i)} < q_i\delta_j$; this was a demultiplication effect in which j received a negative spillover from i. When $I_{ij} = 0$, $S_j^{(i)} = q_i\delta_j$; the multiplier coefficient was 1, and only a background spillover existed that j received from i.

It is worth noting that tourism spillovers are bidirectional processes from i to j or from j to i; the values of the two spillovers could even be unequal. In this article, we regarded the level of tourism spillover $S_j^{(i)} + S_i^{(j)}$ generated and received by the two cities as a conjugate value of the two regions, which we used to measure mutual benefit or mutual loss.

Defining Variables

In Equation (2), q_i denotes the tourism scale of region i, which we measured using the total number of domestic tourists. Inbound tourists were ignored for two reasons: First, the proportion of inbound tourists in China is comparatively small (about 7.1% in 2008); and second, the cities of Beijing, Xi'an, Shanghai, Guangzhou, and Shenzhen are best loved for inbound tourists (Ma & Li, 1999); thus, the spillover effects would be much weaker for longer distance among these cities.

$G_{ij}^{(l)}$ in Equation (2) denotes the tourism grade gap between regions i and j, which we calculated as follows:

$$G_{ij}^{(l)} = \left| \ln \frac{l_i}{l_j} \right| \tag{4}$$

where l_i, l_j denote the tourism attraction level in regions i and j, respectively. Here we used the Baidu index to evaluate l_i and l_j. Baidu is a Chinese-language Internet search engine. According to the China Search Engine User Behavior Study in the Year 2009 (China Internet Network Information Center [CNNIC], 2009), by the end of June 2009, the number of search engine users in China had reached 235 million, and Baidu occupied a share of 77.2%. Baidu provides a "user attention" index, which is calculated from a weighted sum of frequency of various keywords in the Baidu search engine. By entering the name of one city following the word *tourism*, we could obtain the user attention index, representing the tourism attraction level of this city.

$G_{ij}^{(k)}$ denotes the type difference between regions i and j, which we calculated as follows:

$$G_{ij}^{(k)} = \ln \frac{k_i + k_j}{2} \tag{5}$$

where k_i and k_j represent the intensity of destination heterogeneity of regions i and j, respectively. The intensity of destination heterogeneity represents the identifiability of the tourism destination, the value of which we derived from the Baidu index according to the daily average value of user attention from November 2, 2008, to November 2, 2009. Here we proposed an empirical rule: The value was set to 1 when the Baidu index of one region was under 100, 1.5 when the index ranged from 100 to 200, 2 corresponding to 200–300, 2.5 corresponding to 300–400, 3 corresponding to 400–500, 3.5 corresponding to 500–600, and 4 when the index was larger than 600.

The geographical distance between two tourism regions is r_{ij}, expressed here by transportation distance, which we obtained from Google Maps (http://ditu.google.cn/).
$\delta_j, \delta_j^{(l)}, \delta_j^{(k)}$ are parameters that are related to the intrinsic learning capability of region j (in which δ_j is a normalization parameter and its value can be either $\delta_j^{(l)}$ or $\delta_j^{(k)}$), in terms of S. Li and Wang's (2009a) definition:

$$\delta_j = C_j^{\alpha} \tag{6}$$

$$\delta_j^{(l)} = C_j^{\alpha_l} \tag{7}$$

$$\delta_j^{(k)} = C_j^{\alpha_k} \tag{8}$$

where C_j represents the economic development level of tourism region j, which we measured by per capita GDP (generally speaking, the higher the level of economic development, the greater the ability to learn); we called $\alpha, \alpha_l, \alpha_k$ the exponents of learning capacity, which had to be quantified.

Parameter Estimation

Equation (2) includes two kinds of parameters, in which $\alpha, \alpha_l, \alpha_k$ are related to the parameters of learning capacities $\delta_j, \delta_j^{(l)}, \delta_j^k$, and β is a spatial damping parameter. Tourism spillovers among cities usually come up within a certain range of territorial scope; the value of β could be set as 0.00446 according to the study done by Z. Wang et al. (2002). Therefore, we had to estimate the power exponent of learning capacities $\alpha, \alpha_l, \alpha_k$.

Estimation of α_k

We used extreme assumptions to estimate α_k. Referring to the definition of the spillover index and learning capacity in Equations (3) and (8), we could describe $\delta_j^{(k)}$ and α_k as follows:

$$\delta_j^{(k)} = \frac{I_{ij} + (\frac{1}{\delta_j^{(l)}} G_{ij}^{(l)})^2 + \beta r_{ij}}{G_{ij}^{(k)}} \tag{9}$$

$$\alpha_k = \frac{\ln \delta_j^{(k)}}{\ln C_j} \tag{10}$$

Bottazzi and Peri (2003) found that knowledge spillover generated by research and development activities has remarkable localization features that do not spread beyond 300 km. With respect to tourism, Wu et al. (1997) found that the radius of "change travel" is usually no more than 250 km, meaning that the distance between two tourism regions that combined to share the same market would not exceed 500 km. But with the development of tourism economics in China, S. Li and Wang (2009b) suggested that the distance is usually less than 600 km (measured in spherical distance). According to S. Li, Wang, and Wang's (2005) statistical study, the average ratio of intercity transportation distance and spherical distance was about 1.31 in China in the early 2000s; consequently, the 600-km spherical distance is equivalent to 786 km of transport distance. Therefore, the transportation distance between two cities falling into the interval of [600, 786] km becomes a limit value for generating tourism spillover. That is, when $r_{ij} \in [600, 786]$ km, $(\beta = 0.00446)$, even with the same scale $(l_i = l_j, G_{ij}^{(l)} = \ln 1 = 0)$, the maximal type difference $(k_{xy} = 4, G_{ij}^{(k)} = \ln 4 \approx 1.3863)$, and the highest learning capacity $(C_j$ with the highest value), the spillover effects between two regions would be negligible, and in this case the spillover index $I_{ij} = 0$. On the basis of the above values and Equation (9), we determined that $\delta_j^{(k)} \in [1.930, 2.529]$. Furthermore, we obtained the value of the power exponent of tourism-type difference $(\alpha_k \in [0.0583, 0.0822])$ based on the data of Shenzhen city, which in 2007 had the highest per capita GDP of 79,645 yuan (Shenzhen Statistics, 2008). Finally, we set the α_k value by mean as $\alpha_k = (0.0583 + 0.0822)/2 \approx 0.070$.

Estimation of α_l

The case study of Shandong Province (S. Li & Wang, 2009a) already estimated the parameter α_l. We improved the estimation from a single value estimation to an interval estimation. The estimation was based on four tourism cities in Shandong Province, namely, Jinan, Zibo, Weifang, and Qingdao cities. The facts show close cooperation among these four cities. It is believed that such cooperation would give rise to both tourism spillover and economic spillover among these cities. Jinan and Qingdao cities are located along the most famous tourist routes, such as the Confucian Landscape and the Golden Coast. Zibo and Weifang cities are located between Jinan and Qingdao; Zibo is famous as the hometown of Liaozhai and Weifang as the Kite City. Zibo and Weifang are connected with Jinan and Qingdao by the Jinan-Qingdao expressway. In late 2007, the Construction Department of Shandong Province released the *Jinan Metropolitan Area Plan*, which put forth that Jinan and its bordering six cities (including Zibo) would jointly form a "1 + 6" integrated urban development area (Liu, 2008), in which the conception of "Metropolitan Area Plan" is included. Since 2007, Weifang has proposed an "integration with Qingdao" strategy, and the Qingdao-Weifang Week has been held annually since then. These two cities also cosigned the *Promote Action Plan of the Integrated Development of Qingdao and Weifang*, as well as a series of other documents that would obviously promote the integrated development of the two cities (Cong, Meng, & Fu, 2009), in which the plan of "Promote Action Plan of the Integrated Development of Qingdao and Weifang" is proposed.

It is worth pointing out that Zibo city prefers developing regional economic cooperation with Jinan city, whereas Weifang city tends to carry out cooperation with Qingdao city. Thus, we assumed that the tourism spillover from Jinan to Zibo city would be greater than that from Qingdao to Zibo, whereas for Weifang city, the tourism spillover from Jinan would be less than that from Qingdao. We then obtained two inequalities as $S_{Zibo}^{(Jinan)} > S_{Zibo}^{(Qingdao)}$ and $S_{Weifang}^{(Jinan)} < S_{Weifang}^{(Qingdao)}$.

Numbering Jinan, Zibo, Weifang, and Qingdao from 1 to 4 according to their relationship to tourism spillover, we substituted Equation (7) into Equation (2), and after further transformation, we obtained

$$\alpha_l < \frac{1}{2 \ln C_2} \ln \left(\frac{\ln (q_4/q_1) + \delta_2^{(k)}(G_{42}^{(k)} - G_{12}^{(k)}) + \beta(r_{12} - r_{42})}{(G_{42}^{(l)})^2 - (G_{12}^{(l)})^2} \right) \tag{11}$$

Table 2. Data for Weifang, Zibo, Jinan, and Qingdao Cities.

| City (No.) | Learning Capacity | Tourism Scale | Grade Gap | Type Gap | Distance Gap | |
	Per Capita GDP in 2007 (C, yuan)	Total Number of Domestic Tourists in 2007 (q, 10,000)	Baidu Index (l)	Intensity of Destination Heterogeneity (k)	Distance From Zibo (r, km)	Distance From Weifang (r, km)
Jinan (1)	39,261	1,990	260	2	117	215
Zibo (2)	43,499	1,325	110	1.5	—	—
Weifang (3)	23,349	1,414	101	1.5	—	—
Qingdao (4)	45,399	3,259	1,100	4	263	160

Note. The data of per capita GDP and the total number of domestic tourists are from the China regional economy statistical yearbook 2008 (National Bureau of Statistics, 2009). The Baidu index is adopted from the daily average value from November 2, 2008, to November 2, 2009 (in which we replaced the term *Weifang tourism* with *Weifang Kite Festival* in the search). Distance data come from driving distances on the Jinan-Qingdao Expressway provided by Google Maps.

$$\alpha_l > \frac{1}{2\ln C_3}\ln\left(\frac{\ln(q_4/q_1) + \delta_3^{(k)}(G_{43}^{(k)} - G_{13}^{(k)}) + \beta(r_{13} - r_{43})}{(G_{43}^{(l)})^2 - (G_{13}^{(l)})^2}\right) \tag{12}$$

We then obtained $0.0531 < \alpha_l < 0.0817$ and took the mean value as $\alpha_l = (0.0531 + 0.0817)/2 \approx 0.067$. Table 2 lists the relevant variable values in Equations (11) and (12).

Parameter α

As to the spillover $S_j^{(i)}$ generated by i toward j in Equation (2), the learning capacity δ_j of tourism j, which could be regarded as a sort of normalization parameter, acted as a regulator on the result of the spillover. Its value could be either $\delta_j^{(l)}$ or $\delta_j^{(k)}$. This means that the power exponent of learning capacity could be either $\alpha = \alpha_l$ or $\alpha = \alpha_k$. The above estimation shows that the intervals of α_l and α_k were of the same order of magnitude and fairly approximate, so with the assumption of $\alpha_l = \alpha_k$, we obtained $\alpha = (\alpha_l + \alpha_k)/2 \approx 0.069$. Compared with the estimated value (0.060) of the power exponent of learning ability from S. Li and Wang (2009a), our parameter value estimation showed a slight difference, but the conclusion $\alpha \approx \alpha_l \approx \alpha_k$ was consistent. The value of the power exponent of learning capacity was much less than 1, showing that learning capacity as indicated by per capita GDP and its impact on tourism spillovers lacked flexibility and would change only through a long and slow accumulating process.

Finally, following the definition of learning capacity and the parameters estimation, we were able to simplify the tourism spillovers model as follows:

$$S_j^{(i)} = q_i C_j^{0.069} e^{-\left(\frac{1}{C_j^{0.069}}G_{ij}^{(l)}\right)^2 + C_j^{0.069}G_{ij}^{(k)} - 0.00446\,r_{ij}} \tag{13}$$

Case Study of the Yangtze River Delta Area

The Yangtze River Delta area comprises a triangular-shaped territory of Shanghai, southern Jiangsu province, and northern Zhejiang province in China. The area is not only booming economically but has also become a tourist hotspot. Declarations on regional tourism cooperation in this region, such as the Hangzhou Declaration, the Huangshan Consensus, the Nanjing Declaration, and so forth, were signed at the Tourism City Summit Forum of the Yangtze River Delta from 2003 to 2009.

The number of participating cities in regional tourism cooperation in the Yangtze River Delta has increased constantly during the past several years, starting with 15 + 1 in 2003, growing to 15 + 5 in 2004 and 15 + 10 since 2006, thus acting as an outstanding example of regional tourism cooperation. Two driving forces lie behind such cooperation, including the requirement that regional tourists be able to flow freely and the hope of forming reciprocal tourism destination circles (and tourist routes) to share the positive tourism spillover effects between cities, thereby attracting more tourists from the external market (S. Li & Wang, 2009a) and enjoying the benefits of economies of scale and of scope. Tourism spillover has thus become an important criterion for measuring the effectiveness of cooperation between cities (Gooroochurn & Hanley, 2005).

Obviously, cooperation is effective if the spillover received by a tourism city is positive; otherwise, it is useless for the participating cities. At the same time, the appearance of tourism cooperation among cities has become an important standard for testing whether a measurement model on tourism spillover is reasonable and effective; that is, a classic cooperation should have higher positive spillover effects. For the cities of the Yangtze River Delta, three typical types of regional tourism cooperation have emerged:

1. Shanghai is the central city of Yangtze River Delta on regional tourism, and integration with Shanghai has become an important regional consensus.
2. The two most classic tourist routes are the three-city tour in East China consisted of Shanghai, Suzhou, and Hangzhou, and the five-city tour in East China consisted of Shanghai, Suzhou, Hangzhou, Nanjing, and Wuxi in the Yangtze River Delta.
3. A tourism route titled Famous City, Famous Lake, Famous Mountain, which comprises Shanghai, Hangzhou, and Huangshan cities.

In this section, we calculate the tourism spillover level in the Yangtze River Delta using the improved model (Equation 13) and discuss the results.

Data Sources and Processing

We collected data from 23 tourism cities (Xuancheng city and Chuzhou city in Anhui Province were not listed due to a lack of data on Baidu index) in the Yangtze River Delta consisting of the per capita GDP in 2007, the number of domestic tourists in 2007, the Baidu index using *XX tourism* (*XX* represents the name of city) as a search item, the intensity of destination heterogeneity for each city, and the geographical distance between every two cities (the values are not listed).

Average Level of Tourism Spillover

Table 3 lists the average tourism spillover and background spillover levels both received and generated. We normalized the values using the maximum value method. We also

Table 3. Average Tourism Spillover Levels Among Cities in the Yangtze River Delta.

No.	City	Received		Generated	
		$S_j^{(i)}$	$q_i \delta_j$	$S_j^{(i)}$	$q_i \delta_j$
1	Shanghai	0.717	0.171	1	0.369
2	Nanjing	0.543	0.188	0.359	0.162
3	Wuxi	0.719	0.198	0.271	0.121
4	Changzhou	0.316	0.199	0.077	0.063
5	Suzhou	1	0.192	0.532	0.173
6	Nantong	0.197	0.196	0.032	0.039
7	Yangzhou	0.425	0.194	0.096	0.055
8	Zhenjiang	0.26	0.198	0.062	0.058
9	Hangzhou	0.883	0.194	0.41	0.149
10	Ningbo	0.508	0.198	0.2	0.111
11	Wenzhou	0.133	0.191	0.052	0.079
12	Shaoxing	0.553	0.197	0.161	0.079
13	Jiaxing	0.33	0.199	0.081	0.067
14	Huzhou	0.237	0.196	0.063	0.06
15	Zhoushan	0.455	0.2	0.076	0.046
16	Huangshan	0.51	0.189	0.083	0.034
17	Chizhou	0.134	0.183	0.019	0.023
18	Jingdezhen	0.036	0.19	0.006	0.024
19	Shangrao	0.12	0.181	0.02	0.025
20	Jinhua	0.142	0.194	0.047	0.067
21	Taizhou (in Jiangsu)	0.109	0.196	0.013	0.024
22	Taizhou (in Zhejiang)	0.137	0.192	0.052	0.079
23	Wuhu	0.088	0.196	0.007	0.016

grouped the tourism spillover levels into five classes and compared these with the results of the original model in Figure 1.

As Table 3 and Figure 1 show, we can observe some obvious facts. First, Suzhou and Hangzhou received the highest spillovers (Figure 1a), 1.0 and 0.883, respectively, meaning that these two cities have benefited the most from regional tourism cooperation; as the saying goes, "Paradise in Heaven, Suzhou and Hangzhou on Earth." In the original model, Changzhou, Wuxi, Jiaxing, and Shaoxing were the group of cities receiving the highest tourism spillover (Figure 1b), which deviated from reality. Second, spillover generated by Shanghai was the highest at 1.0 (Figure 1c), which could be recognized as a footnote explaining why other cities in the Yangtze River Delta are eager to cooperate with Shanghai. It also revealed the unshakable status of Shanghai as the regional tourism center. The results of the original model, on the other hand, revealed Yangzhou, Changzhou, Jiaxing, and Shaoxing to be the group of cities generating the highest tourism spillover (Figure 1d). Finally, in the first participating cities (the first 16 cities) in 2003, except for Wenzhou and Nantong, the tourism spillover received and generated was all greater than their corresponding background spillover, and the reciprocal effects among cities were remarkable. For the subsequent participating cities (the next 7 cities), the spillover received and generated was all less than their corresponding background spillover, meaning that those cities' cooperation

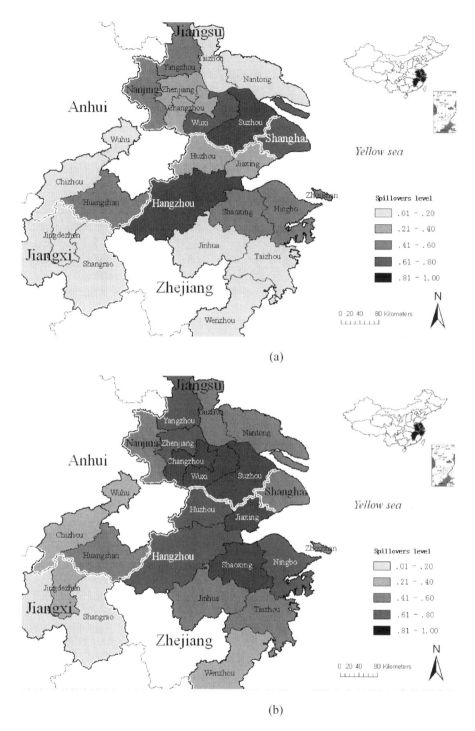

Figure 1. Classification of average spillover levels among cities in the Yangtze River Delta—Comparison between the improved and the original models: (a) improved model, recipient; (b) original model, recipient; (c) improved model, generator; and (d) original model, generator.

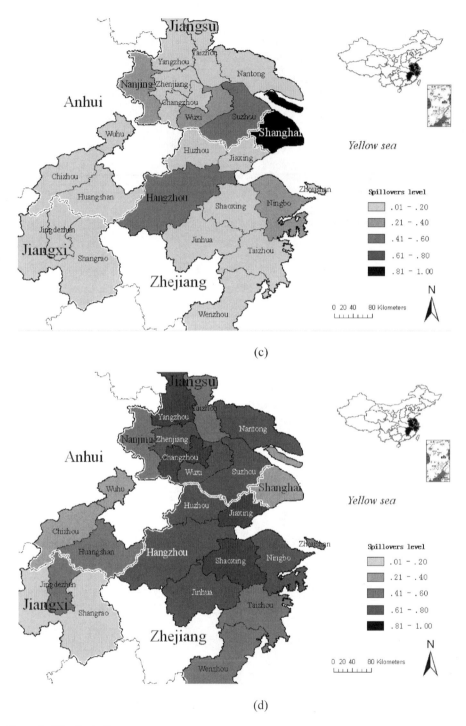

(c)

(d)

Figure 1. (Continued).

with other cities held no profit for themselves. This also indicates that regional tourism cooperation should have a certain boundary and limited copartners.

Tourism Spillover of Typical Cities

In this section we are examining five cities, namely Shanghai, Nanjing, Suzhou, Hangzhou, and Huangshan, because they are the cities most concerned with tourism in the Yangtze River Delta area.

According to the user attention index of the Baidu index (Table 4), we calculated the tourism spillover index and tourism spillover levels (and conjugate values) among

Table 4. Data for the 23 Cities in the Yangtze River Delta.

No.	City	Per Capita GDP in 2007 (Yuan)	Total Number of Domestic Tourists in 2007 (10,000)	Baidu Index	Intensity of Destination Heterogeneity
1	Shanghai	66,367	10,210	850	4
2	Nanjing	44,972	4,489	580	3.5
3	Wuxi	65,212	3,351	390	2.5
4	Changzhou	43,704	1,747	160	1.5
5	Suzhou	67,387	4,792	550	3.5
6	Nantong	29,273	1,072	120	1.5
7	Yangzhou	29,419	1,522	340	2.5
8	Zhenjiang	40,123	1,590	150	1.5
9	Hangzhou	61,258	4,112	1,100	4
10	Ningbo	61,067	3,074	370	2.5
11	Wenzhou	28,387	2,192	200	2
12	Shaoxing	45,244	2,192	320	2.5
13	Jiaxing	47,157	1,850	130	1.5
14	Huzhou	34,596	1,668	100	1.5
15	Zhoushan	42,275	1,285	450	3
16	Huangshan	16,867	943	990	4
17	Chizhou	10,949	632	240	2
18	Jingdezhen	16,899	669	95	1
19	Shangrao	8228	695	320	2.5
20	Jinhua	32,002	1,856	110	1.5
21	Taizhou (in Jiangsu)	26,085	661	80	1
22	Taizhou (in Zhejiang)	30,366	2,174	120	1.5
23	Wuhu	25,933	432	80	1

Note. The data of per capita GDP and the total number of domestic tourists come from the China regional economy statistical yearbook 2008 (National Bureau of Statistics, 2009). Because the Baidu index did not provide data for the search terms *Chizhou tourism* or *Shangrao tourism*, we replaced the two regions with search terms *Jiuhuashan tourism* and *Wuyuan tourism*, both with the highest value in the Baidu index. Because Putuo Mountain is the main tourist destination of Zhoushan tourism and is synonymous, we replaced *Zhoushan tourism* with *Putuo Mountain* as keywords for searching.

Table 5. Tourism Spillover Levels Between Shanghai and Other Cities in the Yangtze River Delta.

No.	City	I_{ij}		$S_j^{(i)}$		
		Shanghai Received	Shanghai Generated	Shanghai Received	Shanghai Generated	Conjugate Value
1	Shanghai	—	—	—	—	—
2	Nanjing	1.452	1.375	0.402	0.385	0.390
3	Wuxi	1.771	1.768	0.413	0.585	0.530
4	Changzhou	0.722	0.624	0.075	0.181	0.148
5	Suzhou	2.299	2.302	1.000	1.000	1.000
6	Nantong	0.688	0.470	0.045	0.151	0.117
7	Yangzhou	1.066	0.906	0.093	0.234	0.189
8	Zhenjiang	0.389	0.268	0.049	0.126	0.102
9	Hangzhou	2.188	2.171	0.768	0.872	0.839
10	Ningbo	1.405	1.389	0.262	0.399	0.355
11	Wenzhou	−0.225	−0.416	0.037	0.062	0.054
12	Shaoxing	1.398	1.320	0.186	0.365	0.308
13	Jiaxing	0.982	0.894	0.103	0.239	0.196
14	Huzhou	0.518	0.329	0.059	0.133	0.109
15	Zhoushan	1.274	1.186	0.096	0.317	0.247
16	Huangshan	1.466	1.195	0.086	0.301	0.232
17	Chizhou	−0.118	−0.492	0.012	0.054	0.041
18	Jingdezhen	−1.774	−2.167	0.002	0.010	0.008
19	Shangrao	0.006	−0.403	0.015	0.058	0.044
20	Jinhua	−0.208	−0.410	0.032	0.063	0.053
21	Taizhou (in Jiangsu)	−0.373	−0.662	0.010	0.048	0.036
22	Taizhou (in Zhejiang)	−0.248	−0.457	0.036	0.060	0.052
23	Wuhu	−0.805	−1.096	0.004	0.031	0.023

cities and normalized the latter by the maximum value (Tables 5 to 9); we then further compared these with the results of the original model (Figures 2 to 6).

The spillover index in Table 5 indicates that Shanghai had a positive spillover effect on most of the first participating cities in 2003 except for Wenzhou, showing an obvious reciprocal effect, but that it also had a negative spillover effect with the subsequent participating cities, rendering cooperation ineffective. In Table 5, Suzhou received the largest spillover (1.0) from Shanghai, meaning that Suzhou could be considered as Shanghai's most anticipated partner. The top three cities with the highest conjugate values of tourism spillover with Shanghai were Suzhou, Hangzhou, and Wuxi (Figure 2), which agrees with the reality that these three cities enjoy close tourism cooperation. The conjugate value between Shanghai and Hangzhou increased from third rank to second after model improvement, which is more in line with people's experience.

The spillover index in Table 6 indicates that Nanjing had a positive spillover effect on most of the first participating cities in 2003 (except for Wenzhou); it also had

Table 6. Tourism Spillover Levels Between Nanjing and other Cities in the Yangtze River Delta.

No.	City	I_{ij}		$S_j^{(i)}$		
		Nanjing Received	Nanjing Generated	Nanjing Received	Nanjing Generated	Conjugate Value
1	Shanghai	1.375	1.452	1.000	0.750	1.000
2	Nanjing	—	—	—	—	—
3	Wuxi	1.489	1.551	0.368	0.827	0.609
4	Changzhou	0.948	0.943	0.112	0.438	0.266
5	Suzhou	1.664	1.739	0.627	1.000	0.859
6	Nantong	0.127	0.036	0.030	0.172	0.095
7	Yangzhou	1.754	1.684	0.218	0.894	0.537
8	Zhenjiang	1.128	1.106	0.122	0.512	0.306
9	Hangzhou	1.292	1.356	0.371	0.678	0.546
10	Ningbo	0.310	0.361	0.104	0.251	0.179
11	Wenzhou	−1.008	−1.091	0.020	0.056	0.038
12	Shaoxing	0.691	0.692	0.108	0.341	0.222
13	Jiaxing	0.134	0.143	0.052	0.198	0.122
14	Huzhou	0.278	0.218	0.055	0.209	0.128
15	Zhoushan	0.153	0.142	0.037	0.196	0.111
16	Huangshan	1.704	1.514	0.128	0.726	0.404
17	Chizhou	0.889	0.654	0.038	0.298	0.156
18	Jingdezhen	−1.100	−1.318	0.006	0.043	0.022
19	Shangrao	−0.500	−0.776	0.010	0.070	0.038
20	Jinhua	−0.767	−0.842	0.021	0.072	0.046
21	Taizhou (in Jiangsu)	0.059	−0.074	0.017	0.153	0.079
22	Taizhou (in Zhejiang)	−0.953	−1.036	0.021	0.059	0.040
23	Wuhu	0.318	0.184	0.015	0.198	0.096

reciprocal effects on Chizhou and Wuhu cities. In particular, Shanghai was the city generating the largest spillover (1.0) on Nanjing, so it could be expected to be Nanjing's most anticipated partner. The top three cities with the highest conjugate values for tourism spillover with Nanjing were Shanghai, Suzhou, and Wuxi, whereas in the original model, the top three cities were Wuxi, Zhenjiang, and Changzhou (Figure 3), which is difficult to explain in reality. For example, the reciprocal effects brought by Shanghai and Suzhou are obviously stronger than Zhenjiang and Changzhou in the tourism cooperation with Nanjing.

The spillover index in Table 7 indicates that Suzhou had positive spillover effects on most of the first participating cities in 2003 (except for Wenzhou), showing an obvious reciprocal effect. As for the spillover level, Shanghai was the city generating the largest spillover (1.0) on Suzhou and thus could be regarded as Suzhou's most anticipated partner. The top three cities with the highest conjugate values of tourism spillover with Suzhou were Shanghai, Hangzhou, and Wuxi, whereas in the original model, the top three cities were Wuxi, Shanghai, and Changzhou (Figure 4); the fact

Table 7. Tourism Spillover Levels Between Suzhou and Other Cities in the Yangtze River Delta.

No.	City	I_{ij}		$S_j^{(i)}$		
		Suzhou Received	Suzhou Generated	Suzhou Received	Suzhou Generated	Conjugate Value
1	Shanghai	2.302	2.299	1.000	1.000	1.000
2	Nanjing	1.739	1.664	0.250	0.516	0.335
3	Wuxi	2.113	2.108	0.272	0.825	0.448
4	Changzhou	1.199	1.120	0.057	0.299	0.134
5	Suzhou	—	—	—	—	—
6	Nantong	0.658	0.486	0.020	0.154	0.063
7	Yangzhou	1.438	1.300	0.063	0.348	0.154
8	Zhenjiang	0.878	0.782	0.037	0.212	0.093
9	Hangzhou	2.021	2.001	0.304	0.738	0.442
10	Ningbo	1.306	1.290	0.111	0.362	0.191
11	Wenzhou	−0.227	−0.382	0.017	0.065	0.032
12	Shaoxing	1.424	1.356	0.089	0.380	0.182
13	Jiaxing	1.168	1.097	0.058	0.294	0.133
14	Huzhou	0.870	0.721	0.039	0.197	0.089
15	Zhoushan	1.147	1.066	0.040	0.283	0.117
16	Huangshan	1.586	1.311	0.045	0.339	0.139
17	Chizhou	0.064	−0.236	0.007	0.070	0.027
18	Jingdezhen	−1.550	−1.849	0.001	0.014	0.006
19	Shangrao	0.050	−0.290	0.007	0.065	0.026
20	Jinhua	0.010	−0.149	0.018	0.082	0.039
21	Taizhou (in Jiangsu)	0.214	−0.009	0.008	0.093	0.035
22	Taizhou (in Zhejiang)	−0.150	−0.314	0.018	0.070	0.035
23	Wuhu	−0.460	−0.684	0.003	0.047	0.017

that the conjugate values of Suzhou and Wuxi were higher than those of Shanghai and Suzhou is also hard to understand.

The spillover index in Table 8 indicates that Hangzhou had a positive spillover effect on most of the first participating cities in 2003 (except for Nantong and Wenzhou) and that Hangzhou also had a reciprocal effect on Shangrao. As for the spillover levels, Shanghai was the city generating the largest spillover on Hangzhou and so could be expected to be Hangzhou's most anticipated partner. The top two cities with the highest conjugate values for tourism spillovers on Hangzhou were Shanghai and Suzhou, whereas in the original model, the top two cities were Ningbo and Wuxi (Figure 5), which is difficult to explain in reality.

Table 9 shows a negative spillover between Huangshan city and about half the first participating cities, showing distinctive characteristics compared with Shanghai, Nanjing, Suzhou, and Hangzhou. As for the spillover levels (Table 9), Shanghai was the city generating the largest spillover on Huangshan and therefore could be

Table 8. Tourism Spillover Levels Between Hangzhou and Other Cities in the Yangtze River Delta.

No.	City	I_{ij}		$S_j^{(i)}$		
		Hangzhou Received	Hangzhou Generated	Hangzhou Received	Hangzhou Generated	Conjugate Value
1	Shanghai	2.171	2.188	1.000	1.000	1.000
2	Nanjing	1.356	1.292	0.195	0.398	0.254
3	Wuxi	1.359	1.372	0.146	0.442	0.232
4	Changzhou	0.447	0.358	0.031	0.156	0.067
5	Suzhou	1.996	2.016	0.394	0.843	0.525
6	Nantong	−0.193	−0.415	0.010	0.070	0.027
7	Yangzhou	0.918	0.762	0.043	0.227	0.096
8	Zhenjiang	0.089	−0.026	0.019	0.106	0.045
9	Hangzhou	—	—	—	—	—
10	Ningbo	1.571	1.571	0.165	0.536	0.274
11	Wenzhou	0.092	−0.100	0.027	0.096	0.047
12	Shaoxing	1.903	1.837	0.164	0.686	0.316
13	Jiaxing	0.762	0.687	0.044	0.218	0.095
14	Huzhou	0.538	0.351	0.032	0.152	0.067
15	Zhoushan	1.462	1.385	0.062	0.435	0.171
16	Huangshan	2.107	1.854	0.087	0.652	0.252
17	Chizhou	0.011	−0.388	0.007	0.067	0.025
18	Jingdezhen	−1.219	−1.640	0.002	0.020	0.007
19	Shangrao	0.699	0.267	0.016	0.127	0.048
20	Jinhua	0.190	−0.014	0.025	0.105	0.048
21	Taizhou (in Jiangsu)	−0.972	−1.272	0.003	0.029	0.011
22	Taizhou (in Zhejiang)	0.026	−0.185	0.025	0.088	0.043
23	Wuhu	−0.807	−1.109	0.002	0.035	0.012

considered as Huangshan's most anticipated partner. The top three cities with the highest conjugate values of tourism spillover with Huangshan were Shanghai, Hangzhou, and Suzhou (Figure 6). This result is in keeping with the tourism route titled Famous City, Famous Lake, Famous Mountain, composed of Shanghai, Hangzhou, and Huangshan. This result also explains the efforts of Suzhou in expecting to cooperate with Shanghai, Hangzhou, and Huangshan in tourism development. In the original model, Jingdezhen city had the highest conjugate value of tourism spillover with Huangshan, whereas Shanghai had the lowest value, as shown in Figure 6. From these results, S. Li and Wang (2009a) suggested that a new tourism circle centering around Huangshan city should emerge.

S. Li and Wang (2009b) also found that in the tourism cities of the Yangtze River Delta, it would be practical to integrate Huangshan into the tourism circle formed by Shanghai, Suzhou, and Hangzhou. The results of the original model showed that Jingdezhen was the most anticipated cooperation partner with Huangshan, but the new model showed that a negative spillover existed between these two cities, probably caused

Table 9. Tourism Spillover Levels Between Huangshan and Other Cities in the Yangtze River Delta.

		I_{ij}		$S_j^{(i)}$		
No.	City	Huangshan Received	Huangshan Generated	Huangshan Received	Huangshan Generated	Conjugate Value
1	Shanghai	1.195	1.466	1.000	0.529	1.000
2	Nanjing	1.514	1.704	0.604	0.654	0.678
3	Wuxi	0.921	1.185	0.249	0.399	0.309
4	Changzhou	−0.011	0.230	0.051	0.150	0.078
5	Suzhou	1.311	1.586	0.527	0.598	0.597
6	Nantong	−0.663	−0.501	0.016	0.070	0.030
7	Yangzhou	0.760	0.873	0.096	0.277	0.146
8	Zhenjiang	−0.118	0.109	0.042	0.132	0.066
9	Hangzhou	1.854	2.107	0.778	1.000	0.909
10	Ningbo	0.600	0.856	0.166	0.286	0.210
11	Wenzhou	−0.038	0.087	0.063	0.126	0.083
12	Shaoxing	0.935	1.140	0.165	0.372	0.229
13	Jiaxing	−0.247	0.041	0.043	0.124	0.065
14	Huzhou	−0.297	−0.067	0.037	0.109	0.057
15	Zhoushan	1.001	1.181	0.104	0.386	0.177
16	Huangshan	—	—	—	—	—
17	Chizhou	1.225	1.129	0.064	0.334	0.130
18	Jingdezhen	−0.225	−0.224	0.016	0.089	0.034
19	Shangrao	1.140	0.994	0.064	0.286	0.120
20	Jinhua	−0.096	0.100	0.050	0.128	0.073
21	Taizhou (in Jiangsu)	−1.237	−1.085	0.006	0.039	0.014
22	Taizhou (in Zhejiang)	−0.627	−0.455	0.034	0.074	0.047
23	Wuhu	−0.474	−0.325	0.008	0.083	0.025

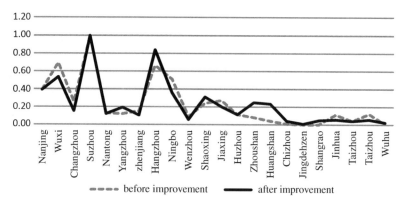

Figure 2. Conjugate values of tourism spillover between Shanghai and other cities in the Yangtze River Delta.

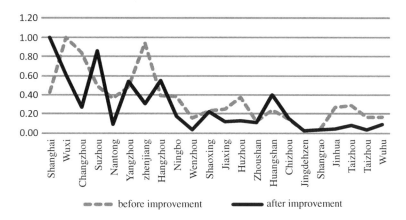

Figure 3. Conjugate values of tourism spillover between Nanjing and other cities in the Yangtze River Delta.

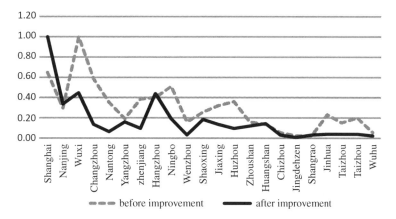

Figure 4. Conjugate values of tourism spillover between Suzhou and other cities in the Yangtze River Delta.

by the different definition of the tourism grade gap. Under the new definition, the tourism grade of Huangshan (the Baidu index) was much higher than that of Jingdezhen, and thus a negative spillover occurred between the two cities. This may also reflect the reality that under the new market conditions, the emerging tourism destinations of Wuyuan and Sanqing Mountain around Huangshan have started to boom, whereas Jingdezhen as a traditional tourism destination has developed more slowly.

Tourism Spillover of City Combinations

Regional tourism pays attention not only to bilateral relations between cities, but also to multilateral relations between them. Therefore, we calculated the conjugate values for the situation of city combinations. The results reveal that for city combination of two cities, the pair of Shanghai and Suzhou combination had the highest conjugate value, indicating that the reciprocal effect between these two cities was the most remarkable in the Yangtze

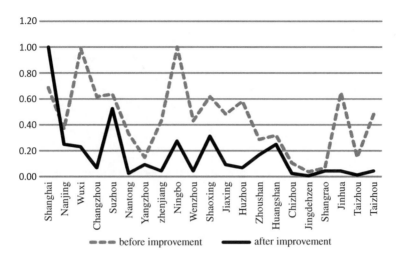

Figure 5. Conjugate values of tourism spillover between Hangzhou and other cities in the Yangtze River Delta.

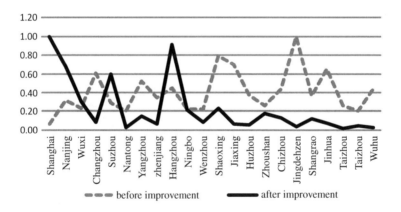

Figure 6. Conjugate values of tourism spillover between Huangshan and other cities in the Yangtze River Delta.

River Delta. Moreover, for a city combination of three cities, the group of Shanghai, Suzhou, and Hangzhou had the highest conjugate value; these also happen to be the cities forming the classic tourist route of the three-city tour in East China. Finally, for the city combination of five cities, the group of Shanghai, Suzhou, Hangzhou, Wuxi, and Nanjing had the highest conjugate value; these happen to be the cities forming the famous classic tourist route of the five-city tour in East China. The above results prove that the conjugate values of tourism spillover could reflect the level of reciprocity among cities, as well as the rationale of our measuring model.

Conclusion and Discussion

In this article, we have improved the measurement model on intercity tourism spillover proposed by S. Li and Wang (2009a) in three respects. First, we developed the model structure by adding the scale of tourism to the original model; this new factor provided a more reasonable expression of the mechanism of tourism spillover. We also found that tourism spillovers had a negative correlation with the grade difference $G_{ij}^{(l)}$ and geographical distance, whereas it showed a positive correlation with the type difference $G_{ij}^{(k)}$ among tourism cities, the learning ability of the tourism city receiving the spillover, and the tourism scale of the city generating the spillover. Second, we also improved the definition on variable indicators. In particular, by introducing the user attention index of the Baidu index, we were able to express the tourism grade gap and tourism-type gap quantitatively and thus more objectively. Furthermore, with respect to the distance gap, we adopted transportation distance in place of spherical distance, thereby bringing the results more in line with the actual situation. And third, we optimized the method for estimating parameters. With respect to the power exponent estimation of learning capacity, we adopted the interval value instead of the single value.

Using this improved model, we then analyzed tourism spillover in the Yangtze River Delta area. The results show the following:

1. Spillover generated by Shanghai city was the highest; thus, it seems that Shanghai possesses an outstanding status as a regional tourism center. The highest spillovers received were by Suzhou and Hangzhou cities, indicating the continuous regional advantages of "Paradise in Heaven, Suzhou and Hangzhou on Earth." A vast majority of the first participating cities benefited from tourism cooperation, whereas the subsequent participating cities were all "more cost than benefit" in such cooperation. Such results suggest that regional cooperation in tourism should have certain boundaries.
2. Shanghai looked forward mostly to cooperating with Suzhou; it was also the most anticipated city for Nanjing, Suzhou, Hangzhou, and Huangshan cities for cooperation. The top two cities with the highest conjugate values of tourism spillover with Huangshan were Shanghai and Hangzhou, making them the internal power source for Shanghai, Hangzhou, and Huangshan in cocreating the world-class golden tourist route of Famous City, Famous Lake, Famous Mountain.
3. The conjugate values of tourism spillover revealed that the city combination formed by the three cities with the highest conjugate values were Shanghai, Suzhou, and Hangzhou. For a combination of five cities, they were Shanghai, Suzhou, Hangzhou, Wuxi, and Nanjing. The results happen to reflect the two classic tourist routes: the three-city tour in East China and the five-city tour in East China as well.

On the whole, the explanatory power of the improved model is much stronger than the original one; the new model also analyzes regional tourism cooperation more effectively. But because the model stems from the knowledge-spillover model, one problem remains to be resolved, namely, knowledge spillovers are always positive, whereas tourism spillovers can be either positive or negative. In our model, we introduced the spillover index as a ruler to judge the sign of tourism spillovers; further, we took $S_j^{(i)} = q_i \delta_j$ as the background spillover of tourism when $I_{ij} = 0$, which solved the problem of how tourism spillovers can be partially either positive or negative. But under such a definition, the physical meaning of background spillover is unclear and needs further study. Second, when measuring the tourism-type gap between two cities, we used the Baidu index as a criterion to decide the intensity of the destination heterogeneity for both simplified and objective purposes; this, however, is a debatable procedure. The tourism grade gap and tourism-type gap between two cities actually reflects the vertical and horizontal differences of tourism products, respectively. If the

Baidu index can be used to measure the former to a certain extent, then the measurement of the latter, which is the horizontal difference (tourism-type gap), should use other, more scientific and objective indicators; this also needs special attention in further study. And third, in the analysis of the Yangtze River Delta, we treated the results of tourism spillover by the method of maximum standardizing, which seemed intuitive and simple for an analysis within one region but would not be conducive to a comparative study on multiregional areas (for example, a comparison between the Pearl River Delta and Bohai Central District); thus, the data processing should be adjusted in different scenarios.

Acknowledgments

This research was funded by the Humanities and Social Sciences Foundation of the Ministry of Education (No. 09YJC790089) and the National Natural Science Foundation of China (No. 41071092, No. 70933002). We gratefully acknowledge Wen Xiong (PhD) and Shu Zhu (PhD) for their helpful suggestions. We also thank three anonymous reviewers for their constructive comments on an earlier version of this article.

References

Arrow, K. J. (1962). The economic implications of learning by doing. *The Review of Economic Studies, 29*(3), 155–173.

Bao, J. (1994). A spatial competitive analysis on the tourism development of stone forest karst landforms. *Economic Geography, 14*(3), 93–96.

Bao, J., & Liang, F. (1991). A spatial competitive analysis on the tourism resources development of coast and bench: A case of bench development in Maoming city. *Economic Geography, 11*(2), 89–93.

Bottazzi, L., & Peri, G. (2003). Innovation and spillovers in regions: Evidence from European patent data. *European Economic Review, 47*, 687–710.

Bretschger, L. (1999). *Growth theory and sustainable development* (pp. 79–94). Aldershot, NH: Edward Elgar.

Caniëls, M. C. J., & Verspagen, B. (2001). Barriers to knowledge spillovers and regional convergence in an evolutionary model. *Evolutionary Economics, 11*, 307–329.

Chen, J., & Bao, J. (1988). A study of tourist behavior and its practical significance. *Geographical Research, 7*(3), 44–51.

China Internet Network Information Center. (2009). *China search engine user behavior study in the year 2009*. Retrieved from http://www.cnnic.net.cn/html/Dir/2009/09/21/5684.htm

Cong, B., Meng, X., & Fu, S. (2009, September 30, the first Edition). Opening cermony of "2009 Weifang Week" was held in Qingdao. Retrieved from Weifang Daily at http://wfrb.wfnews.com.cn/html/2009-09/30/content,129207.htm

Deng, Y., Wang, Z., & Li, S. (2004). A study based on GIS of a computable model of spatial planning of tourism regions. In W. Zheng (Ed.), *Geo-computation on urban and regional planning: Urban tourism sustainable development* (p. 243). Beijing, China: Science Press.

Gooroochurn, N., & Hanley, A. (2005). Spillover effects in long-haul visitors between two regions. *Regional Studies, 39*(6), 727–738.

Grossman, G. M., & Helpman, E. (1991). Trade, knowledge spillovers and growth. *European Economic Review, 35*, 517–526.

Grossman, G. M., & Helpman, E. (1993). *Innovation and growth in the global economy* (pp. 16–21). Cambridge, MA: MIT Press.

Lazzeretti, L., & Capone, F. (2009). Spatial spillovers and employment dynamics in local tourist systems in Italy (1991–2001). *European Planning Studies*, *17*(11), 1665–1683.

Li, F., & Huang, Y. (2008). An analysis of spillovers of inter-regional urban tourism economy: A case of urban cluster in the Pearl River Delta. *Tourism Tribune*, *23*(5), 23–28.

Li, S., & Wang, Z. (2009a). Computable models on regional spillovers of tourism industry: A case study of the Yangtze River Delta. *Tourism Tribune*, *24*(7), 18–26.

Li, S., & Wang, Z. (2009b). Computable models on the temporal and spatial scale of an optimum tourism destination circle. *Acta Geographica Sinica*, *64*(10), 1255–1266.

Li, S., Wang, H., & Wang, Z. (2005). A study on tour time planning of domestic sightseeing travel itineraries. *Human Geography*, *20*(2), 51–56.

Liu, Z. (2008). Shangdong "integration" makes strides in 2008. Retrieved from Qingdao Daily at http://ribao.qingdaonews.com/html/2008-01/03/content_214932.htm

Lucas, R. E. (1988). On the mechanics of economic development. *Journal of Monetary Economics*, *22*(1), 3–42.

Ma, Y., & Li, T. (1999). *Spatial analysis of the inbound tourism flow to and in China* (p. 136). Beijing, China: Science Press.

Mankiw, G. N. (2009). *Principles of economics* (5th ed.). Microeconomics Volume (p. 211). Beijing, China: Peking University Press.

National Bureau of Statistics. (2009). *China regional economy statistical yearbook 2008*. Beijing, China: China Statistics Press.

Romer, P. (1986). Increasing returns and long-run growth. *Journal of Political Economy*, *94*(5), 1002–1037.

Shenzhen Statistics. (2008, April 10). *The 2007 statistics bulletin of the National Economic and Social Development of Shenzhen*. Retrieved from http://www.sztj.com/main/xxgk/tjsj/tjgb/gmjjhshfzgb/200804101586.shtml

Wang, Y. (1993). A study on tourism development of Mencius' native place. *Geography and Geo-Information Science*, *9*(2), 50–52.

Wang, Z., Gong, Y., & Liu, L. (2003). A research to [*sic*] R&D spillovers between China and the United States. *Studies in Science of Science*, *21*(4), 396–399.

Wang, Z., Jiang, Y., Wang, Y., Li, S., Wang, Y., & Weng, G. (2002). Tourism area model and the applications based on GIS. *Tourism Tribune*, *17*(2), 57–62.

Wang, Z., Liu, H., & Liu, L. (2003). An analysis of GDP spillovers of China's east, center and west regions. *Economic Science*, *1*, 5–13.

Wu, B., Tang, J., Huang, A., Zhao, R., Qiu, F., & Fang, F. (1997). A study on destination choice behavior of Chinese urban residents. *Acta Geographica Sinica*, *52*(2), 97–103.

Urban Morphology and Tourism Planning: Exploring the City Wall in Pingyao, China

城市形态和旅游规划: 探索中国平遥城墙

FEIFAN (PHILIP) XIE
KAI GU

The article presents a case study of spatial morphology in Pingyao, Shanxi Province, to illustrate the significance of architectural heritage, particularly distinctive features of the city wall. It traces three stages of intramural and extramural changes under governmental policies as tourism has become a means of economic growth. Urban tourism has a profound impact on the transformation of the danwei units and preservation of historic buildings. The use of the city wall as a historical landmark promotes a sense of place and authenticity. This article ends by suggesting that the integration of spatial morphology with tourism planning will foster a better understanding of the complex interplay of urban form and function.

本文通过研究山西省平遥古城的空间形态，阐明建筑遗产，特别是城墙特色的重要性，并探索旅游业在政府政策下成为经济发展手段对古城内外带来的转变。城市旅游对单位的变化和历史建筑物的保存都具有深远的影响。以城墙作为历史地标能够促进地方感和原真性。在结尾部分，本文建议结合空间形态和旅游规划，以更好地了解城市形态和功能两者之间复杂的相互影响。

Introduction

The extant research on urban morphology focuses upon the study of the city as human habitat and has included a number of disciplines, such as geography, planning, and architecture (Burgers, 2000; Vance, 1990). The study of the relationship between urban morphology and tourism originated in Britain as resort morphology (Gilbert, 1949) and has commonly been utilized to describe the form and function of towns since the advent of space commercialization. Morphology posits an evolutionary cycle of the town and tracks a dynamic complexity of changes in various time periods. The growing literature on urban morphology pursues very different models ranging from static (Crang, 2000), to historical (Moudon, 1997), to integrated (Conzen, 2009; Whitehand, 1992). These studies offer an important decision-making process for regional planning and improve the existence of elements that create urban form, such as old districts, commercial streets, and development zones.

Feifan (Philip) Xie is Associate Professor of the Sport Management, Recreation and Tourism Division at Bowling Green State University, Bowling Green, OH, USA (E-mail: pxie@bgsu.edu).
Kai Gu is Lecturer of the School of Architecture and Planning at the University of Auckland, Auckland, New Zealand (E-mail: k.gu@auckland.ac.nz).

Policies for urban regeneration are generally inspired by exploiting the cultural potentials of urban historic districts (Jansen-Verbeke & Lievois, 1999). Urban tourism, as an integral part of revitalization, has transformed the landscapes within a space–time framework. Although the resulting morphological and socioeconomic implications vary in different cities, urban morphology has increasingly become instrumental to understand tourism impacts on the national and local scales. Moudon (1997) proposed that urban form is often defined by physical elements, such as buildings, streets, and open spaces. The study of urban form can be understood at various levels of resolution. Most important, urban form reflects historical elements of the city that undergoes continuous transformation and replacement. Thus, form, resolution, and time constitute the three fundamental components of urban morphological research.

Given the importance of historical elements in urban morphology, there is an increasing interest in incorporating morphology with tourism studies in recent years (Gospodini, 2001, 2004); however, the significance of applying morphology to urban tourism remains neglected by tourism researchers (Liu & Wall, 2009). Furthermore, architectural heritage has been discussed in tourism literature, but little work has been carried out explaining how it relates to urban development (Lasansky & McLaren, 2004). Gospodini (2001) suggested that architectural heritage reflects differences among cities and provides cities with a sense of historical and cultural authenticity. It not only provides a frame of reference that articulates the physical composition of an urban area but also represents a place identity embedded with images and memories for tourist consumption. Architectural heritage is not limited to old houses but landmarks, such as city walls, characterized by their tourist–historic functions (Bégin, 2000). These landmarks have integrated into the contemporary socioeconomic life of a city in which the past and present are inexorably intertwined.

This article aims to introduce the urban morphology associated with the city of Pingyao, an ancient walled city in Shanxi Province. It draws on the city wall to characterize three periods of Pingyao's urban changes. The intramural and extramural morphologies reflect a shifting pattern of tourism planning, which becomes the significant historico–morphological marker for the city. The city wall serves as a reference point for Pingyao's gradual emergence as a major tourist destination in China. The unique social–economic development, geographical conditions, and cultural traditions of its 14th-century city wall merit academic research. Thus, the purpose of this article is twofold. The first is the introduction of urban morphology in the context of China as well as the sources that can be used in its investigation in urban tourism. The second is to assess the historical development of the city wall in Pingyao. The impact of tourism development in Pinyao associated with the wall has been detailed.

Urban Morphology and City Walls

There is a growing and substantial literature about urban morphology in China (K. Gu, 2001; Liu, Zhan, & Deng, 2005; Xu, 2000; Yan, 1995). The majority of research focuses on spatial changes and urban land expansion during the economic reform era (Lu, 2006). Tourism planning is viewed as an essential component of economic development which improves tertiary services. Bégin (2000) conducted research in Xiamen, China, and identified that Chinese cities had gone through three stages of morphology; that is, renovation, expansion, and redevelopment. The old central core of the city tends to be too condensed to develop a modern central business district (CBD). Consequently, an initial form of "recreational business district" or a "tourist cultural district" was engendered due to the mixture of traditional residential areas and emerging business districts. Ashworth (1989) argued that there exists a transition zone between the newly developed business district and the old town. The transitional morphology can be seen in the glittering office buildings in contrast to the dilapidated urban cores. In China, the transition zone can be found in Maoist-era residential and industrial campuses (Bégin) versus the newly developed districts (*xingqu*). The dividing line between these stages of urban morphology tends to be marked by administrative boundaries or historical landmarks, such as the city wall.

Chinese cities are experiencing massive urban changes that are the result of commercialization. Struggles between preservation and development continue as tourism becomes an effective means of economic growth. Influenced by urban designs for sweeping changes in the old core of the city, local governments face challenges due to simultaneous pressures to modernize the city and preserve its historical architecture. Commodification, such as tourism, has profoundly impacted spatiotemporal changes in urban cores and caused tensions between heritage preservation and urban conservation. One of the major issues is authenticity and sense of place in urban design (Ouf, 2001). Gospodini (2001) proposed that urban morphology faces three properties in relation to tourism development; that is, the preservation of aspects of the city's past, authenticity in terms of spatial morphology, and richness in meaning. The architectural heritage of the city should not be viewed as static but evolves in various periods of time. It represents *genius loci*, the spirit of place, defining a city's identity.

The concept of "critical regionalism" proposed by Tzonis and Lefaivre (1990) upholds the individual and local architectonic features against the mainstream of the society. Many local characteristics may reflect critical-regionalist design, such as material, plan form, wall surface, construction mode, etc. The emphasis is on the authenticity of the architectural elements. Frampton (1983) argued that critical regionalism represents the particularities of place with nostalgic reconstructions of vernacular architecture or urban elements. Herr (1996) and Powell (2007) suggested that by studying heritage architecture in Ireland and the United States, these elements are idiosyncratic and emblematic for regional traditions, which require an extensive study. The medieval walled cities in Europe and North America, such as Quebec City (Evans, 2002), have become an instant symbol of critical regionalism. The walls are used to promote national identity and to market its cultural heritage. They constitute a major contribution to the historical grain of a city and have significant implications for planning, especially conservation. It is noted that differences between the East and the West regarding heritage building conservation approaches exist. For example, cultural heritage in Asian cities is largely shaped by philosophies and religious systems that emphasize the intangible rather than the tangible. Those differences are manifested in the 1994 Nara Documents and 2003 Hoi An Protocols.

Tourism can be used as a means to legitimize or to authenticate public culture (P. Xie, 2003). Public culture can be refashioned by the needs of tourism to symbolize reconstruction of the existing entity. Hollinshead (1999) called this kind of modification "the legerdemain of tourism" (p. 267), where material symbolism has been constantly construed in various time periods. Heritage architecture is widely seen as representative of local culture and identity; however, history shows that the architecture is built or renovated to suit the local needs for political, economic, and sociocultural purposes. In many cases, this selective reinterpretation of architecture serves to legitimize a governmental viewpoint on those aspects of the past that are important to remember or to market. Chan (2005) examined the multiple meanings of building the temple, Huang

Da Xian, for Mainland Chinese, Chinese in Hong Kong, and Taiwanese. As a heritage temple, the Mainland Chinese regard Huang Da Xian as an ideal place to practice religious activities and to develop pilgrimage tourism. Conversely, for overseas Chinese, the construction of the temple is viewed as a nostalgic search for roots and authenticity. Finally, the Chinese governments utilized the temple as a symbol of nationalism to reinforce a Chinese identity. AlSayyad (2001) called this kind of regeneration "engazement" (p. 4)—a process through which the tourist gaze transforms the built environment into a cultural imaginary. In other words, the gaze is not the same everywhere but its spatiotemporal dimensions change from place to place. Heritage identities have been reinterpreted by different stakeholders for the purpose of tourism development.

Various aspects of city walls have been the subject of research including their values in urban tourism planning (Knapp, 2000; Le, 2005). City walls are arguably the most prominent heritage landscape feature in a traditional Chinese city (Whitehand, Gu, & Whitehand, 2011). During the 20th century, many city walls in China, such as Beijing, were demolished and their sites became important thoroughfares encircling the core of the city (Ruan, 2003). The restoration of the existing walls serves a multitude of purposes from the socioeconomic and heritage perspectives. In particular, tourism remains a catalyst of change in the process of restoration and urban regeneration. The revival of ancient walls and their conversion into tourist attractions are often seen as "theatres of memory" (Samuel, 1994, p. viii) in which a region's historic and cultural past is salvaged and reshaped. The restoration encompasses a sense of regional identity and, most significantly, rejuvenates a sense of place attachment in heritage architecture (H. Gu & Ryan, 2008). Tourism represents a powerful option for preserving these walls and an effective means of making a visible cultural identity.

The importance of the conservation of city walls has received attention from the urban planners and government officials since the 1980s. For example, in Xi'an, restoration of the city wall and development of a park outside the wall began in 1983 (J. Wang, Ruan, & Wang, 1999). In Beijing, there were two projects to restore the city walls and create city-wall parks at the beginning of the 21st century. One was the Ming City Wall Park—a 1.5-km strip with an area of 12.2 ha (Y. Zhang, 2008). Another was the Imperial City Wall Park, which is 2.8 km in length and has an area of 7.5 ha (Dong, 2006). Similarly, in Shanghai, where the 16th-century wall had been demolished almost entirely between 1912 and 1914, an Ancient Wall Park was created in 2002 (Whitehand et al., 2011). These are just a few examples of the widespread reinstatement of historical fortification zones in China that were colonized for other uses during earlier periods.

Research Setting

Pingyao was the original birthplace of the banking and financial system in China (Xiong, 2003). A representative culture, *Jin Shang* (Jin Merchant or Shanxi business people), was embedded in commercial activities in Pingyao when the city was the financial center in the 19th century. Geographically, Pingyao is situated on the gently sloping plain between the River Huiji and the River Liugen in central Shanxi. It is one of the very few cities that still retain large parts of its traditional layout and fabrics. In particular, it is one of the few Chinese cities that still retain its city wall. The perimeter of the city is 6.4 km long, which surrounds the earliest and largest intact city wall in China. The number of gates has remained the same despite the large increase in the size of the walled area: two in each of the eastern and western stretches of the wall and one in each of the northern and southern stretches (Du, 2002). The wall on the north, east, and west sides is straight except in the northeast corner, whereas the wall on the south side follows the former winding course of the River Zhongdu, later realigned and renamed the River Liugen. The wall is 8–12 m wide at its base, 3–6 m wide at its top, just over 10 m high, and protected by a moat. Textures made from the wall and streets inside the city look like a geometric pattern on a tortoise shell, as a result, Pingyao is nicknamed the "tortoise city" (Xiong).

After the Communist Party took power in 1949, Pingyao was transformed into an industrial city, a hub for textile and agricultural machinery manufacturing. Publicly owned residential and industrial campuses, *danwei*, comprised of housing and community buildings, were created both within the walled city and beyond the walls. The 14th-century wall, towers, and gates suffered considerable damage at various times, especially during the Cultural Revolution of 1966–1976 (Committee for Pingyao Gazetteer, 1999). Tourism planning has been an integral part of master urban plans and conservation for Pingyao since the early 1980s. It has been particularly highlighted in the urban master plans in 1982 (Pingyao Urban and Rural Planning Bureau, 2006); the conservation plan in 1989 (Shanxi Research Institute of Urban and Rural Planning and Design, 2005); the provincial plan in 1999 (Pingyao Development and Reform Bureau, 2009), and provincial urban design in 2005 (Shanxi Research Institute of Urban and Rural Planning and Design, 2005). The marriage of urban planning and tourism has been viewed as a driving force to revive this historical city. In 1986, Pingyao was added to the List of Precious Chinese Historico–Cultural Cities (*lishi wenhua mingcheng*) and was inducted into United Nations Educational, Scientific and Cultural Organization's (UNESCO) list of World Heritage Sites (WHS) in 1997. This status is perceived to bring enormous prestige at both the global and national levels, as well as impacting future planning decisions at the local level (Smith, 2002). The city has swiftly become a popular tourist destination to experience cultural heritage, urban landscape and traditional *Jin Shang* culture.

This historical core of Pingyao had a population of approximately 35,000 in 2001 (Xiong, 2003). The significance of the walls has drawn tourists internationally. Urban tourism plays a vital role in the improvement of both the local economy and the physical environment. A number of previous courtyard houses or institutions were redeveloped and converted for commercial uses. Concomitantly, there has been a widespread reinstatement of historical transition zones that were colonized for other uses in many Chinese walled cities prior to the 1980s. The restoration of city walls began to be actively pursued by the planning authorities in Pingyao (Pingyao Development and Reform Bureau, 2009). Large-scale landscaping and housing clearance projects have been implemented in the zones immediately adjacent to the city wall. The new developments in the past two decades have mainly concentrated in the areas associated with the 14th-century city wall. The rapid transformation of the urban landscape, mainly driven by tourism development, poses great challenges for the preservation of the cultural continuity and authenticity of a historic city.

The development of the city wall can be categorized into three major stages: (a) 1949 to the early 1980s: The wall worked as a symbol of demarcating residential areas and industrial zone. The impact of tourism was negligible since travel was widely viewed as a political activity. (b) 1980 to 1999: Pingyao evolved from a sleepy industrial city into a vibrant destination for cultural and heritage tourism. Tourism began to exert great influence on urban planning as the wall was seen as an authentic heritage asset for marketing and promotion. (c) 2000 to present: Conservation of walled city has gained attention and support from local government and tourism planners alike. The wall is now viewed as a significant cultural marker for the city of Pingyao. Commercial real estate development has been restricted in order to preserve architectural structures. Tourism has become a major source of income for the city.

Methodology

The research was based upon extensive reviews of urban planning documents in Pingyao. It draws on qualitative and quantitative data that were collected as part of a longitudinal and ongoing study of Pingyao as a heritage tourism destination. Fieldwork was conducted in three stages from 2005 to 2009. First, governmental documents were compared to the historico–morphological shifts in recent decades. Various agencies, such as Pingyao Urban and Rural Construction Bureau and Shanxi Research Institute of Urban and Rural Planning and Design were visited in order to obtain updated data on city planning. Historical documents in three periods were examined to understand the transformation of the walls surrounding the city. Maps of changing morphology in these periods were drawn and compared.

In the second stage, changes of urban tourism planning on streets and districts were carefully recorded and plotted with the goal of assessing the variation of urban forms. The tourism business district (TBD) offering a geographical concentration of facilities and attractions was identified. The distribution of the informal sector, such as hawkers, street vendors, and itinerant sellers, was mapped since the majority of the sector spread to adjoining streets and city walls.

In the third stage, selected local officials in urban and tourism development were interviewed and their attitudes toward heritage preservation were observed in 2008 and 2009. Tourism-related professionals were invited to discuss the problems and prospects of the city wall as a source of urban tourism. A recent proposal from the Pingyao government including a physical development plan and implementation guidelines was collected to reflect the changing policies toward tourism development.

Stages of Tourism Development

The Creation of Danwei (1949 to Early 1980)

Prior to the Second World War, Pingyao was essentially a preindustrial city. Profound changes to the social and economic organization of the city began to occur in 1949. A traditional service and administrative center began to be transformed into an industrial city in accordance with the ideology of the new Communist China (Y. Xie & Costa, 1991). Socialist industrialization between the 1950s and the 1970s significantly changed the physical environment of Pingyao. A key feature of this transformation was the creation, mainly between the mid-1950s and early 1980s, of *danwei*, or residential and industrial campuses. *Danwei* was an integral component of a centrally planned economy in which financial resources were planned by entire sectors (Ding & Gerrit, 2003). Communities were created by local governments to revamp the old core of the city and to implement social projects. Public housing was established to provide accommodation for the working class. Entire communities were constructed all at once, enabling workers to live close to their work. A railway line linking Taiyuan and Jiexiu and a railway station on the northwest side of Pingyao were built in early 1950s. The construction of this station limited city expansion in the northwest sector of the city, instead attracting the growth of *danwei* to the west of the walled city for citizens requiring direct access to transportation.

The creation of *danwei* has been the fundamental socio-spatial unit of urban China under socialist policies and has had an influential impact on morphology. Normally walled enclosures each contain a workplace, such as a hospital, school, or factory; residential accommodation for those employed in the workplace and services; and often include a communal dining hall. The wall served as a divider between self-sufficient *danwei*. Outside the city wall, *danwei* largely occupied previously rural land, forming a major extension of the extramural residential belt. Before 1949 this part of the belt comprised little more than the glacis, the moat, eight religious or quasi-religious sites, and a military ground (Whitehand et al., 2011). *Danwei* were added to surround the extramural area in large numbers, mainly to the west of the wall. At the same time, large areas of high-density housing were created and public buildings erected in places separating the open area outside the wall from the surrounding rural area, especially to the south of the walled city but also to a lesser degree on its eastern side. Bray (2005) suggested that *danwei* functions not only as a major purveyor of employment, wages, and other material benefits for the majority of urban residents but also an institution through which the population was housed, regulated, policed, and protected as a community.

Tourism planning was nonexistent since it functioned as political propaganda during the creation of *danwei*. Few governmental organizations paid attention to the wealth of heritage buildings. H. Zhang, Chong, and Ap (1999) proposed that prior to 1978, the Chinese government used tourism solely to serve the needs of "socialism rebuilding." *Danwei* was designed largely for the purpose of working class who clustered near factories and offered an easy access to stores. It also presented politics of identity in a region where industrialization was highly prioritized. *Danwei* was widely viewed as a modern socialist product that was realized in both formal and functional terms while simultaneously conveying an ideological charge that relied on the reinterpretation of deeply rooted traditions and the continuity of identity. In contrast, intramural buildings in the old core of the city were denigrated as instances of the insufficient architecture, devoid of social consciousness, that had been produced by and for the dominant "bureaucratic feudalism." Deterioration of intramural buildings was due to negligence, poor maintenance, and an emphasis on *danwei* development. Vernacular architectural forms and decorative elements were abandoned. Most temples in Pingyao were readapted and converted into elementary and high schools after 1949. For example, the *Wen Miao* (the Temple of Civil Culture) was transformed to Pingyao Middle School, which is the biggest school in the city, and the Taoist temple became the Bureau of Food Administration (S. Wang, 2008). The original social and religious functions of the temples have disappeared and been forgotten.

However, the creation of *danwei* unintentionally helped to preserve the vernacular architecture in the old core of the city as *danwei* housing became viable for the majority of workers. It was virtually impossible to build factories in or to convince workers to commute to the inner city. The majority of owners of the houses in the old core of the city fled after the Communist Party took power. Local policies sought to reoccupy and reconfigure extant buildings rather than building new ones. Land distribution and political agitation to solve the housing deficit resulted in a chaotic system. New residents living on government subsidies quickly filled these houses in the inner city deemed inadequate by Western standards. It was not uncommon to have four to six families inhabiting one old house without proper sewage or tap water. The lack of maintenance aggravated living standard in the old core of the city as more residents moved to the neighborhoods of *danwei*.

Modernization and Tourism Development (1980 to 1999)

Tourism, which had previously been considered a political activity, emerged as a new pivot of economic development from 1986 to 1991. Local government sought to construct a new political identity in which tourism played a significant part. From 1992 to 1999, the provincial government regulated tourism as part of a market economy model and offered a wide range of freedom and flexibilities. Pingyao benefited from commercial ethos as tourism planning was implemented. The previously blank walls of the *danwei* were eventually replaced by continuous shop fronts bustling with petty-commerce vendors and private businesses. Local government officials and developers in Taiyuan, the capital of Shanxi Province, began to recognize that Pingyao, especially its city wall, had major potential for tourism. After Pingyao was designated on UNESCO's list of World Heritage Sites in 1997, the wall instantly became a valuable landmark to preserve the ancient inner city.

The wall's role as a mere line of demarcation defining *danwei* became a thing of the past; instead, it represents an authentic heritage asset and imaginable physical setting in urban planning. Tourism was widely viewed as a way of deconstructing identities for the city of Pingyao. The intramural and extramural were marked by front stage (where *danwei* was clustered) and back stage (where the old core of the city remained intact) for a growing number of tourists. The collective memory of industrialization reflected in *danwei* has been replaced by a sense of place stimulated through conservation of heritage architecture inside the city. Karimi (2000) used the term "traditional anchor elements" to describe urban characters that possess a high degree of commercial and social meaning and accommodate major activities in a given destination. These anchor elements, such as the temple of the City God, Taoist temples, the *Wen Miao*, and main streets, initially seem to be unrelated to tourism but are affirmed by the images and representations of ancient Pingyao reproduced for domestic and international tourists (S. Wang, 2008). Heritage architecture inside the city has been subjected to insistent and prolonged pressures from government planning where old buildings can be rejuvenated for a different purpose. The political change signaled the beginning of a dramatic upheaval in how architecture was understood and practiced.

Profound changes have taken place in Pingyao since 1980 such that the wealth of heritage architecture and the wall have been recognized as important assets for local culture and heritage. Architecture was not always regarded as a formative part of the city's cultural heritage until a stream of tourists was surprised by the vernacular buildings, a reflection of Pingyao's economical and constructive apogee. The original functions of these buildings have been restored under the support of local government. For example, the *Wen Miao* was revived as the symbolic architecture in the old core of the city as the high school was relocated. The replacement of *danwei* with a commercial housing market gives local residents greater freedom of location, but it has also led to the deconstruction of communities in which work, leisure, and commerce are closely integrated (Ding & Gerrit, 2003). *Danwei* was regarded as stylistically backward in terms of the conditions and functions of housing. The areas adjacent to the wall have been transformed into a mixed-use complex as shops catering to tourism have grown exponentially.

The promotion of traditional *Jin Shang* culture, once forgotten by local residents, has become a focus for tourism planners. The film *Raise the Red Lantern* was shot in a location about 30 km from Pingyao in 1992. Despite the distance from Pingyao, the brick-walled compound and housing style featured in the film have induced many domestic tourists to visit the city (Stringer, 2001). The influence of the film was so strong that Pingyao decided to solidify the city's new image as the birthplace of red lanterns. Old buildings dealing with banks and merchants were quickly restored to ensure tourists understand the history of *Jin Shang*. Although the city itself provides little physical evidence about the nature of *Jin Shang*, it has nevertheless become a marketing tool to attract more tourists.

Urban Tourism and Commercialization (2000 to Present)

Pingyao's tourist success resides as much in the physical form of the architecture as in the methods of dissemination and promotion of that form. The induced effects of the successful film and revived regionalism have refashioned planning adjacent to the city wall. Local government has invested heavily to restore these buildings as the number of tourists has risen significantly. The heritage architecture, once occupied by local residents, has transformed into hotels or bed and breakfasts that are marketed as "living museum" for tourists. For example, the well-known Yide guesthouse was converted from a courtyard house built in 1736. It provides air conditioning, heating, and private bathrooms to accommodate tourist needs. Other courtyards have been turned into museums, such as Baichuan Tong and Rishengchang, where old banks were located.

There are two major impacts of the wall in urban tourism development in 2000s. First, by 2006, large amounts of single-story, but high-density housing that had recently begun to mushroom on the south side, began to be demolished in order to reopen views of the wall. Forces of transformation have changed the extramural areas into "green belt" to beautify the old core of the city. In the spring of 2009, a new multistory building, some 900 m west of the wall and highly visible from afar, was in the process of having four stories removed (Whitehand et al., 2011). The first impact is an increase in regulations that has resulted in the demolition or reconstruction of several buildings in the city. The strict regulations encompass building height, façade, materials, signs, and architectural designs. The local government has negotiated the reduction in height with real estate developers because the buildings reduce its visibility from the walled city.

Another tourism impact on the wall involves the traditional CBD. In contrast to Western cities, where the expansion of CBD was a major influence on the development, virtually all of the traditional CBD in Pingyao is situated along the 14th-century wall, next to a large residential zone. The concept of CBD in Pingyao has, over the last two decades and especially since the mid-1990s, become increasingly tourist oriented, to the extent that tourist trade is now its prime function. Tourism has revived the CBD area as a new commercial core to cater to tourists and provide shopping opportunities. As a result, the original *danwei* districts have further shrunk and tourism businesses have extended significantly into the interiors of street blocks.

The wall has transformed into a boundary dividing the tourism zone and the non-tourism zone. It has morphed into a marker and a gateway to define tourist flows. Residents living inside the wall, who were previously employed in other ways, are now working for tertiary sectors and traditional *danwei* units have been commercialized. There is a growing debate questioning whether the architectural renovations are truthful in the sense of originality. Cultural continuity and authenticity have become issues as an increasing number of buildings inside the wall has been turned into tourist attractions. S. Wang (2010) argued that the problem in Pingyao is whether the city retains its "spatial spirit" as its past has been rescripted to serve contemporary tourism needs. Numerous courtyard houses have been transformed to cater to the curiosity of tourists, whereas historical accuracy is of relative interest to urban planners. The temples are open for tourists for a fee where the original rituals and performance become Disneyfied. Emphasizing *Jin Shang* culture allows Pingyao to construct interesting heritage sites and architectures. However, this culture has never been materialized in reality as various stores compete for the governments' sanction as the birthplace of *Jin Shang*.

The involvement of tourism has had a profound impact on the urban setting. Figure 1 shows the evolutionary urban morphology in Pingyao since the establishment of the wall in the 14th century. The encircled wall defines *danwei* and intramural heritage architecture. The main intramural zone is a mixture of temple sites, many of them redeveloped from *danwei*, along the northwest of the walled city. There are roads bordering the city wall, particularly the roads inside the wall and outside the moat, and the other encircling roads now became practically complete ring road. With the advent of tourism, this entire zone is being beautified, notably by tree planting in areas just inside and outside the wall. Large areas of this unit were previously occupied by agriculture on the northern side, military barracks and related uses on the western side, and housing on the southern side. *Danwei* occupied the west and east sides, just outside the wall. These distinctive components have given the city a distinctive character, which should be an important consideration in determining planning priorities, especially at a time of major urban growth and accompanying pressures for urban conservation (Whitehand et al., 2011).

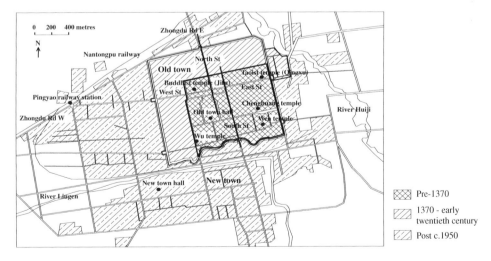

Figure 1. Urban morphology in Pingyao. *Note.* From *Chinese Urban Form: A European Perspective* (pp. 731–736), by J. W. R. Whitehand and K. Gu, 2003, Bari, Italy: Uniongrafica Corcelli Editrice.

Research Implications

Morphology in Pingyao epitomizes the shift of urban development in China. Urban transformation in Pingyao bears similarities to other Chinese cities: As in other cities, Pinyao's urbanization is marked by the emergence of a CBD and the rise of the TBD. Simultaneously, the socio-spatial template inherited from previous era, such as the influence of *danwei*, continues to shape postreform urban development (Lu, 2006). This article provides a mapping of urban transformation by highlighting tourism development, which has significantly impacted city morphology. Tourism development centered on the ancient walls should be viewed as the development of "urban tourism precincts" (Hayllar, Griffin, & Edwards, 2008, p. 9), where a number of attractions aggregate alongside tourism-related services, providing Pingyao with a particular spatial, sociocultural, economic identity. Six decades of Chinese socialist policies have altered the way Pingyao use public spaces and accommodate the growing number of tourists.

As far as the city wall is concerned, the proliferation of the *danwei* between the mid-1950s and early 1980s was exceedingly significant. Extramural development indirectly helped preserve the intramural buildings and architecture. However, spatial changes occurred as tourism became a more viable source of economic growth in the late 1980s. The ancient wall has evolved and been developed in a variety of ways and contexts ranging from the demarcation of *danwei* to the preservation of the old core of the city with a strong tourist element. The utilization of the wall in urban tourism reflects its commercial value and serves as the delimitation and symbol of the World Heritage Site. The local government's effort to reduce the number of stories in tall buildings and to increase the visibility of the walled city highlights the importance of preserving the landscape for tourism.

Although the city wall has existed for centuries, the changes inside and outside provide an interesting case study for the impact of tourism on urban morphology. The wall is an expression of cultural identity and a representation of critical regionalism in Pingyao, which increasingly becomes a neutral and interchangeable unit that facilitates tourism development. The wall should be viewed as a line of demarcation, imaginable physical setting, and a marker to define tourist flows in three different time periods. The balance between the preservation of architectural heritage and economic development has been a crucial problem. Architectural heritage sites, such as temples, have been reconverted to their original use; however, the *genius loci* has disappeared due to the encroachment of tourism. The traditional rituals and ceremonies that occurred in these temples were replaced by admission fees for a view, which have changed the meanings of these rituals. The courtyard and traditional civil dwelling houses were transformed into hotels and bed and breakfasts to cater to tourists. S. Wang (2008) suggested that historical preservations based upon the European model need to be modified in the context of China. The revisions and displacements of architectural heritage have challenged the process of preservation. Due to tourism's significance to urban planning, future studies of tourism should integrate concerns about urban morphology and vice versa. The concepts of authenticity and sense of place should be considered in tourism marketing.

The historic city of Pingyao is in a state of exceptional flux. From the morphological perspective, the urban landscape is a historical phenomenon: past, present, and future are indissolubly linked (Whitehand & Gu, 2007). In particular, intramural and extramural zones have experienced greater pressures to change for the sake of tourism development. Major urban renewal and tourism projects have taken place in both zones as a result of the dynamic relationship between a shifting economic priority and authenticity of architectural heritage. Pingyao's city wall embraces the elements of critical regionalism despite its mixed use of public spaces and responses to different governmental policies. The wall reflects a distinctive blend of urban tourism, economy, and social changes in the context of modern China.

References

AlSayyad, N. (2001). Prologue. In N. AlSayyad (Ed.), *Consuming tradition, manufacturing heritage* (pp. 1–33). New York, NY: Routledge.

Ashworth, G. (1989). Accommodation and the historic city. *Built Environment, 15*(2), 92–100.

Bégin, S. (2000). The geography of a tourist business: Hotel distribution and urban development in Xiamen, China. *Tourism Geographies, 2*(4), 448–471.

Bray, D. (2005). *Social space and governance in urban China: The danwei system from origins to reform.* Palo Alto, CA: Stanford University Press.

Burgers, J. (2000). Urban landscapes on public space in the post-industrial city. *Journal of Housing and the Built Environment, 15*(2), 145–164.

Chan, S. (2005). Temple-building and heritage in china. *Ethnology, 44*(1), 65–79.

Committee for Pingyao Gazetteer. (1999). *Pingyao xianzhi* [Gazetteer of Pingyao]. Beijing, China: Zhonghua Shuju.

Conzen, M. (2009). How cities internalize their former urban fringes: A cross-cultural comparison. *Urban Morphology, 13*(1), 29–54.

Crang, M. (2000). Urban morphology and the shaping of the transmissible city. *City, 4*(3), 303–315.

Ding, C., & Gerrit, K. (2003). Urban land policy reform in China. *Land Lines, 15*(2), 1–3.

Dong, G. (2006). *A 50-year evolutionary record of the ancient city of Beijing.* Nanjing, China: Southeast University Press.

Du, L. (2002). *History of the old town of Pingyao.* Beijing, China: Zhonghua Shuju Press.

Evans, G. (2002). Living in a world heritage city: Stakeholders in the dialectic of universal and particular. *International Journal of Heritage Studies, 8*(2), 117–135.

Frampton, K. (1983). Toward a critical regionalism: Six points for an architecture of resistance. In H. Foster (Ed.), *The anti-aesthetic: Essays on postmodern culture* (pp. 16–30). Seattle, WA: Bay Press.

Gilbert, E. (1949). The growth of Brighton. *The Geographical Journal, 114*(1/3), 30–52.

Gospodini, A. (2001). Urban design, urban space morphology, urban tourism: An emerging new paradigm concerning their relationship. *European Planning Studies, 9*(7), 925–934.

Gospodini, A. (2004). Urban morphology and place identity in European cities: Built heritage and innovative design. *Journal of Urban Design, 9*(2), 225–248.

Gu, H., & Ryan, C. (2008). Place attachment, identity and community impacts of tourism—The case of a Beijing Hutong. *Tourism Management, 29*(4), 637–647.

Gu, K. (2001). Urban morphology of China in the post-socialist age: Towards a framework for analysis. *Urban Design International, 6*(3/4), 125–142.

Hayllar, B., Griffin, T., & Edwards, D. (2008). *City spaces—Tourist places: Urban tourism precincts.* Oxford, England: Butterworth-Heinemann.

Herr, C. (1996). *Critical regionalism and cultural studies.* Gainesville, FL: University Press of Florida.

Hollinshead, K. (1999). Tourism as public culture: Horne's ideological commentary on the legerdemain of tourism. *International Journal of Tourism Research, 1*, 267–292.

Jansen-Verbeke, M., & Lievois, E. (1999). Analysing heritage resources for urban tourism in European cities. In R. Butler & D. Pearce (Eds.), *Contemporary issues in tourism development* (pp. 81–107). London, England: Routledge.

Karimi, K. (2000). Urban conservation and spatial transformation: Preserving the fragments or maintaining the "spatial spirit." *Urban Design International, 5*(3–4), 221–231.

Knapp, R. (2000). *China's walled cities*. Oxford, England: Oxford University Press.

Lasansky, M., & McLaren, B. (2004). *Architecture and tourism: Perception, performance and place*. New York, NY: Berg Publishers.

Le, J. (2005). *History of Chinese architecture*. Beijing, China: Tuanjie Press.

Liu, J., & Wall, G. (2009). Resort morphology research: History and future perspectives. *Asia Pacific Journal of Tourism Research, 14*(4), 339–350.

Liu, J., Zhan, J., & Deng, X. (2005). Spatial-temporal patterns and driving forces of urban land expansion in China during economic reform era. *Journal of Human Environment, 34*(6), 450–455.

Lu, D. (2006). *Remaking Chinese urban form*. New York, NY: Routledge.

Moudon, A. (1997). Urban morphology as an emerging interdisciplinary field. *Urban Morphology, 1*, 3–10.

Ouf, A. (2001). Authenticity and the sense of place in urban design. *Journal of Urban Design, 6*(1), 73–86.

Pingyao Development and Reform Bureau. (2009). *Report on the completion of a comprehensive environmental remedy project (first phase) for the fringe area of the ancient city of Pingyao*. Unpublished manuscript.

Pingyao Urban and Rural Planning Bureau. (2006). *Reflections on the performance of Pingyao Urban and Rural Planning Bureau*. Unpublished manuscript.

Powell, D. (2007). *Critical regionalism*. Chapel Hill, NC: The University of North Carolina Press.

Ruan, Y. (2003). *Documenting urban conservation*. Beijing, China: Zhongguo Jianzhu Gongye Press.

Samuel, R. (1994). *Theatres of memory*. London, England: Verso.

Shanxi Research Institute of Urban and Rural Planning and Design. (2005). *Pingyao gucheng baohu jianjie* [A brief introduction to city conservation in Pingyao]. Unpublished manuscript.

Smith, M. (2002). A critical evaluation of the global accolade: The significance of world heritage site status for Maritime Greenwich. *International Journal of Heritage Studies, 8*(2), 137–151.

Stringer, J. (2001). Global cities and the international film festivel economy. In M. Shiel and T. Fitzmaurice (Eds.), *Cinema and the city* (pp. 134–144). Oxford, UK: Blackwell Publishers.

Tzonis, A., & Lefaivre, L. (1990). Why critical regionalism today. *A & U Architecture and Urbanism, 236*(5), 23–33.

Vance, J. (1990). *The continuing city: Urban morphology in Western civilization*. Baltimore, MD: John Hopkins University Press.

Wang, J., Ruan, Y., & Wang, L. (1999). *The theories of historical urban preservation*. Shanghai, China: Tongji University Press.

Wang, S. (2008). A mirror with two sides: Heritage development and urban conservation in the ancient city of Pingyao, China. *Historic Environment, 21*(3), 22–26.

Wang, S. (2010). *In search of authenticity in historic cities in transformation: The case of Pingyao, China* (Asia Research Institute Working Paper Series No. 133). Singapore: National University of Singapore.

Whitehand, J. W. R. (1992). Recent advances in urban morphology. *Urban Studies, 29*(3/4), 619–636.

Whitehand, J. W. R., & Gu, K. (2003). Chinese urban form: A European perspective. In A. Petruccioli, M. Stella, & G. Strappa (Eds.), *The planned city?* (pp. 731–736). Bari, Italy: Uniongrafica Corcelli Editrice.

Whitehand, J. W. R., & Gu, K. (2007). Extending the compass of plan analysis: A Chinese exploration. *Urban Morphology, 11*(2), 91–109.

Whitehand, J. W. R., Gu, K., & Whitehand, S. (2011). Fringe belts and socio-economic change in China. *Environment and Planning B, 38*(1), 41–60.

Xie, P. (2003). Managing aboriginal tourism in Hainan, China: Governmental perspectives. *Annals of Leisure Research, 6*(3), 279–302.

Xie, Y., & Costa, F. (1991). Urban design practice in socialist China. *Third World Planning Review, 13*(3), 277–296.

Xiong, W. (2003). *Pingyao: The living ancient city* (Unpublished master's thesis). Texas Tech University, Lubbock, TX.

Xu, Y. (2000). *The Chinese city in space and time: The development of urban form in Suzhou.* Honolulu, HI: University of Hawaii Press.

Yan, X. (1995). Chinese urban geography since the late 1970s. *Urban Geography, 16*(6), 469–492.

Zhang, H., Chong, K., & Ap, J. (1999). An analysis of tourism policy development in modern China. *Tourism Management, 20*(4), 471–485.

Zhang, Y. (2008). Steering towards growth: Symbolic urban preservation in Beijing, 1990–2005. *Town Planning Review, 79*, 187–208.

The Impacts of Heritage Tourism on Public Space in Historic Towns: A Case Study of Lijiang Ancient Town

Xiao-bo Su* , Chun-yuan Huang

National University of Singapore

Abstract:

Heritage tourism is increasingly important to the historic towns in China. It has become a crucial force to boost the local economy and prompt urban conservation. Up to now most of the literature about the impacts of heritage tourism concerns the cultural and social aspects of heritage sites but seldom addresses the issue of public space, especially the impacts of tourism on human activities and public space in terms of harmony and compatibility, which is one of the key issues concerning the heritage authenticity. This paper uses Lijiang Ancient Town of Yunnan province as an example to explore the impacts of heritage tourism on the public space of heritage sites from a commercial perspective. The data are mainly collected through in-depth interviews and on-site observations. It is argued that the profit-driven heritage tourism often leads to the dissociation of the harmony and compatibility between human activities and public space in the process of commodification. This directly results in the lost of cultural and social significance in public space and museumization. It also influences the authenticity of Lijiang Ancient Town as a world heritage site. Therefore, heritage tourism should not aim at making a profit alone, but should strengthen the compatibility between human activities and public space and enhance the social and cultural significance of public space.

* Corresponding author

Xiao-bo Su, PhD candidate, Department of Geography, National University of Singapore, Email: suxiaobo_2000@yahoo.com.

Chun-yuan Huang, Master candidate, Lee Kuan Yew School of Public Policy, National University of Singapore, Email: chy_huang@yahoo.com.cn.

1. Introduction

In a broader sense, urban public space refers to the space which is open to the use by all instead of certain groups of people; particularly, it is the space in which people can conduct social activities and it includes streets, squares, parks, green fields, mountains and streams (Liang & Wu, 1998). Lynch (1960) defines the legibility of urban public space as the following five elements: paths, edges, districts, nodes and landmarks. According to Lynch, local residents and visitors will be able to identify urban public space with the help of these five elements. Most of the existing historic towns in China are small but embody a high density of buildings, lacking green fields and parks. Squares are usually combined with streets. In addition, no great mountains can be found in these towns because they are built on plateaus. This paper mainly focuses on urban space in its narrow sense, i.e. the streets, streams, courtyards and buildings defining urban space in historic towns. These are the main components of heritage in historic towns (Lu, 2001).

The public space in historic towns is very different from that of a metropolis. Compared with modern metropolises, the public space in historic towns are able to demonstrate local culture and traditions and provide the local people with many places for socialization. Thus, community culture can be widely acknowledged and passed on to the future generations. The harmonious living environments of historic towns offer people who live in metropolitan cities a place to escape temporarily from their hectic life. In addition, the historical significance embedded in public space can raise a sense of nostalgia. Therefore, historic towns can attract a large number of tourists (Bao & Su, 2004). For example, Zhouzhuang, a small town with an area of 0.24km^2 in Jiangsu province, received 2.08 million tourists in 2001 (Zhou, 2002). Commodification is a direct impact of huge tourist flows to historic towns. Many tourist-oriented businesses are thus established, leading to the collapse of the original commercial structure and the alteration of cities' nature. The impacts of these changes on both public space and the everyday life of local people in historic towns are unpredictable. Taking Lijiang Ancient Town in Yunnan province as the example, this paper explores the impacts of heritage tourism on public space by analyzing the transformation of commercial structure and urban function in the process of commodification. The main argument is that with the maximization of economic profit as a main objective, heritage tourism would distract the harmony between public space and human activities, undermine the socio-cultural meanings of public space and lead to museumization of historic towns.

2. Literature Review and Data Collection

Urban Heritage Tourism

A number of scholars have studied the impacts of tourism on historic towns. In general, they believe that many historic towns are facing culture shocks and other changes while achieving economic growth (Frenkel & Walton, 2000; Moore, 1995; Parlett, Fletcher, & Cooper. 1995). For instance, Hoyle (2001) argues that tourism played a significant role in regenerating the waterfront area in the town of Lamu but also aroused a lot of controversy in relation to exploitation, cultural attrition and occasional violence due to the juxtaposition of wealthy visitors and poor locals. Jamison (1999) studies the relationship between tourism and ethnicity in Malindi, a small town with a population of 35,000 in Kenya, stressing that tourism is a vehicle for the locals to re-interpret their identity, especially for those who rely on tourism or whose businesses are influenced by tourism. In addition, the impacts of tourism on the business environment in destinations are also widely studied. In the case study of Stone Town in Zanzibar, Marks (1996) analyzes the contradiction and uncertainty of tourism, with findings showing that between 1983 and 1993 when the place was being developed as a destination, commercial land use rose three times and economic benefits prompted the building of private houses which accounted for nearly 10% of the total number of houses. Moreover, considerable overseas and domestic investment was generated by the tourism industry in Stone Town, giving rise to the rapid growth of hotels and guesthouses. New buildings and commercial activities exerted tremendous pressure on the limited land and infrastructure of the town, resulting in inflating land price and construction costs. However, Pearce (1999) investigates the relationship between the land price and the retail shop-owners' attitude and behavior along one of the sightseeing roads in Christchurch in New Zealand and comes to the conclusion that the renovation of the sightseeing road has limited impacts on the land price and urban restoration of Christchurch. These case studies provide various viewpoints of the role of heritage tourism in urban development. However, as far as urban conservation is concerned, the aforementioned studies only concern the socio-cultural aspects, without touching the topic of public space, let alone exploring the harmony between public space and human activities.

In the process of urban conservation and tourism development, the conflicts between conservation and development are always difficult to resolve. The main reason is that during urban conservation, the facades of historic buildings are often embellished in order to emphasize their appearances; the embellishment of these buildings are mainly done for tourism purpose without considering the traditional community life, resulting in damaging the authenticity of heritage (Maclaren & Des, 2001). The historic district in Singapore is a typical example. Having analyzed the dilemma of conservation and redevelopment in Kampong Glam, Yeoh and Huang (1996, p. 421), point out that:

> *"Conflict arises because gazetted monuments and conservation areas often slice up the organic form and texture of cultural hearths in an arbitrary fashion, legislating boundaries between a defended zone perceived to be of historical value and an excluded landscape which is threatened with excision."*

In the case of the Chinatown in Singapore, Henderson (2000) argues that to a certain extent, the authenticity of many physical heritages can be maintained after renovation, but it is not easy to restore the traditional lifestyle prevailing in the streets. Not only the locals, but also tourists are unwilling to return to the previous congested condition. However, the problem is that what kind of authenticity and whose authenticity should be presented to tourists. Government officials and the tourism board intend to create an environment which preserves the past and displays the tradition in a compromising fashion. However, as Henderson (2000) states, the authenticity of Chinatown has been carefully selected or even twisted to avoid widespread disputes and censure of the citizens. This model may make Chinatown more attractive to tourists and they will be willing to spend time and money in Singapore, but hardly strengthen the sense of place among Singaporeans.

The abovementioned conflicts between conservation and development also exist in Lijiang Ancient Town. Tourism has brought both positive and negative socio-cultural impacts to the town after tourism began to experience rapid growth in 1996. Yang (2002) explores the tourism industry and the fate of the town, arguing that due to commodification, the town and the local Naxi culture is facing unprecedented culture clashes from the outside world and the risk of museumization. Studying the transformation of Naxi music in the context of tourism development, Yang (2001) accentuates that the Naxi music "exists only in the commercial context". As the Regional Advisor for Culture in Asia Pacific of UNESCO, Peters (2001) examines the conflicts between tourism and cultural heritage conservation in Lijiang from an anthropological perspective, pointing out that treating cultural tourism as a new way to boost the economy will contribute to the uncoupling of tourism and conservation. The reasons, according to Peters, include: 1) the local traditional lifestyle is under the threat of tourism; 2) the local economy tends to rely on tourism; and 3) the revenue generated from tourism cannot cover the heritage conservation costs.

Until now, there is limited literature on the impacts of tourism on the environment of historic towns, especially the physical landscapes. Many studies of urban tourism concentrate on employment, tourist consumption and tourist behaviour (Parlett et al., 1995; Pearce, 1999; Stabler, 1998). Research on the impacts of tourism on urban regions is not common and the actual effect of tourism on urban development and restoration has seldom been verified. One of the main reasons is that it is a very complicated and difficult task to evaluate the overall impact of tourism on cities (Law, 1992; Lutz & Ryan, 1996; Stabler, 1998). Law (1992, p. 607) further argues that "most impact studies are limited to economic matters. They rarely consider the impact upon the renewal of the physical environment, the role of visitors in maintaining or creating amenities valued by residents…". From the perspective of commodification, the paper analyzes the impacts of heritage tourism on the public space of historic towns and provides an insight to the interaction between tourism development and urban conservation.

Data Collection

The data are mainly collected from on-site observations conducted in March, 2003, September to December, 2004 and June, 2005. The main research methods include in-depth interviews and participant observation with the purpose of exploring the relationship between human activities and public space in Lijiang. The interviewees covered local residents, tourists, tourism managers and government officials. The average duration for the interviews varied from 50 to 90 minutes and the total number of respondents was 20. In addition, some key respondents were interviewed more than once. Questions such as how they comprehend public space and how they evaluate the change of public space in the process of tourism development were discussed. All the interviews were permitted to be recorded and were transcribed afterward by the authors in order to obtain accurate answers. On-site observation was conducted in two ways: one was to gain hands on experience of the public space in Lijiang Ancient Town by the authors and the other was to observe how business owners, residents and tourists make use of public space. During this process, more than 1,200 photos were taken to capture the relationship between human activities and public space. Apart from these first-hand data, secondary source such as newspaper articles and related literature were used to gather the information.

3. The Characteristics of Traditional Public Space in Lijiang Ancient Town

This paper examines Dayan ancient town, also commonly known as Lijiang Ancient Town in Lijiang County. Historically, the town was an important economic and political centre of the Naxi ethnic minority group. Located in the northwest of Yunnan Province, the town was built between the end of Song Dynasty and the beginning of Yuan Dynasty (the end of the 12th century to the middle of the13th century) with an area of 3.8km². The distinctive character of the town, according to Jiang (1997), is that streams and streets intermingled together. To the north of the town lies the Black Dragon Pool which is the main water source of the town. The water makes its way from the north to the south until reaching the entrance of the town where the water is subdivided into three tributaries flowing to the east, the middle and the west. These three tributaries link up the entire town. Sifang Square is the centre of the town and together with the five main streets of Xinghua, Wuyi, Qiyi, Xingyi and Guangyi, they form a framework which extend to all parts of the town. The residential buildings represent the architectural style of Naxi. The Naxi architecture has absorbed the characteristics of the architectural styles of Han, Bai and Tibet with the Naxi traditional Jing-gan style (log-cabin construction) of wooden houses as the basis (Jiang). The typical family dwellings are "three gabled buildings with a garden wall" and "four abodes with five patios" (Zhu, 1988). Due to the unique cultural background and townscape, Lijiang Ancient Town has been inscribed on the list of World Cultural Heritage Site by UNESCO in December 1997 and become a must-see attraction in Lijiang city.

In traditional unplanned towns, the self-determined configuration of urban space clearly reflects the collective behavior and ideology of the locals. The construction activities in which the whole communities involve ensure the continuation of traditional experiences. Therefore, harmonious combination of the public space and the natural environment, the organic succession of urban forms and the co-ordination and consistency of setting and environment constitute a satisfactory spatial structure. The public space in Lijiang Ancient Town has been existed for several hundreds of years. It was determined by the governing body and the grass roots and conformed to the pattern of an organic city (Wang, 1999). Even now, one can still easily recognize the features of the streets and lanes and be affected by the uniqueness and characteristics of the public space, especially the streets, streams and courtyards.

Street and Stream

As a core and tangible component in historic towns, the street plays an important role in organizing the sights and is a space with complex and interrelated meanings (Lillebye, 1996). Through "reading" the signs of streetscape, people can experience the cultural dynamics of historic towns: the citizens, their social relationships, behavior and psychology, and the long-accumulated cultural connotations (Zhou & Ma, 1993). In the town, the doors of the shops and houses at the sides of the streets can be disassembled, thus extending the space of passers-by's activities into the houses and residents' activities on the streets. This results in the formation of mixed value-added spaces, encouraging people to socialize on the streets and intermingle with indoor human activities. Streets then become the extension of private life as well as places for public activities. Through the transportation network, streets not only construct a harmonious neighborhood, but also a social network with multiple functions including habitation, production, shopping and relaxation (Zhou & Ma). In general, the width of the streets in Lijiang Ancient Town ranges from 3.5 to 5 meters, a pleasant scale. The height of one-storey buildings along the streets is about 2.5 to 2.8 meters and that of two-storey buildings is 5 meters. The proportion of the width and height is appropriate; people will feel enclosed but not packed together when walking on the streets. The streets allow people to keep a distance of 1.5 meters from each other to avoid a sense of insecurity when walking by strangers. Therefore, the functions of streets in Lijiang include: laying out and linking up the entire town, providing space for organizing social activities, presenting the natural features of the landscape, displaying visual images of art and the characters of public space (Jiang, 1997).

The streets and streams are the skeleton and essence of the public space in Lijiang Ancient Town. The water runs through the streets, blurring the boundaries between the fluid and the solid. People can either appreciate the flowing water or converse with others without feeling bored and idling around. Table 1 elaborates the features of water in the town. From the Table, it is clear that water has been incorporated into the public space and attaches great importance to the community. The water in Lijiang Ancient Town is the reason why it is called 'the town of canals in highland'. The bridges, flowing water and Naxi people are most appealing for tourists.

Table 1. The Features of Water in Lijiang

Water and streams in the town	Functions	Features			
		Landscape	Intimacy	Nature	History
Inflow of Water	Moistening the air, extinguish fire	Integrating with everyday life	People can feel the existence of water	The flowing of water reflects vibrancy of the town	
Configuration	Forming the layout of the town, adding variety and amusement	Interweaving with streets	Running through courtyards, streets and alleys	The sound of water gives a sense of "nature"	The most distinguished feature
Incorporation into the environment	Creating space for public activities	An important part of everyday life	Activities near the canals improve interpersonal relationships	Forming a complete water system	The core of everyday life in the town
Enhancement of cultural significance	Increasing a sense of place and belonging	Part of historic landscape			An important element in social history and the history of the town

Adapted from (Zhao, 1995)

Courtyard

Since China experienced a long history of feudalism, the residential structure in the town also underwent a sluggish and inflexible development process. Eventually, courtyard-style houses were formed, which are confined and enclosed. An enclosed courtyard can create a kind of private, peaceful and safe living environment. The outside of the residential houses in Lijiang may look like humble walls or shops, but inside the courtyards is a vibrant and colorful environment in which the Naxi people actually live. This environment also reflects Naxi people's adoration of life and their belief that life is eternal like the natural environment (Jiang, 1997). Naxi people have a passion for gardening. They take it as a way to approach the nature and beautify their surroundings for relaxation. In addition, a courtyard is also an important public space for family gatherings, wedding parties and neighbor visits. In the words of a local lady, a courtyard "is an open soul, but leaves certain privacy to oneself. That is to say, it is like a self-owned land containing rich cultural meanings and one's feelings as well" (personal interview, 2004-10-18).

4. The Impacts of Tourism Commodification on Public Space

The direct impacts of tourism on Lijiang Ancient Town is commodification. After 1996, the town became well-known all over the world and the local government made endeavor to boost tourism. As a result, Lijiang attracted a huge number of visitors. In 2004, tourist arrivals reached 3.6 million (Lijiang Statistic Bureau, 2005). One of the authors investigated the functions of buildings along the main streets in the town in August 2002 and found that among the total 979 units surveyed, 69.66% targeted tourists as customers, 19.92% targeted both tourists and the locals and 10.42% the locals, in the approximate proportion 7:2:1. Therefore, it is found that an approximate 90% of commercial units were related to tourism of which about 70% directly related to tourism. The commercial units in the town were largely dependant on tourism and bear high relevance to tourism (Bao & Su, 2004). Bao and Su define this kind of commercial phenomenon driven by tourism as tourism commodification because "the number of tourist shops is large enough to outnumber the shops that target the locals as customers and the goods are beyond the locals' purchasing power" (Bao & Su, p. 428).

Heritage Tourism and Commodification in Lijiang Ancient Town

The business environment under commodification is clearly different from the traditional business environment in Lijiang Ancient Town. Goullart (1955, p. 33) went into details to describe the bars and open markets in the town during the 1940s, reflecting the relations between the customers and the shop-owners:

> "Anyone could have a drink at any shop, but some villagers acquired preferences for particular shops. These regular and faithful customers grew intimate with the lady owner and always gave her the first option on whatever they were bringing to the market for sale. Similarly the lady favored them with special discounts on whatever they wanted to buy from her. Actually their relations were beyond clients and shop-owner. The lady also acted as their broker, banker, postmaster and confidante".

From Goullart's description, it can be seen that the commercial environment was very good. The relationship between customers and shop-owners and among shop-owners is very friendly; they make a living together. Such integrity rooted in the commercial culture is closely related to the Naxi culture since in reality Naxi people are practical and realistic, faithful, courteous and value etiquette. However, with the rapid growth of tourism in 1996, this commercial integrity has changed dramatically under the influence of the tourism industry and foreign businessmen. A survey was conducted in March 2003 to investigate randomly the price of a tourism commodity,

Panasonic 2CR5, a special kind of battery for cameras in 7 shops of different locations (Table 2). The prices in brackets refer to the prices offered by shop-owners after bargaining.

Table 2. The Price List of 2CR5

Location	Guanmen Entrance (local)	Tianyuliufang Gateway (non-local)	In front of Mufu Palace (non-local)	Dongda Street (non-local)	Cuiwen Lane (non-local)	A Cake Shop in Dongda Street (local)	Xinyi Street (local)
Unit Price (Yuan)	50	68	58 (50)	68 (60)	50 (45)	48	75
Price marked	yes	no	no	no	yes	yes	no

It can be seen from Table 2 that the 4 shops which did not mark the price of the battery were all operated by non-locals. Uncertain price inflicted risks on tourist consumption and the quality of the battery could not be guaranteed. According to a camera shop-owner who sold the same type of Konica battery at the entrance of the town said that most of the Panasonic 2CR5 batteries sold in the town were counterfeit. A tourist who has visited Lijiang for several times complained:

> "Integrity is used to be the most important aspect of doing business in Lijiang, but this is not the case any more. Fake goods such as sliver ware and jewellery are everywhere. I am not saying that there are no genuine goods here, but they are too hard to find" (Personal interview, 2004-10-14).

A Taiwanese shop-owner also pointed out that "more and more fake goods are sold here" (personal interview, 2004-10-14). With the growth of tourism, an increasing number of foreign merchants are flowing into the town while local business owners are leaving the town at the same time (Yamamura, 2004). The merchants in the town are no longer honest, although it is a violation of the traditional Naxi culture.

A further comparison of the commercial environment in different periods can illustrate the impingement of tourism on Lijiang Ancient Town. The commercial activity of Lijiang has its most glorious time in the Tea-horse route during the Second World War. Various historical documents have recorded the flourishing commercial activities at that time, such as the text quoted above from Goullart. Table 3 compares the commercial environment between the Tea-horse route period and the present under tourism commodification, showing that the local commerce has almost dismantled and has been superseded by tourist-oriented services and commodities. The nature of the town has also changed in response to the change. Although the physical elements of public space like streets, streams and courtyards still exist in the town, the living landscapes-human activities-are totally altered. A Naxi scholar in the town expressed his anxieties:

> *"As far as the current situation is concerned, the number of aboriginal residents in the town is decreasing. This historic town is nothing but an empty shell although this Wuyi Street, the street we are now living in, has basically retained its authentic appearance. In the past we frequently came across our friends and acquaintances on the street; now we can't be sure if we can run into one because many of them have moved out of the town to some remote places. ...we don't celebrate the traditional festivals (in the town) any more, which definitely causes negative impacts on preserving our traditional culture and ethnic language"* (Personal interview 2005-06-24).

The disappearance of acquaintances and friends and traditional festivals, which are the important elements of community life, will speed up the formation of an 'empty shell'. On the other hand, a huge influx of tourists and foreign merchants, as well as tourism commodification give rise to numerous unfaithful businesses which go against the traditional Naxi culture. The combination of these changes speed up the formation of museumization of public space in Lijiang Ancient Town.

Table 3 The comparison of Lijiang's commercial environment in different periods

	Present situation under tourism commodification	Tea-horse route period
Number of shops	Over 1000	More than 1200 at the peak
Shop size	Apart from hotels, the shops are small with limited fixed capital and liquidity	Large-scale businesses and over 20 shops had branches outside the town
Main commodities	Tourism products	Daily necessities, Chinese medicine, sliver and bronze ware
Main customers	Tourists	Peasants, local inhabitants, Tibetans, Xiaguan, Kunming and foreign traders
Features of customers	Lack of trust on merchants; seldom revisiting leading to low degree of customer loyalty; strong purchasing power; monotonous purchasing habit	Strong faith and customer loyalty; buying various goods necessary for daily use
Features of merchants	Mainly non-locals with poor credibility; poor relationship with their clients	Mainly locals with credibility; close relationship with their clients

	Present situation under tourism commodification	Tea-horse route period
Features of the town	Attracting many tourists; being used by merchants for tourist businesses; commercial activities are disconnected with the locals, resulting in the lack of vitality in the town	Because of the special geographic location and cultural background of Lijiang, numerous traders and peasants went to Lijiang to do business, which dealt with the locals' everyday life
Role of the town	Tourist attraction; carrier of tourism businesses	A junction in the Tea-horse route; a carrier of trade and commerce
Nature of the town	Tourist city	Commercial city; suitable for living

Source: Geng, 2000

Commodification and Museumization of Public Space

A city is a place of collective memory. The memory of different components of a city can provide major leads to understand the whole urban structure (Yang & Wu, 1999). Wars, disasters and foreign cultures in the past altered Lijiang Ancient Town. However, the local people are under the deep influence of the Naxi culture, which enabled them to rebuild their ruined hometown and incorporate other cultures into their own to reconstruct the town. Due to the Naxi culture, the town continues to retain its appearance and in turn, functions as a tradition bearer of the Naxi culture. In every region, an ethnic group's cultural tradition and its evolution will exert impacts on urban space distribution and development, resulting in the formation of unique cultural characteristics of urban space. These characteristics may be reflected in the physical landscapes which bear and sustain the local history and culture on the one hand; on the other hand, these characteristics will be developed according to the alteration of residents' behavior and their cultural value. In return, the urban space will affect the behavior and cultural value of the people living in it. During tourism growth, a huge number of tourism businesses have been set up in Lijiang Ancient Town. They not only changed the town's commercial function, but also have immense impacts on the town's public space such as streets, streams and courtyards.

Street

The decorations used for better displaying commodities and services have changed the building facades and the connotation of the streets. For those shops which are unable to afford large-scale marketing activities, signboards, different ways of displaying commodities and extending the shopfront are some of the effective means to lure customers. Under the current policies and regulations, shop owners can advertise their goods by putting up signboards to distinguish themselves from others, using English, Chinese and Dongba languages on signboards, displaying goods on glass shelves, using high-powered lights at nights and so on. These strategies over-emphasize the commodities sold in shops, thus reducing the exposure of historic buildings and weakening the building's role on the streets. The buildings are nothing more than walls and the space enclosed by the walls on the streets. In addition, shop owners have strong intention of delineating their proprietary space and strengthening their right to use the buildings once they rent them, thus discouraging the expansion of activities on the streets into the buildings. A wide variety of goods arouses a sense of compression and uneasiness. The whole streets are converted into public passages and shopping areas which are filled with restlessness and indifference prevailing in the modern commercial world and lack local cultural connotations (see Figure 1 and Figure 2). Miss He, a Naxi lady who mentioned that she found the streets 'a little irritating' because:

> *"...this is not Lijiang. It's too crowded. Previously the town was quiet. You could easily tell who was a stranger and who was a local on the streets. Now it is impossible. Eight people out of ten you run into are tourists and only two are locals. That is why you get the feeling that there are fewer Naxi people now in the town" (Personal interview 2004-11-9).*

A tourist from Beijing pointed out directly that "there is no difference between the town and a shopping mall except that it has no skyscrapers in it. As time passed, no one will be interested in visiting a town like this" (personal interview 2004-10-20).

Figure 1 Guanmenkou of Qiyi Street

Figure 2 The Streetscape of Dongda Street

Congestion and noise lead to the deterioration of public space quality and the inhabitants have to use the public space less frequent. The noise and polluted air produced by flocks of people on the streets make it difficult for the residents and tourists to stop for a while. It is observed that apart from Sifang Square where some tourists would stop walking and take a rest, people on other main streets would not stop except for taking photos occasionally. According to Mr. Tang, a local resident:

> *"Life in the town was peaceful and quiet (when I was young). But now, I would rather take the small lanes than the main streets. If I have to run some errands, I prefer the small lanes that people seldom use and then take the same route back. ... Previously, you could buy anything you need in the busy main streets (in the town). But now, all you can find are tourism commodities. If I need to buy daily necessities, I have to take a bus and walk for a long time"* (Personal interview 2004-10-08).

On the other hand, the buildings along the main streets had been carefully restored in order to demonstrate the Naxi architectural culture to visitors. Aiming at applying for the title of world cultural heritage site, on August 9, 1996, the Lijiang County government determined to demolish the buildings which are violating the town's value. The plan was to "demolish all buildings made of concrete or brick along Dongda street and rebuild them according to the Naxi architectural style" ("Gucheng Dongda Street," 1996). In fact, the facades of these redeveloped buildings are more exquisitely and skillfully built than the original Naxi buildings, with the purpose of displaying the Naxi culture. However, these buildings are separated from the community as they serve for tourism functions only. Public space serves for tourists and merchants rather than the local residents and gradually detaches itself from the local society and culture. In addition, the role that public space plays as the carrier of the Naxi culture has started to fade away.

Stream

Streams facilitate the local residents' everyday life and are the main water source for daily usage and fire service. There are many wells in different places of the town. Water surfaces and the streets are level, "forming space for the locals to engage in public activities which encourage harmonious interpersonal relationships" (Yan & Li, 2002, p. 3). However, the water quality in streams is deteriorating. The environmental monitoring report in June 1, 2003 revealed that the water quality index of the river upstream of the town entrance was 65, which belonged to the third category and indicated that the water was slightly polluted; the water index of downstream dropped to 30, which belonged to the fifth category, meaning the water was seriously polluted ("Water Environment," 2003). According to this report, the streams were severely contaminated when flowing downstream through the town. The water is no longer suitable for daily usage; instead it becomes an important ornament of the town ("Yao Rang Gucheng," 2004). The harmonious scenes that residents socialize beside the streams are disappearing and are replaced by tourists jamming along the streams to take photos, drink beer or twiddle their thumbs. The bars in Cuiwen Lane and Shuangshi Lane alongside the western river adjacent to Sifang Square are particularly serious. The dinning tables of the bars are so packed that the view of the river is completely blocked. The high consumption and hubbub put many locals, especially the elderly off going there to enjoy the beautiful scene of the river.

Streams are also culture carriers, but this function is gradually weakening. For example, residents in the town are accustomed to releasing lights in streams as a way to memorize their ancestors during Zhongyuan festival in mid June of the Lunar calendar. In May 2000, a government-owned company, Naxi Cultural Development Company determined to package this festival as a tourism program in order to fully exploit Lijiang's cultural resources and encourage tourist participation. The company arranged to sell stream lights every night in different locations of the town at a price of 10 yuan per unit. However, the stream light activity of the senior residents organized every year by the Xinghua Street committee was cancelled in 2004. According to a staff of the committee, "there is no need for us to organize this kind of activity any more since the company organizes this activity every day" (personal interview 2004-11-03). A local resident commented that "now every day is Zhongyuan festival; the cultural atmosphere is destroyed". However, a manager of the company held a different viewpoint:

> *"This problem is not about the concept of the festival, but how you understand it. ... We only concern how to encourage tourists to take part in our traditional activities in the long term. ... If we didn't embark on this project, or this commercial activity to introduce this local cultural activity, no one would have the chance to see it any more. In my opinion, the cultural industry is to preserve the culture by using economic means" (Personal interview 2004-11-2).*

To the local residents, releasing stream lights does not have cultural significance any more. Also, the possibility of expressing this cultural tradition via public space is very remote. In fact, releasing stream lights has become an instrument to demonstrate the 'Naxi culture' to tourists and make a profit. This demonstration, however, has disassociated with the territorial significance of Naxi society. Streams as a form of public space have become a carrier of commercial culture for quick profits. This kind of commercial culture also influences individual resident's behavior and willingness through public space, drifting them and their own tradition apart.

Courtyard

The residential readjustment for tourism radically changes the original feature of courtyard-style houses. With the growth of tourism, the strong demands for shops along the streets force many residents to rebuild their houses. As a result, the houses along the streets are turned into shopfronts which are mostly rented by non-local merchants. When the walls along streets are pulled down to become shopfronts, it makes great changes to the whole building. Previously, what behind the shopfronts were living rooms or bedrooms used and owned by families. Now in order to lease out the units, the whole buildings are divided into several parts and the doors to inner courtyards are bolted for different commercial usage (see Figure 3). Pulling down the walls and bolting the doors divide the whole residential houses into parts, thus losing the original features and the completeness of courtyards. To adapt to the tourism development, residential houses are being renovated, regardless of whether it is done for the sake of function or embellishment. The most crucial alteration is that the previously inner private living space becomes an exposed commercial space. A female tourist from Hunan Province pointed out:

> *"There were many well-preserved buildings in the town. However, because of tourism and the building of guesthouses, these buildings were used to achieve their commercial values. The previous architectural spaces were damaged to some extent. In the process of renovation, the original historical significance is vanished substantially. I suppose this is impossible to avoid"* (Personal interview 2004-10-16).

Figure 3 The alteration of residential houses along the streets in Lijiang Ancient Town

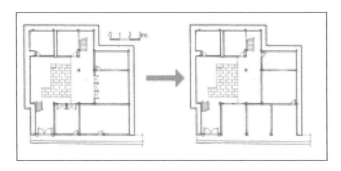

Source: Gao, 1997

The cleavage of residential buildings leads to the disappearance of private space. The noise and pollution brought by the huge influx of tourists and the encroachment of tourist consumption and visit on the resident's private life directly affect the inhabitants of the town. Mr. Yang, a local resident told us a story of his neighbor:

"Since the people moving in are total strangers with different social backgrounds, you can't trust them too easily. For example, there is a bar directly opposite to our houses and it opens until 1 to 2 in the morning. It creates much noise and tumult that my neighbor had to move out (to a new city), though he carefully retained his traditional lifestyle and cherished his own house very much" (Personal interview 2004-10-18).

The vanishing of public space makes it highly difficult for people to communicate with each other. Without private space and socialization, people lose internal balance. Escaping to a new city is a good alternative because at least one can be guaranteed an enclosed private space.

Apart from the direct negative impacts of tourism, leasing houses to foreign merchants is another influential factor which causes the local residents to leave Lijiang Ancient Town. However, some locals, especially those senior residents, would like to return to their courtyards to sit back and enjoy the sunshine while reminiscing the life that they had lost. Mr. He, an old Naxi folk moved out to settle down in a new city after he signed a 10-year contract with a couple from Hebei Province to rent them his house as a guesthouse in September 2004. The guesthouse owner said, "The landlord is very friendly. The old couple frequently visits here to chat with us. But we are not very close" (Personal interview 2004-11-24). With regard to why he comes here frequently, the old man mentioned: "I like here. Previously I came to the town every day. But later I couldn't make it because it took me around half an hour to get to the town from where I live now. The new city is very cold. As to the town, it has more than 800 years of history. So it is a very good place. The wind is not strong here, beautiful sunshine in the courtyard and the water is better. It's cold and the wind is strong there (the new city)" (Personal interview 2004-11-24). There are many other similar cases like this. Another Naxi old folk even said that he was excited and felt the "freshness" of it every time he returned to the town since it was always beautiful and changed so swiftly (personal interview 2004-10-04). Without doubt, this "freshness" causes a sense of estrangement between those Naxi people who moved out and the ancient town. On the other hand, their sentiment and nostalgic feelings motivate them to return to the town to 'visit'. Eventually, these locals, who are supposed to be the guardian angels of the town, are more or less the same as tourists.

Rapopport (1992) argues that in many situations, environment may influence human being through many cues. People rely on these cues to justify or interpret social dynamics and occasions in order to react appropriately. In other words, social occasions affect people's behavior while physical environments provide cues. Public space is the outcome of the interaction between human activities and physical landscapes which not only involve the physical elements of space but also cultural context including social culture, historical events and human activities. All human beings grow up in a certain social culture which deeply affects their behavior and choice based on personal decisions. Historically, the urban public space in Lijiang Ancient Town including streets, streams and courtyards have significant psychological impacts on the inhabitants because it makes proper socialization possible and enhances their sense of place. However, the current public space under tourism commodification is unable to provide cues for the locals to comprehend their traditional culture. The living environment in the town forces them to leave. Also, in order to make a profit, more and more inhabitants lease their houses to non-local merchants and settle down in a new place. In the end, Lijiang Ancient Town will become an empty shell in which the physical elements are delicately restored and preserved, resembling the display items in museums and lacking a real sense of community life. This process is called museumization. Relph (1976, p. 101) points out that museumization is to preserve, reconstruct and idealize history, arguing that "such places strive for accuracy of replication in their visible detail, but so long as they meet the general demand for historical atmosphere it does not seem to matter whether they are genuine relics or complete fakes and facades." Similarly, Getz (1994) argues that developers tried very hard to restore the details directly visible to the eye to create a historic atmosphere for tourists, instead of accentuating the authenticity of historical tradition, not to mention enhancing the tourist's understanding of the cultural and historical landscapes cherished by the locals. Commodification directly leads to the dissociation of public space and residents' social life, resulting in losing a sense of identity to public space and the gradual disappearance of traditional cultural significance. The public space in Lijiang Ancient Town has thus been turned into an elite landscape disconnected from the local community by officials, planners and developers (Teo & Huang, 1995).

5. Conclusion

The public space in Lijiang Ancient Town is being reconstructed under tourism commodification. During the process of commodification, a large portion of public space has been altered without considering the locals' everyday life. The cultural and historical connotation is gradually withering away and the authenticity of heritage is undermined. Duang, Li, Li, Yang, Zhou, & Duang (2000, p. 16) comments on Lijiang's tourism development:

> "The prices of commodities are low due to competition. To make good profits, shop owners cheat tourists and sell fake and low-quality goods. ...The rapid growth of tourism has pushed the prices of many goods up in Lijiang and affected some local people's quality of life; that's why they're always complaining. ...Many native people run businesses with non-local merchants in the old town because of the high profits. The commercial and tourism atmosphere is too strong that it is eating into the traditional culture. With the emergence of tourism and modern culture, traditional architectural style, festivals, virtue, language, costume, religion, traditional handicrafts and folk art are dying out and changing, causing the old town to reach a cultural crisis."

Tourism commodification alters the urban function of Lijiang Ancient Town. The traditional commercial culture is facing great challenges and streets are gradually converted into places for making commercial profits. The role that streams perform as a cultural carrier is disappearing and courtyard-style houses where people socialize and have a private moment are divided into several parts for commercial use. In addition, the symbolism of Naxi culture is emphasized. For example, the buildings in the Naxi architectural style in Dongda Street that give prominence to the facades and the traditional Naxi decorations have been taken out to mass produce souvenirs. As a result, Lijiang Ancient Town becomes a symbol of the Naxi culture and a place for the tourist to "perform" and consume (Yang, 1997). Naxi culture and the culture carrier of public space, i.e. Lijiang Ancient Town, have turned into a symbol of tourism consumption (Wang, 1999). As a result, the disassociation of the town's public space and the traditional community life will destroy the town's cultural significance. The town is facing the danger of museumization, which is a huge challenge to the conservation of the town.

Traditional buildings must keep pace with the social development in order to survive. Being the social and cultural capital, traditional houses are being reconstructed and rebuilt in order to adapt to new family structures and life styles, and eventually conform to the contemporary life (Lu, 2001). In fact, urban conservation not only promotes cities as tourism attractions, but also generates huge benefits through restoring historic buildings. Some benefits are directly generated from the rising commercial values of the buildings while some are not measurable with money. For example, people can obtain satisfaction and pleasure from a preserved building without paying any money (Garrod, Willis, Bjarnadottir, & Cockbain, 1996). In reality, a vibrant city should allow economic development, strengthen social integration, ensure a safe and healthy living environment and enhance the citizens' sense of belonging and identity (Zhang, 2001). Therefore, heritage tourism and urban conservation in Lijiang Ancient Town should not be profit-oriented only, but should consider building harmony between public space and human activities and enhancing the cultural and social significance of public space in order to ultimately create a vibrant city.

It is possible to obtain some effective measures from the perspective of an organic city. Being an organic city, a historic town has a form which will grow, develop, mature, but will not die. A healthy urban form can solidify itself through achieving a dynamic balance and keeping its self-adjusted characteristics. When this "organic order" is disturbed, the urban form will fall sick. When urban development exceeds a certain level, the self-adjusted function ceases to work and all elements have the same tendency, the disease becomes contagious or even malignant (Wang, 1999). It appears that Lijiang Ancient Town has some of the above "symptoms" and has come to a crossroads - either worsening or recovering. To recover, the heritage management in Lijiang should consider the following two options: 1) to consciously control or even place a restriction on tourism in order to retain economic and cultural integration and strengthen the residents' sense of identity on public space. 2) to continuously encourage heritage tourism as an economic means to rebuild the Naxi culture and public space which acts as a carrier so that they can be incorporated into tourism.

It should be ensured that tourism is a catalyst to conservation and cultural transformation. This method has been adopted in many destinations and proved to be successful (Smith, 1989). On the basis of urban conservation, the 800-year-old Lijiang Ancient Town may achieve steady and healthy development during the process of integrating and resisting external "diseases" in the future.

Acknowledgement

Some of the data in this paper were collected when the authors were pursuing their Master degrees at the Sun Yat-sen University. The authors would like to thank Professor Bao Ji-gang, Dr Dai Guang-quan and Associate Professor Peggy Teo from the Department of Geography, National University of Singapore for their encouragement. The authors' gratitude also goes to the two anonymous referees of this journal for providing constructive comments. The errors and faults in the paper should, of course, be ascribed to the authors alone.

References

Duang, S. T., Li, X., Li, H. B., Yang, L. S., Zhou, H. K., & Duang, P. H. (2000). *Culture heritage management and tourism: Models for co-operation among stakeholders: A heritage protection and tourism development case study of Lijiang ancient town China.* Bhaktapur, Thailand: United Nations Educational, Scientific and Cultural Organization (UNESCO Bangkok).

Frenkel, S., & Walton, J. (2000). Bavarian Leavenworth and the symbolic economy of a theme town. *Geographical Review, 90*(4), 559-585.

Garrod, G. D., Willis, K. G., Bjarnadottir, H., & Cockbain, P. (1996). The non-priced benefits of renovating historic buildings: A case study of Newcastle Grainger Town. *Cities, 13*(6), 423-430.

Getz, D. (1994). Event tourism and the authenticity dilemma. In W. F. Theobald (Ed.), *Global tourism: The next decade* (pp. 313-329). Oxford, U.K.: Butterworth-Heinemann.

Goullart, P. (1955). *Forgotten kingdom*. London: Murray.

Henderson, J. (2000). Attracting tourists to Singapore's Chinatown: A case study in conservation and promotion. *Tourism Management, 21*(5), 525-534.

Hoyle, B. (2001) Lamu: Waterfront revitalization in an East African port-city. *Cities, 18*(5), 297-313.

Jamison, D. (1999). Tourism and ethnicity: The brotherhood of coconuts. *Annals of Tourism Research, 26*(4), 944-967.

Law, C. M. (1992). Urban tourism and its contribution to economic regeneration. *Urban Studies, 29*(3/4), 599-618.

Lillebye, E. (1996). Architectural and functional relationships in street planning: An historical view. *Landscape and Urban Planning, 35*(2/3), 85-105.

Lutz, J., & Ryan, C. (1997). Impacts of inner city tourism projects: The case of the International Convention Centre, Birmingham, U.K.. In P. E. Murphy (Ed.), *Quality management in urban tourism* (pp.41-52). Chichester, U.K.: John Wiley & Sons.

Lynch, K. (1960). *The image of the city*. Cambridge, MA: Technology Press.

Maclaren, F. T., & Des, M. E. (2001)。亚洲历史城市中心区遗产保护的真实性：在有关解释和成就中的假像。国外城市规划，4，9-21。

Marks, R. (1996). Conservation and community: The contradictions and ambiguities of tourism in the Stone Town of Zanzibar. *Habitat International, 20*(2), 265-278.

Moore, R. S. (1995). Gender and alcohol use in a Greek tourism town. *Annals of Tourism Research, 22*(2), 300-313.

Parlett, G., Fletcher, J., & Cooper, C. (1995). The impact of tourism on the Old Town of Edinburgh. *Tourism Management, 16*(5), 355-360.

Pearce, D. G. (1999). Assessing the impact of urban casinos on tourism in New Zealand. *Tourism Economics, 5*(2), 141-159.

Peters, H. A. (2001). Making tourism work for heritage preservation: Lijiang, A case study. In C. B. Tan, S. C. H. Cheung, & Y. Hui (Eds.), *Tourism, anthropology and China: In memory of Professor Wang Zhusheng* (pp.313-333). Bangkok, Thailand: White Lotus Press.

Relph, E. (1976). *Place and placelessness*. London: Pion.

Smith, V. L. (Ed.). (1989). *Hosts and guests: The anthropology of tourism* (2nd ed.). University of Pennsylvania Press.

Stabler, M. (1998). The economic evaluation of the role of conservation and tourism in the regeneration of historic urban destinations. In E. Laws, B. Faulkner, & G. Moscardo (Eds.), *Embracing and managing change in tourism: International case studies* (pp. 235-263). London: Routledge.

Teo, P., & Huang, S. (1995). Tourism and heritage conservation in Singapore. *Annals of Tourism Research, 22*(3), 589-615.

Wang, N. (2000). *Tourism and modernity: A sociological analysis* (1st ed.). NY: Pergamon.

Yamamura, T. (2004). Authenticity, ethnicity and social transformation at world heritage sites: Tourism, retailing and cultural change in Lijiang, China. In D. R. Hall (Ed.), *Tourism and transition: Governance, transformation, and development* (pp. 185-200). Wallingford, U.K.: CABI Publishing.

Yeoh, B. S. A., & Huang, S. (1996). The conservation - Redevelopment dilemma in Singapore: The case of the Kampong Glam Historic District. *Cities, 13*(6), 411-422.

阿摩斯·拉普卜特 (1992)。建成环境的意义：非言语表达方法 (黄兰谷等译)。北京：中国建筑工业出版社。

保继刚，苏晓波 (2004)。历史城镇的旅游商业化研究。地理学报，59(3)，427-436。

顾彼得 (1992)。被遗忘的王国 (李茂春译)。昆明：云南人民出版社。

古城东大街全面拆建，"百花"命运待安排 (1996 年 9 月 24 日)。丽江日报，1。

蒋高宸 (1997)。丽江：美丽的纳西家园。北京：中国建筑工业出版社。

丽江市统计局 (2005 年 3 月 7 日)。2004 年丽江市国民经济和社会发展统计公报。丽江政务。2005 年 10 月 31 日，取自：http://www.lijiang.gov.cn/pubnews/doc/read/tjgb/180333379.133960031/index.asp

梁幼侨，巫纪光 (1998)。传统欧洲与亚洲城市公共空间布局比较研究。华中建筑，3，61-66。

陆志钢 (2001)。江南水乡历史城镇保护与发展。南京：东南大学出版社。

牛耕勤 (2000)。茶马古道上的纳藏贸易之道。丽江文史，19，62-78。

水环境检测公报 (2003 年 7 月 1 日)。丽江日报，3。

严爱琼，李和平 (2002)。丽江古城建成环境特色探讨。工业建筑，8，1-4。

杨慧 (2002)。旅游发展与丽江古城命运的思考。中央民族大学学报 (哲学社会科学版)，1，69-72。

阳建强，吴明伟 (主编)(1999)。现代城市更新。南京：东南大学出版社。

杨曦帆 (2001)。商业社会中的传统艺术。民族艺术研究，1，71-74。

杨正文 (1997)。复兴与发展：黔东南苗族社区的变迁态势。西南民族学院学报 (哲学社会科学版)，4，19-24。

要让古城常年保持清水长流 (2004 年 7 月 9 日)。丽江日报，1。

张松 (2001)。历史城市保护学导论：文化遗产和历史环境保护的一种整体性方法。上海科学技术出版社。

赵芸 (1995)。丽江古城的空间构成与保全。云南工业大学硕士论文, 未出版。

邹怡，马清亮 (1993)。江南小城镇形态特征及其演化机制。载于仲德昆（主编），小城镇的建筑空间与环境。天津科学技术出版社。

周庄：从历史走向未来 (2002)。人民日报。2005 年 10 月 31 日，取自：http://www.china.org.cn/chinese/CU-c/100377.htm

朱良文 (1988)。丽江纳西族民居。昆明：云南科技出版社。

Leisure in an Urban Environment—A Perspective of University Students

大学生对城市休闲的看法

SHAN YANG
HONGGEN XIAO
CHAU YEUNG TSE

This inductive analysis examines Hong Kong university students' perceptions of leisure through in-depth interviews around open-ended questions pertinent to their participation and experience. Grounded theory methodology was followed through a systematic procedure of open coding, axial coding, and selective coding in order to make sense out of the interview transcripts. The study finds that participants' perceptions of leisure are (in)formed by personal emotions (e.g., mood, enjoyment, comfort) and expected impacts (e.g., health, being "re-created," well-being, self-development); they think that leisure is activity oriented; leisure participation is primarily determined by the amount of free, unobligated time the participants have; and their choices of leisure activities are influenced by their expected impacts. Leisure participation is grouped into four categories of activities: physical, social interaction, entertainment, and learning, from which participants experience an impact, either positive or negative, and on the basis of which subsequent decisions are made for future leisure activities. The benefits of leisure are categorized into four types: physical health, social interaction, self-development, and psychological well-being. By implication, constructions of leisure in a non-Western context could lend to discussions on the meaning of leisure and its association with quality of life and work.

本文透过跟香港大学生的深入访谈，以开放式的问题了解他们对休闲的参与和体验，并探讨其对休闲的看法。本文运用扎根理论方法，通过开放性编码、主轴性编码和选择性编码等归纳式的系统程序来分析访谈结果。本研究发现，参与者对休闲的看法是由其个人情绪（例如，心情，享受，舒适度）和预期影响（例如，健康，被"再创造"，福祉，自我发展）形成。他们认为休闲是具有活动导向的；参与休闲与否主要决定于参与者的自由时间或非劳动时间；而他们的预期影响则会左右其休闲活动的选择。参与休闲可按活动性质分为四类：体育，社会互动，娱乐和学习。参与者体验这些活动带来的正面或负面影响，并在这个基础上策划未来的休闲活动。休闲的好处也可以分为四类：身体健康，社会互动，自我发展和心理健康。总的来说，研究休闲在非西方语境里的含义及其跟生活和工作质量的关联，具有重要意义。

Shan Yang is a candidate for a Master of Accountancy at Chinese University of Hong Kong, New Territories, Hong Kong, China (E-mail: s1010150400@mailserv.cuhk.edu.hk).

Honggen Xiao is Assistant Professor of the School of Hotel and Tourism Management at The Hong Kong Polytechnic University, Kowloon, Hong Kong, China (E-mail: hmhgxiao@polyu.edu.hk).

Chau Yeung Tse is a candidate for a Master of Finance at The Hong Kong Polytechnic University, Hung Hom, Kowloon, Hong Kong, China (E-mail: 10609370g@polyu.edu.hk).

Introduction

Hong Kong has been commonly acknowledged as one of the world's leading financial centers. At the same time, it is also rated as one of the most stressful places in the world, according to a clinical psychological report recently released by the University of Hong Kong (Messing, 2009). The pace of life in this metropolis is so fast that its residents often feel rushed and exhausted. The role of leisure in achieving work–life balance has been important and central to both intellectual discussions and policy practices (Leisure and Cultural Services Department, 2008). Leisure has become critical to individuals' sense of self, in increasing quality of life and in improving psychological well-being of the urban residents. According to Kleiber and Kirshnit (1991), leisure is essential in the sense of human development because it provides opportunities for the promotion of new skills and the formation of social relationships and new identities. Also, leisure is a key domain in the quality of life of an individual as it maintains one's life in equilibrium through promoting pleasure to counterbalance stress.

Many studies have tried to define and measure leisure, a notion emerged from the Western cultural context and evolved over the years into a distinct field of study. Comparatively, systematic research on leisure in the "other" cultural contexts has been inadequate (Iwasaki, Nishino, Onda, & Bowling, 2007). Nonetheless, perceptions of leisure are highly influenced by an individual's cultural background. By adopting an international/intercultural perspective to the study of leisure, a fuller understanding of the notion can be possibly attained (Lee, Oh, & Shim, 2001). Moreover, understanding residents' perceptions of leisure from their own cultural perspective can help stake-holders (e.g., governmental departments of culture and leisure, leisure service providers, and other associated organizations) implement policies and practices pertinent to leisure activities and service deliveries. In this research, the meaning of leisure for residents in Hong Kong was inductively explored through in-depth interviews.

This study has three objectives: to (a) identify Hong Kong residents' perceptions of leisure by allowing the study participants to demonstrate "their understanding and knowledge" about leisure; (b) identify major activities that the interview participants have engaged in during their free/unobligated time in order to understand their leisure participation; and (c) examine the benefits of leisure on participants' life and work. In the following discussions, the article begins with a review discussion on the meaning (s) and perceptions of leisure, which is followed by a presentation of the methodology adopted for this undertaking. Subsequently, through an inductive process, a conceptual model is derived from the participants' "constructions" and the meaning(s) they attach to the notion of leisure. Implications and limitations of the study are also reflected.

The Meaning of Leisure for Residents in Hong Kong

Leisure is essential to the life and work of urban residents; it constitutes an important part of their lifestyles, well-being, and quality of life, particularly for people in a busy metropolis (Kaplan, 1979; Llyod & Auld, 2003). In an earlier study, Shaw (1985) stated that leisure is part of the everyday life of a modern individual. In addition, Pieper (1952) referred to culture as a distinct context within which leisure is pursued and practiced. Notably, how people perceive leisure in their life and/or what meaning(s) they attach to it have remained a major area of interest in the leisure studies community (Godbey, 1994; Horna, 1994; J. Kelly & Godbey, 1992; R. Kelly, 1996).

The Meaning(s) of Leisure

Perceptions of leisure vary by age, gender, time and location, cultural background, and the education level of an individual. In the classic introductory texts (Godbey, 1994; Iso-Ahola, 1980; Kaplan, 1979; J. Kelly & Godbey, 1992; Neulinger, 1974; Shaw, 1985), leisure typically connotes (a) free time away from paid work, (b) activities carried out in unobligated time, (c) the function of a social class who have to work to earn leisure, (d) the privilege of those who can afford to have others work for them (or the leisured class), and (e) a state of existence or state of being encompassing "freedom from . . ." (constraints or escape) as much as "freedom to . . ." (participation or emancipation). In ancient philosophy, Aristotle regarded leisure as a state of being in which a leisure activity is performed for its own sake. In the classical notion of leisure, work is seen as boring and monotonous. Leisure, on the other hand, is happy and enjoyable and is often associated with a cultivation of the mind, spirit, and character (De Grazia, 1962).

In Veblen's (1899) classic text, titled *The Theory of the Leisure Class*, he suggested that leisure is closely related to a social class. He argued that in Europe during the feudal and Renaissance periods as well as the Industrial Age, the possession and visible use of leisure became the hallmark of the upper class. Though this idea may be outdated, the wealthy or privileged class in the modern society still continues to enjoy a wide variety of expensive and prestigious leisure activities.

A common approach to this notion is the definition of leisure as unobligated or free time or the surplus of time remaining after practical necessities of life have been attended (Godbey, 1994). This perspective on leisure excludes the time devoted to essential life-maintenance activities such as sleep, eating, or personal care. Both economists and sociologists find such a definition useful in their approach to leisure as an economic and social behavior.

Another perspective is to approach leisure as "activities" that people engage in during their free time. In this regard, leisure is often associated with recreation and tourism when it occurs outside a usual home environment. Arguably, it can be any activities and in any forms that an individual indulges in of her own free will—to relax and rest, to amuse or entertain herself, and to engage in a learning experience. It is also concerned with the outcomes of a leisure activity, as mentioned by Austin and Crawford (1996), ". . . experiences are growth producing, leaving participants with feelings of accomplishment, confidence, and pleasure" (p. 9).

Moreover, the notion of leisure is also seen as a state of being. Such a conception emphasizes the perceived freedom of an individual in a psychological state of mind, which constitutes both the notion of freedom to (or proactive participation) and that of freedom from (i.e., escape from constraints) in her leisure participation to achieve self-enrichment. Neulinger (1974) stated that "to leisure means to be oneself, to express one's talents, one's capacities, and one's potentials" (p. 15). Leisure activities are therefore seen as part of a whole life, in which the individual explores her capabilities and self-fulfillment. In addition, some researchers conceive leisure in terms of its contribution to spiritual expression or religious values.

Leisure, Quality of Life, and Well-Being

The idea of having a good quality of life (QOL) has been a huge concern for individuals, communities, and government in an urban environment. Prior research has established a positive relationship between leisure and QOL (Baldwin & Tinsley, 1988; Iso-Ahola, 1980; R. Kelly, 1996). Iwasaki (2007) proposed four mechanisms that can facilitate the meaning-making and enhancement of QOL: (a) positive emotions and well-being experienced from leisure; (b) positive identities and self-esteem gained from leisure; (c) social and cultural connections and a harmony developed through leisure; and (d) the contribution of leisure to learning and human development across the lifespan. Bartko and Eccles (2003) identified a linkage between leisure participation and well-being. Trainor, Delfabbro, Anderson, and Winefield (2010) suggested that adolescents achieve improved psychological well-being through structured leisure activities.

Much of the discussion on QOL and well-being centers around the benefits of leisure for distinct (or different types of) participants. For example, for mentally disabled people, Craik and Pieris (2006) found that leisure was valued in terms of meeting individual and unique needs for mental health. For their study participants, life is made much more meaningful with (or in) leisure. Similarly, García-Villamisar and Dattilo (2010) supported the notion that participation in recreation activities positively reduces stress and enhances QOL of adults with autism spectrum disorder. In addition, Tinsley, Colbs, Teaff, and Kaufman (1987) reported on benefits of leisure for the elderly in urban places. Their study noted that older women alluded to social interactions and companionship as a lure of participation and/or leisure pursuits. Focusing on senior users of urban parks, Hung and Crompton's (2006) study confirmed the benefits of leisure for the elderly through maintaining/improving their physical health as well as satisfying their social and psychological needs for interaction and companionship. Sivan (2003) reported in a study on the role of leisure in youth development in Hong Kong; she found that leisure helped young people strike a balance between academic pursuits and social involvement. In terms of stress and coping through leisure, Stanton-Rich and Iso-Ahola (1998) suggested that the higher the level of leisure satisfaction, the lower the level of emotional exhaustion and hence the higher the personal accomplishment for the participants.

Leisure and Recreation in Hong Kong

Though Hong Kong is widely known as a paradise for food and shopping, its leisure facilities and recreational space are also notable. In addition to restaurants, stores, and horse-racing courts, the special administrative region has an extensive country park network, with 24 country parks and 17 special areas totaling 44,000 hectares, and many trails for hiking. It also has four marine parks and one marine reserve totaling 2,430 hectares to facilitate water-based recreation. According to a Hong Kong household survey on residents' leisure time use by the Census and Statistics Department (CSD, 2003), about 50.5% of the population participated in leisure activities in the 3 months prior to the survey. To break down by frequency of leisure participation, about 52.7% of the respondents participated at least once a week; 30.7% less than once a week but at least once a month; 11.7% less than once a month but at least once every 3 months; and 4.9% less than once every 3 months. Collectively, some 1.4 million residents participated in leisure activities on a weekly basis. The average duration of time was 2.2 hours spent for recreational or sports activities and 2.8 hours for other leisure and social activities. On weekends, persons aged 15 and over spent on average 5.6 hours on free time/leisure activities. As of the 2003 survey, some 43.3% or 2,423,000 persons aged 15 and over participated in recreational/sports and leisure activities. In addition, a study by a consulting firm (Synovate, 2005) noted that Hong Kong's affluent are also taking their leisure seriously, with substantial increases in the number of leisure participants. For example, this study found that there was a 162% increase in the number of people jogging, a 59% increase in the number of people swimming, and a 112% increase in participation in aerobics in recent years.

In modern Chinese cities, leisure behavior and participation display distinct cultural characteristics in contrast to rural contexts. According to Su, Shen, and Wei (2006), there were significant differences in the general pattern of leisure involvement and subjective perceptions about leisure life between urban and rural elderly residents in China. Whereas rural elderly residents were more occupied by care-giving and housework responsibilities, their urban counterparts were more actively involved in interests and hobbies, social interactions, and recreational activities that entertain personal interest. Overall, their study found that urban elderly residents were more satisfied with their leisure activities than rural residents.

As a metropolis, recreational facilities and leisure participation are of paramount importance for residents maintaining a busy lifestyle. In addition, because space in an urban environment is usually limited, leisure facilities are built in consideration of enhancing QOL of the residents, achieving economic returns, and facilitating lifelong learning (Verduin & McEwen, 1984). However, very often the goals of enhancing the image of a city and fostering economic growth have overshadowed the role of public leisure spaces in providing experiences to enhance the QOL of urban residents (Llyod & Auld, 2003). Built on the above discussions, this analysis attempts to explore Hong Kong residents' perceptions of leisure and to examine the meaning(s) they attach to leisure participation and leisure pursuits.

A Qualitative Approach to Unveil the Meaning(s) of Leisure

In this study, a qualitative approach is adopted to disclose the meanings and perceptions of Hong Kong residents toward leisure. Such an inductive approach has been widely used in leisure studies and is found to be of particular relevance to the scrutiny of leisure experiences. For example, Jamal and Hollinshead (2003) called for more use of qualitative inquiries in tourism studies; Samdahl and Jekubovich (1993) demonstrated the use of such approaches to enhance our understanding through bringing out the richness and texture from the contextualized data (Samdahl, 1999). Also, as Denzin and Lincoln (1994) alluded, qualitative research could provide a crucial lens to help scholars understand phenomena in a different and often complementary perspective. In regard to leisure perceptions, a qualitative approach allows a researcher to probe, through open-ended questions, and achieve an in-depth understanding of the meaning and impacts that the interview participants attach to leisure participation, expressed in their own terms and from their own perspectives.

Preparing for and Conducting the Interview. The instrument of this research was an in-depth interview, which mainly consisted of three open-ended and other probing (or follow-up) questions related to the topic. Planning for the interview started with setting objectives for this study. Preliminary discussions were held among the authors, and consensus was reached on the dimensions of the main interview questions, which were overarched by the study objectives: "What comes to your mind when I mention leisure to you?" "What kinds of leisure activities do you participate in?" "What influence(s) does leisure participation bring to you?" Probing questions around these broad queries were prepared, either prior to or during the interview, due to their open-ended nature and the dynamics and interactions between the interviewer and the interviewee. The questions were pilot tested with a non-tourism-related student before the actual interview to check for validity and neutrality and to ensure that no leading elements or ambiguities were embedded in the question wording.

In-depth interviews were conducted with three students from a local university in Hong Kong, each lasting about 45 minutes. One participant was a female student, aged 23, with a bachelor's degree in hotel management; another, a male student of the same age, was continuing his education on social policy and administration after a few years' work experience; the third was a male degree student, aged 21, from a department of management in a faculty of business at a local university. The interviews were conducted in the students' residences, because these are generally regarded as pleasant and relaxing environments where interview participants can "feel at home" to express their views on leisure. Confidentiality and the purpose of research were conveyed at the beginning of the interview. Informed consent and permission to record the interviews were obtained from the participants; field notes were taken during the interview where and when nonverbal communication occurred or meaningful observations were made on the topic under study.

Because the participants were all native speakers of Cantonese, the interviews were conducted in this popular local dialect in Hong Kong and were later translated into English for coding and analysis. The translation was reviewed and checked back-to-back by two students from the Department of Chinese and Bilingual Studies to ensure that "loyalty" to the original text was maintained in the translation. Some minor changes were suggested and subsequently incorporated into the final transcripts. Because the interview participants also read English, the translated version of the transcripts was later shared with them as a "member check" to ensure that the researchers interpreted their meanings correctly.

Inductive Analysis of the Interview Data. In this study, data analysis followed a grounded theory methodology. This approach was regarded as suitable for the study because of its feature as a general method of making constant comparisons to develop or generate theory initially from the data (Glaser & Strauss, 1967). A systematic procedure of open coding, axial coding, and selective coding was followed as mentioned by Strauss (1987) in order to allow theory to emerge from the data. According to Strauss, open coding is the initial stage of unrestricted coding of the data and is to be devoid of (or free from) sensitizing concepts; axial coding consists of intense analysis done around one category of conceptual codes at a time to result in cumulative knowledge about the relationships between the category and other categories, to achieve best fit; and selective coding pertains to coding toward a core to result in the identification of themes or theories (Xiao & Smith, 2004). These coding stages were performed individually in each interview and were followed by group discussions among the researchers in order to merge the open and axial codes in the final stage of sense-making out of the data.

Operationally, both manifest and latent contents in the transcripts were open coded. In vivo codes were occasionally used in the instances of directly quoting a term or expression, in the interviewee's own words, from the transcripts. Also, the researchers tried to determine whether and to what extent a piece of data and a corresponding code assigned answer the question relevant to the research objectives. Comparative codes such as "relax," "fun," "shopping," and "traveling" were identified during the group discussions. These codes were then subject to an intense analysis in the stage of axial coding when categories of such codes are identified.

In addition, the relationships among the open codes were identified during axial coding, especially for those codes that bear common properties and appear to "go together." An intercoder consistency check was performed to watch for the use of tags and labels and conceptual and thematic categories, to make sure that a conceptual diagram induced from the process is grounded in the three transcripts. Typically, in the axial coding stage, a category was revolved around an "axis" (or conceptual code). In this analysis, for example, four major categories of leisure activities (physical exercise, entertainment, social interaction, and self-development) were identified. Transcripts and notes were read and reread to determine and confirm that these categories fit the data and vice versa. In this analysis, the grounded theory approach provides not only a means for deriving theoretical explanations but also one for processing the qualitative data. Thus, while confronting the data, the researchers discovered a strong relationship between the three core concepts (perceptions, types of activities, and impacts of leisure).

Hong Kong Residents' Perceptions of Leisure

Typical of the grounded theory approach, methodological processes and outcomes in terms of findings are indistinguishable in this study. Hong Kong residents' perceptions of leisure are unveiled along the process of open coding, axial coding, and selective coding. Inductively, a construction of the meanings of leisure is also derived, through selective coding, from the participants' perceptions.

Open Coding. The initial step was to identify conceptual codes from the interview transcripts (i.e., tags, labels, in vivo codes, keywords or phrases). Inductively, 27 codes were used to represent perceptions and/or meanings of leisure addressed in interview question 1; 26 codes retained for activities and leisure participation referred to in interview question 2; and 23 codes identified for impacts, influences and/or benefits from leisure, as implied in interview question 3 (Tables 1, 2, and 3).

Axial Coding. In this stage, categories were constructed. By looking for similarities and differences among the open codes, distinct categories were identified through axial coding (Tables 4, 5, and 6).

Table 1. Open Codes for Perceptions and Meanings of Leisure.

Relax	Relax mentally	No need to work	No work
Enjoy	Comfortable	Do whatever	Break
Sleep	Happy	Weekend	Family
Activities	Alone	Home	Travel
Important	Badly in need	Improve efficiency	Reading
Refreshing	Escaping	Away from daily life	Ease
Freedom	Beach	Adjust attitude	

Table 2. Open Codes for Activities and Leisure Participation.

Watch drama alone or with friends	Surf internet	Take photos	Traveling
Read novels and comics	Dating girlfriend	Go to theme parks	Play pool
Sharing information about leisure activities with friends	Taking a shower	Call friends	Sleeping
Have dinner with family or friends	Go shopping	*Yumcha*	Go to bars
Stare blank; do nothing	Go hiking	Listen to music	Be alone
Read magazines and news	Watch movies	Talking with family	Swimming
Recollect memories	Play basketball		

Table 3. Open Codes for Impacts, Influences, or Benefits of Leisure.

Feel happy	Enjoy	Keep up-to-date	Get excited
Learn better	Refreshing	Have better relationship with family and friends	Better mood
Good for health	Feel energetic	Broaden knowledge	Relax
Awake	Feel fun	Away from daily life	Learning
Broaden vision	More sociable	Physical and mental benefits	Balancing life
Review the past	Recharge	Discover new things	

Table 4. Perceptions and Meanings of Leisure.

Positive Emotion	Activity Oriented	Impact Expected
Relaxation, enjoyment, comfort, happiness, something important, badly in need, or refreshing	Travel, reading, being alone, beach, sleeping, activities, break, home, no work/no need to work, weekend, family, doing whatever	Freedom, improving efficiency, ease, being away from daily life, attitude adjustment, escape, mental relaxation

Selective Coding. After organizing codes into categories, higher level thematic codes or core codes were attempted. The relationships among the three main interview questions were generated from the data after systematic coding or thinking-through. A conceptual diagram was derived in an attempt to construct the meaning of leisure through data reduction and categorization of the participants' perceptions (Figure 1). The relationships among theoretical categories are proposed and visually represented to make sense of the interview data.

The conceptual framework shows that the participants' perceptions of leisure are (in)formed by personal emotion and expected impacts; the informants also think that

Table 5. Leisure Activities and Participation.

Participation Span	Categories of Leisure Activities	Types of Leisure Activities and Participation	
Short	Physical activities	Sports (swimming, basketball, pool)	
	Entertainment	Listening to music	Staring blank, doing nothing
		Reading novels and comics	Taking a shower
		Watching movies/drama	Dating girlfriends
		Surfing the Internet	Visiting theme parks
		Taking photos	Sleeping, being alone
	Social interactions	Going to the bar	Having dinner with family and friends
		Calling friends	Sharing information about leisure activities with friends
		Shopping	
		Hiking or traveling	
		Yumcha	
			Talking with family
	Learning	Reading, Recollecting memories	Surfing the Internet, Watching movies
Long	Multidimensional activities	Traveling	

Table 6. Impacts, Influences, and Benefits of Leisure.

Types of Impacts	Codes of Impacts, Influences, and Benefits
Physical health	Good for health, staying awake, physical benefits
Psychological well-being	Feeling happy, enjoyment, excitement, feeling refreshed, better mood, relaxation, feeling energetic, feeling fun, being away from daily life, mental benefits, recharging, balancing life
Social interaction	Better relationship with friends and family, more sociable
Self-development	Broadening knowledge, broadening vision, reviewing the past, discovering new things, learning

leisure is an activity-oriented pursuit. The choice of leisure activities is primarily determined by residents' participation span (or length and amount of time they have for leisure) and, secondarily, leisure participation is influenced by the expected impacts or outcomes. In other words, the informants expect to have an impact, regardless of positive or negative, from their leisure participation. Such benefits or influences will in turn inform future decisions or choices in terms of leisure activities and participation. In this cycle, residents' perceptions are (in)formed by, or modified through, leisure participation and benefits received. In this study, all of the informants

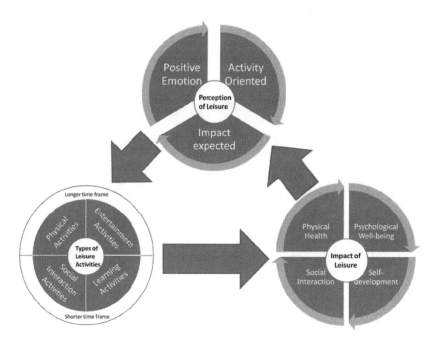

Figure 1. Construction of the meaning of leisure from the participants' perceptions (color figure available online).

have reported positive and beneficial experiences resulting from their participation or engagement in leisure.

In observing the categories and impacts of leisure, one should assume that there are no simple cause-and-effect linkages between categories. Several categories may operate simultaneously when an individual makes decisions about leisure preferences and participation. These categories are discussed in the following section, with in vivo codes or quotes from the participants to support the theorizing.

A Construction of the Meaning(s) of Leisure

Residents' Perceptions of Leisure. The meaning of leisure is rather consistently perceived across the interviewees. According to the interviews, the informants' first impression of leisure is formed by personal emotions, activities or participation, and expected impacts or outcomes. This finding confirms Neulinger's (1974) notion that leisure connotes activities or participation with both intrinsic motivations and perceived freedom on the part of an individual. On one hand, a leisure activity itself constitutes a main source of attraction, from which an urban resident experiences a sense of freedom, life satisfaction, and rewards or learning. On the other hand, urban individuals perceive themselves intrinsically as a source of action for the much needed "re-creation" and/or "playfulness." Such a goal- or work-related orientation in Hong Kong resident's perceptions of leisure brings the notion in close vicinity to the "recreational mode" in Cohen's (1979, p. 183) phenomenology of tourist experience, which is notably attained from a place outside their usual home environment. Arguably, the high volume of pleasure travel from Hong Kong every year to its neighboring countries or regions is indiscernible from the enormous call for leisure and recreation by its residents.

In relation to personal emotions, terms such as *relax, comfort, enjoyment, freedom of choice*, and *refreshing* were frequently used to describe their impression of leisure in the interviews. Positive notes of emotions implied that the interviewees have a pleasant feeling toward leisure. They agreed that leisure is the time when they can get away from work and daily life; on the contrary, they also associated leisure negatively with unpleasant feelings such as "pressure,","stress," and/or "tiring." It was found that the interviewees had a feeling of both anticipation and emancipation toward leisure, as implied in their perceptions of the notion as unobligated or discretionary time.

Apart from emotional notes, an interesting finding was that the interviewees tended to associate leisure with a special time of the day or a special activity they were engaged in. "No need to work" is a common description of leisure throughout the interviews. Specifically, two interviewees used *holiday, travel, weekend*, and *vacation* to distinguish their leisure and nonleisure time use. In addition, the interviewees also intuitively used activities to associate with their leisure time. As noted in Table 5, these encompass an array of physical, entertainment, and social activities. Understandably, these activities and (dis)satisfaction from leisure participation convey a sense of concreteness to an otherwise abstract notion.

Another point to note about Hong Kong residents' perceptions of leisure is the expected impacts or outcomes of a leisure pursuit. For example, interviewees used words such as *freedom, ease, adjust attitude*, and *improve efficiency* to express the impacts they had felt from leisure participation. They also mentioned a "mental impact" in the release of stress or work pressure, which is consistent with the findings of Bartko and Eccles (2003), who reported a positive correlation between leisure and quality of life and psychological well-being for adolescents.

Leisure Activities and Leisure Participation. There are varieties of leisure activities mentioned during the interviews. It was found that length of free time or "time frame" was a common concern that influenced the interviewees' choices of leisure activities. Two of the interviewees used duration terms (e.g., *long* or *short* leisure period) as a benchmark to determine the leisure participation and activities they would like to choose. Interestingly, a correlation between duration of leisure and types of activities was observed from the interviews: The shorter the length of time for leisure, the more personal the chosen activities were. For example, two interviewees mentioned that they would stay alone and do some reading or listen to music if their leisure during a certain time of the day or week was really short and limited. Arguably, though free time use and leisure participation have been extensively researched in the Western context (Cushman, Veal, & Zuzanek, 2005; Zuzanek & Smale, 1997), the above observation points to an interesting proposition in a distinctly Asian (or Chinese) context for further testing or measurement on the relationship between length of free time and types of leisure activities participated.

Another dimension of the activity construct is leisure participation away from home. Notably, travel is one of the most frequently mentioned activities by the inter-viewees. Nonetheless, it is not on the top priority list to choose if unobligated time is short and remains a constraint, because the interviewees did not want to "feel rushed" during their leisure. However, this feeling is inconsistent with their expected outcome or impacts from leisure. Thus, leisure activities can also be understood as outcome-based choices, in which the benefits or impacts should be consistent with the basic perceptions of leisure.

Moreover, two interviewees mentioned that they chose a particular leisure activity not because of the activity per se but because of the impacts it can have on their well-being. For instance, one of the male interviewees mentioned that he would not swim or play in the pool unless he was with his friends for the sake of socializing or fun. Leisure activities can thus be categorized into four domains of participation according to their potential impacts: physical, social interaction, entertainment, and learning activities.

Benefits of Leisure Participation. Notably, in Figure 1, physical health refers to relaxation, recreation, and fitness such as swimming mentioned by the above-mentioned interviewee. It is interesting to note that two interviewees did not mention physical activities throughout the interview. Though there has been some research in the Anglophone community about physical activity and leisure (Mannell, Kaczynski, & Aronson, 2005), future studies could explore whether residents in a metropolis perceive regular physical activities as leisure and the extent to which they participate, particularly when these activities occur indoor in a leisure facility such as gyms, health clubs, or indoor swimming pools.

Another dimension in the impact construct is psychological well-being, which includes a desire for change in environment and routine, as well as a relief from boredom and stress. Prior studies have noted the role of leisure as a coping strategy when participants are under pressure or stress (Folkman, Lazarus, Dunkel-Schetter, DeLongis, & Gruen, 1986; Iwasaki & Mannell, 2000). In much the same vein, this analysis supports the observation that leisure activities contribute to both physical and psychological well-being of an individual through relieving boredom, stress, and tension; increasing relaxation and mental health; and pursuing enjoyment, interests, and pleasure (e.g., photography, movie-going, or listening to music, as often referred to in the study interview).

Additionally, in light of Iwasaki (2007), this study adds to the discussion on leisure and quality of life from a distinctly urban and cultural context. We examine the perceptions of leisure through in-depth interviews and how urban participants make sense of leisure participation as well as its association with quality of life and work in a non-Western context. Furthermore, whereas Iwasaki's research was more about the linkage between leisure and quality of life, our analysis focuses on perceptions, meaning, and benefits of leisure participation.

As an echo to Havitz and Mannell (2005), social interaction enhances involvement and quality of experience in leisure participation. As a construct in this perception study, it refers to interactions or exchanges with friends and family in a leisure context in order to maintain kinship or renew friendships, as indicated by codes such as "dinning out with family," or "*yumcha* [drinking tea] with friends" in this study. Self-development or learning is often accompanied by discovering new things through activities such as photography or traveling, as mentioned by the interviewees. In light of leisure benefit studies, our analysis, in large part, supports a prior construct by Verduin and McEwen (1984) in which the benefits of leisure were construed in five dimensions, namely, social, relaxation, educational, psychological, and aesthetic benefits. Notably, the last dimension of benefits was not identified in the present study.

In summary, perceptions, participation, and impacts (or benefits) form a cycle in the construction of the meanings of leisure for residents in Hong Kong. Succinctly put, the sense-making process of the study participants begins with perceptions (regardless of whether they are positive or negative); it then proceeds to leisure activities and participation in accordance with their perceptions. Impacts (or benefits) derived from leisure participation serve as both an outcome (expected or unexpected) and a confirmation or disconfirmation in the meaning-making of leisure, which will have implications for an individual's future leisure behavior (e.g., choice of activities and leisure participation).

Conclusion

This inductive analysis appears to warrant the following observations. First, leisure is activity oriented in the mind of the study participants and involves the emotions of and benefits for a participant. All the interviewees perceive some positive benefits from their leisure activities (regardless of how often their participation is). Second, in our (the researchers') sense-making process, a grounded theory approach allows us to synthesize leisure activities reported by the participants into four impact-related categories: physical health, psychological well-being, social interaction, and self-development. Third, it also appears warranted to note that in our (and indeed the participants' own) construction of the meaning of leisure, a cycle of perceptions, participation, and impacts or benefits has emerged in their sense-making of leisure (dis)satisfaction, experience, and behavior.

In addition, it is interesting to note that there is a high level of consistency or recurrences across the interviewees' perceptions. Despite its many dimensions, leisure is rather unanimously perceived as a notion encompassing relaxation, enjoyment, and comfort. Travel is mentioned as a common leisure activity; however, residents in Hong Kong are not likely to engage in this as a routine or daily activity unless they have an adequate amount of free time and the awareness of a need to be fulfilled outside this special administrative region.

Notably, this perception study could have implications for leisure and cultural policy in Hong Kong, as well as for destination marketing of leisure travel targeting at this metropolis. Probing into what residents think about leisure could inform policies of free time use and the provision of leisure facilities or the delivery of leisure services. By extension, such knowledge could also help the planning and management of service businesses and industries in an increasingly expanding leisure economy. Specific to leisure tourism, findings as such may be useful in luring and accommodating pleasure travelers from this region. Take urban tourism as an example. It may be essential for destination marketing and management to consider convenience, accessibility, security, and even tranquility (or excitement) of an attraction for leisure travelers, because they have a relatively high expectation for a comfortable, recreational, and relaxing experience. Such concerns for pleasure, entertainment, and leisure as a means of coping with stress may also hold for individual properties such as resort hotels catering to this golden horde from the crowds.

Trustworthiness, Limitations, and Future Inquiries

Trustworthiness of this analysis was attended to in notable ways. As prescribed by the grounded theory methodology, the inductive process (of both data collection and analysis) has lent to a detailed description to convey the needed richness and texture of an analysis (Lincoln & Guba, 1985). In a qualitative inquiry, Creswell and Miller (2000) referred to this as the creation of "verisimilitude, or statements that produce for the readers the feeling that they have experienced, or could experience, from the events being described in a study" (p. 129). Thus, credibility could be established through the lens of readers. In addition, analytic triangulation was performed through meetings and discussions among the researchers along the way of conducting, transcribing, and coding the interviews. Notably, the study participants were communicated for "member-check" of the translated version of the interview transcripts. Moreover, in the coding and sense-making process, objectivity and sensitivity were maintained as much as possible through "increasing our awareness to help us control intrusion of bias into the analysis while retaining sensitivity to what is being said in the data" (Strauss & Corbin, 1998, p. 43).

Nonetheless, it is important to note that subjectivity is typical of a qualitative inquiry; readers are therefore cautioned about the context of the study and perspectives of the authors (or researchers) embedded in this analysis and interpretation. Limitations are noted as follows. Specifically, the limited resources available for this exploratory inquiry did not allow a prolonged engagement with the study participants. The researchers' backgrounds, skills, and knowledge of the topic under study may have unconsciously resulted in disparities or differences in interpreting the data and in reaching consensus at a higher level of coding. Additionally, in the preparation and interview stage, the study was somewhat guided by an assumption that the interviewees have actually (or already) participated in some leisure activities. Yet, the interview started with leisure perception and all interviewees mentioned some types of leisure activities they participated before the activity/participation question was asked. Furthermore, the three interviews were conducted by three different researchers, in which interview dynamics may have influenced participants' responses (despite our use of field journals or interview notes). Also, demographic features of the participants (e.g., young university students) may render this set of observations more relevant to this target group than other residents in Hong Kong. Nonetheless, in this last connection, a similar caution of applying the sample representation logic to this analysis should be noted. Though we look for commonalities or recurrences in coding the interviews, generalization of the report to a wider resident population is not the intent of this analysis. Nonetheless, this inductive analysis identifies a number of elements typical in a participant's perception and sense-making of leisure participation. These elements, as visualized in the conceptual diagram and reflected in the discussion, could be interesting points for future inquiries. Take the "emotion" element as an example. An interesting line for future studies could be to explore the formation of emotions in the process of leisure perceptions.

Arguably, leisure studies are a niche community in the social sciences academia in this special administrative region, and the recent launching of a Hong Kong chapter of the World Leisure Organization marks an encouraging start. Though this research lends to discussions on residents' perceptions of leisure in Hong Kong, much remains to be understood about free time use, leisure behavior and participation, and leisure and quality of life or well-being in Asia's World City. The conceptual diagram derived from this analysis could be a point of departure for further assessment or replication to test or quantify the relationships between leisure perception, leisure participation, and benefits in this cultural context.

References

Austin, D., & Crawford, M. (1996). *Therapeutic recreation: An introduction* (2nd ed.). Boston, MA: Allyn & Bacon.

Baldwin, K., & Tinsley, H. (1988). An investigation of the validity of Tinsley and Tinsley's (1986) theory of leisure experience. *Journal of Counseling Psychology*, *35*(3), 263–267.

Bartko, W., & Eccles, J. (2003). Adolescent participation in structured and unstructured activities: A person-oriented analysis. *Journal of Youth and Adolescence*, *32*(4), 233–242.

Census and Statistics Department. (2003). *Thematic household survey report No. 14: Time use pattern, pattern of participation in unpaid activities, and pattern of participation in social activities*. Hong Kong SAR, China: Author.

Cohen, E. (1979). A phenomenology of tourist experiences. *Sociology*, *13*, 179–201.

Craik, C., & Pieris, Y. (2006). Without leisure . . . "It wouldn't be much of a life": The meaning of leisure for people with mental health problems. *British Journal of Occupational Therapy*, *69*(5), 209–216.

Creswell, J., & Miller, D. (2000). Determining validity in qualitative inquiry. *Theory Into Practice*, *39*(3), 124–130.

Cushman, G., Veal, A., & Zuzanek, J. (2005). *Free time and leisure participation: International perspectives*. Seattle, WA: CAB International.

De Grazia, S. (1962). *Of time, work and leisure*. New York, NY: Twentieth Century Fund.

Denzin, N., & Lincoln, Y. (1994). Introduction: Entering the field of qualitative research. In N. Denzin & Y. Lincoln (Eds.), *Handbook of qualitative research* (pp. 1–18). Thousand Oaks, CA: Sage.

Folkman, S., Lazarus, R., Dunkel-Schetter, C., DeLongis, A., & Gruen, R. (1986). Dynamics of a stressful encounter: Cognitive appraisal, coping, and encounter outcomes. *Journal of Personality and Social Psychology*, *50*, 992–1003.

García-Villamisar, D., & Dattilo, J. (2010). Effects of a leisure program on quality of life and stress of individuals with ASD. *Journal of Intellectual Disability Research*, *54*(7), 611–619.

Glaser, B., & Strauss, A. (1967). *The discovery of grounded theory: Strategies for qualitative research*. Chicago, IL: Aldine.

Godbey, G. (1994). *Leisure in your life* (4th ed.). State College, PA: Venture Publishing.

Havitz, M., & Mannell, R. (2005). Enduring involvement, situational involvement, and flow in leisure and non-leisure activities. *Journal of Leisure Research*, *37*(2), 152–177.

Horna, J. (1994). *The study of leisure: An introduction*. Oxford, UK: Oxford University Press.

Hung, K., & Crompton, J. (2006). Benefits and constraints associated with the use of an urban park reported by a sample of elderly in Hong Kong. *Leisure Studies*, *25*(3), 291–311.

Iso-Ahola, S. (1980). *The social psychology of leisure and recreation*. New York, NY: McGraw Hill.

Iwasaki, Y. (2007). Leisure and quality of life in an international and multicultural context: What are major pathways linking leisure to quality of life? *Social Indicators Research*, *82*, 233–264.

Iwasaki, Y., & Mannell, R. (2000). Hierarchical dimensions of leisure stress-coping. *Leisure Sciences*, *22*, 161–183.

Iwasaki, Y., Nishino, H., Onda, T., & Bowling, C. (2007). Leisure research in a global world: Time to reverse the Western domination in leisure research? *Leisure Sciences*, *29*, 113–117.

Jamal, T., & Hollinshead, K. (2003). Tourism and the forbidden zone: The underserved power of qualitative inquiry. *Tourism Management*, *22*(1), 63–82.

Kaplan, M. (1979). *Leisure, lifestyle and lifespan: Perspectives for gerontology*. Philadelphia, PA: W. B. Saunders.

Kelly, J., & Godbey, G. (1992). *The sociology of leisure*. State College, PA: Venture Publishing.

Kelly, R. (1996). *Leisure*. Melbourne, Australia: Allyn & Bacon.

Kleiber, D., & Kirshnit, C. (1991). Sports involvement and identify formation. In L. Diamant (Ed.), *Mind–body maturity: Psychological approaches to sports, exercise, and fitness* (pp. 193–211). Washington, DC: Hemisphere.

Lee, J., Oh, S., & Shim, J. (2001). The meaning of leisure: Conceptual differences between Americans and Koreans. In G. Kyle (Ed.), *Proceedings of the 2000 northeastern recreation research symposium* (General Technical Report NE-276, pp. 145–149). Newtown Square, PA: U.S. Department of Agriculture, Forest Service, Northeastern Research Station.

Leisure and Cultural Services Department. (2008). *Annual report of 2008.* Hong Kong SAR, China: Author.

Lincoln, Y., & Guba, E. (1985). *Naturalistic inquiry.* Beverly Hills, CA: Sage.

Llyod, K., & Auld, C. (2003). Leisure, public space and quality of life in urban environment. *Urban Policy and Research, 21*(4), 339–356.

Mannell, R., Kaczynski, A., & Aronson, R. (2005). Adolescent participation and flow experience in physically active leisure and electronic media activities: Testing the displacement hypothesis. *Loisir et Societe/Society and Leisure, 28,* 653–675.

Messing, D. (2009). *Business in Hong Kong: One of the most stressful cities in the world.* Retrieved from http://www.associatedcontent.com/article/2128307/business_in_hong_kong_ one_of_the_most.html

Neulinger, J. (1974). *The psychology of leisure.* Springfield, IL: Charles C. Thomas.

Pieper, J. (1952). *Leisure: The basis of culture.* New York, NY: New American Library.

Samdahl, D. (1999). Epistemological and methodological issues in leisure studies. In E. Jackson & T. Burton (Eds.), *Leisure studies: Prospects for the twenty-first century* (pp. 119–133). State College, PA: Venture Publishing.

Samdahl, D., & Jekubovich, N. (1993). Patterns and characteristics of adult daily leisure. *Loisir et société/Society and Leisure, 16,* 129–149.

Shaw, S. (1985). The meaning of leisure in everyday life. *Leisure Sciences, 7*(1), 1–24.

Sivan, A. (2003). Has leisure got anything to do with learning? An exploratory study of the lifestyles of young people in Hong Kong universities. *Leisure Studies, 22*(2), 129–146.

Stanton-Rich, H., & Iso-Ahola, E. (1998). Burnout and leisure. *Journal of Applied Social Psychology, 28*(21), 1931–1950.

Strauss, A. (1987). *Qualitative analysis for social scientists.* New York, NY: Cambridge University Press.

Strauss, A., & Corbin, J. (1998). *Basics of qualitative research: Techniques and procedures for developing grounded theory* (2nd ed.). Thousand Oaks, CA: Sage.

Su, B., Shen, X., & Wei, Z. (2006). Leisure life in later years: Differences between rural and urban elderly residents in China. *Journal of Leisure Research, 38*(3), 381–397.

Synovate. (2005). *Synovate survey shows Hong Kong affluent tuning in and toning up.* Retrieved from http://www.synovate.com/news/article/2006/10/synovate-survey-shows-hong-kong-affluent-tuning-in-and-toning-up.html

Tinsley, H., Colbs, S., Teaff, J., & Kaufman, N. (1987). The relationship of age, gender, health and economic status to the psychological benefits older persons report from participation in leisure activities. *Leisure Sciences, 9,* 53–65.

Trainor, S., Delfabbro, P., Anderson, S., & Winefield, A. (2010). Leisure activities and adolescent psychological well-being. *Journal of Adolescence, 33*(1), 173–186.

Veblen, T. (1899). *The theory of the leisure class.* New York, NY: Macmillan.

Verduin, J., & McEwen, D. (1984). *Adults and their leisure: The need for lifelong learning.* Springfield, IL: Charles C Thomas.

Xiao, H., & Smith, S. (2004). Residents' perceptions of Kitchener–Waterloo Oktoberfest: An inductive analysis. *Event Management, 8*(3), 161–175.

Zuzanek, J., & Smale, B. (1997). More work—Less leisure? Changing allocations of time in Canada (1981 to 1992). *Loisir et Société/Society and Leisure, 20,* 73–106.

A Residential Survey on Urban Tourism Impacts in Harbin

Yu Wang
Leeds Metropolitan University, UK

Gang Li*
University of Surrey, UK

Xuemei Bai
Dongbei University of Finance and Economics, China

Abstract:

Tourism is becoming more and more important in the global economy, and its long-term prosperity is desired by every tourism destination. Prosperity, however, cannot be achieved successfully without the involvement of those influenced by the industry, so, evaluating residents' perceptions of tourism and involving them in as many aspects of planning and policymaking as possible are important steps in creating sustainability in tourism destination development. In attempting to fill in the research gaps in social impact analysis of urban tourism development in the Chinese context, a face-to-face survey was carried out to explore residents' perceived impacts of tourism development in Harbin, a famous tourist destination in north-eastern China. The findings of this survey suggest that residents' reaction towards local tourism development varies between different interest groups. Age, income and personal connections with local tourism were found to influence residents' perceptions to some extent.

* Corresponding author
Yu Wang, School of Tourism, Hospitality and Event, Leeds Metropolitan University, UK, Email: mollyyuwang@hotmail.com.
Dr Gang Li, Lecturer in Economics, School of Management, University of Surrey, UK, Email: g.li@surrey.ac.uk.
Prof. Xuemei Bai, Professor of Statistics, Department of Statistics, Dongbei University of Finance and Economics, Dalian, China, Email: xmbai@dufe.edu.cn.

城市旅游对当地居民的影响—哈尔滨实证分析

王俞
英国利兹都市大学

李刚
英国萨里大学

白雪梅
东北财经大学

摘要

旅游业现已日渐成为世界经济的重要组成部分。每一个旅游目的地都渴望实现其自身长期而稳定的繁荣发展，而这一目标的顺利实现不能脱离受旅游业发展影响的各方面利益群体的参与。因此，了解旅游地居民对当地旅游业发展所持的观点并及时进行评估以及尽可能地让他们参与到当地旅游业发展的规划和政策制定过程中是实现旅游目的地可持续性发展目标的重要步骤。然而，目前关于旅游业发展的各类影响研究在城市旅游范畴内还很薄弱。这一点尤其体现在对中国旅游发展影响问题的研究中。为了弥补这两方面的研究不足，研究者以中国北方著名的旅游城市哈尔滨为例，以面对面问卷调查的方式对旅游业发展给当地居民所带来的影响进行了调查。调查结果表明受调查者的背景，尤其是居民的年龄、收入情况以及和当地旅游业的关连性等特点都会不同程度地影响其对当地旅游业发展所持的观点。

1. Research Background

The fast worldwide growth of tourism has had an inevitable effect on host perspectives and attitudes towards the industry's development. The intensification is often associated with a variety of negative impacts, which may cultivate an increasingly antagonistic response from local residents towards the tourism industry and tourists (Pearce, Moscardo and Ross, 1996). This can then cause undesirable effects by harming the destination's image and reducing the tourist numbers (Smith, 1978). Fortunately, considerable effort has already been made in trying to discover the host's reactions to local tourism development. Special attention has been paid to observing various kinds of tourism impacts in developing countries (Brunt and Courtney, 1999), because these countries are always experiencing high tourism growth rates (Singh, 1997), which may consequently change local community's perspectives and attitudes towards the industry and tourists over a period of time (Bastias-Perez and Var, 1995).

Surprisingly, despite the fact that China is one of the world's largest developing countries and it is estimated by the World Tourism Organization (WTO) to be the number one world tourism destination country in 2020, very little tourism research has been undertaken in China to investigate how well the host can cope with such rapid growth. The dearth of tourism social impact research in China is probably due to its relatively late entry into the world tourism market, which only became possible since 1978. However, the seemingly sheer contrast between Chinese tourism's short history and its present achievements (with round 98 million international visitors and 878 million domestic tourists in 2002) should only be an encouragement for conducting timely tourism impact research in China in response to such unprecedented growth. Furthermore, due to the differences that existed in social structure and environment, studies conducted in other developing countries will not necessarily reflect the situation in China. All those factors are calling for more research attention on the social impacts of tourism development in the Chinese context.

Along with the increasing popularity of short city breaks, urban tourism is becoming increasingly important. However, to some extent, despite its importance in terms of generating both economic benefits and tourist arrivals, the study of 'urban tourism' as a distinct area within the tourism field is still in its infancy (Gilbert and Clark, 1997). Besides, those findings from outside the urban environment could be misleading due to the potentially different opinions of residents from rural destinations when compared with the opinions of those living in cities (Snaith and Harley, 1999). Bearing in mind the lack of research, the Chinese city resort of Harbin was chosen for this residential survey, in attempting to provide more empirical evidence to existing tourism impact findings in an urban environment. At the time that the research was conducted, Harbin was bidding to hold the 21st Olympic Winter Games in 2010. Having correct understanding of local residents' perceptions, trying to obtain their active support, and developing effective tourism policies, all of these make this research necessary and practical for local tourism management and planning.

2. Research on Tourism Impacts and Residents' Perceptions

In recent years the impact of tourism on local residents has been a growing area of research, as it has become widely recognized that planners and entrepreneurs must take the views of the host community into account if the industry is to be sustainable in the long term (Ap and Crompton, 1998). There are many reasons to support this view, and most of them are based on a belief that a happy host is more likely to welcome the tourist and consequently generate an atmosphere which is conductive for both increased repeat visitors (LeBlanc, 1992) and positive word-of-mouth marketing effect (Pearce, 1994). Since tourism ventures benefit from a "happy" environment, knowing what make residents support or turn against tourism is necessary.

In recognition of the critical role that the host community plays in the tourism development process, many attempts have been made to study residents' attitudes and perceptions towards tourism distinguished by different background features of the local communities. Commonly adopted criteria may include socio-demographic characteristics, economic dependence on tourism, type of employment, and place of residence (Rothman, 1978; Pizam, 1978; Belisle and Hoy, 1980; Ahmed, 1986). Not only were differences found from one destination to another, even within the same community, the local's perceptions were found to be significantly diverse across a variety of socio-economic and demographic indicators (Teo, 1994; Snaith and Harley, 1999). Thus, many have argued that the residents' opinions of the impacts of tourism should not be viewed as homogenous in their support for tourism development (Mason and Cheyne, 2000).

Several models have been developed to help explain the impacts of tourism and their relationship with residents' perceptions. Doxey's 'Irridex model' (Long, Perdue and Allen, 1990), Butler's 'destination life cycle theory' (Butler, 1980), and Ap's 'social exchange theory' (Ap and Crompton, 1993) all offer very useful theoretical bases to understand residents' attitudes towards tourism, although the first two received some criticism for granting certain degrees of homogeneity of attitudes and community reactions to tourism development (Joppe 1996, Brurt and Courtney, 1999).

Recent investigations have suggested that communities have a certain capacity to absorb tourists. If beyond this capacity or threshold, the expansion may result in negative social and environmental impacts and diminishing returns on tourism investments (Wahab and Pigram, 1997). However, research following this concept has not yet given satisfactory answers to questions like "how does one measure the capacity?" Therefore, as Allen and other academics (1988) concluded, the carrying capacity concept has not been implemented successfully. It seems that none of these approaches can be sufficient by themselves in explaining the complicity. To help better understand the reality, those models should be considered as complementary to each other, rather than conflicting approaches when conducting impact studies, since each of them offers insights into the variety of factors that may affect residents' attitudes towards tourism.

It has been argued that among the important macro-trends, the demographic factors, such as population growth, life expectancy and age profile, are vitally important to tourism (Lickorish, 1991). Age, as one of the most easily accessible demographic indicators, has shown its power in differentiating residential perceptions. Previous research results show that a breakdown according to age produced the most varied classification of residents' attitudes of research population, especially in urban areas, as in the case of Darwin, Australia (Bastias-Perez and Var's, 1995) and in Lankford and Howard's (1994) study of Columbia River Gorge. Therefore in this Harbin research, special attention has been paid to comparing the responses from different residential age groups in seeking to generate more targeted information in assisting local tourism authorities' planning decisions. Income level has also been chosen as one of the differentiating criteria for further comparative analysis because of the assumed comparatively high possibility of 'money' influences on opinions of people from developing countries.

3. Harbin Residential Survey

Harbin in brief

This residential survey was conducted in Harbin, a city in the north-eastern part of China. It is the capital of Heilongjiang province and also the largest of the capital cities of China in terms of area. It has a population of above 9 million residents (3 million in the city proper). The city was first established at the end of the 10th century by the Nuzhen people, and they named the area of their settlement "Harbin" meaning "Swan" (Zhao and Li, 1999). By the 1920s, Harbin had become a famous international commercial centre in the Far-East with nearly 200,000 foreign residents from over 30 countries. The names of "Paris in the East" and "Moscow in the East" were given to Harbin show its importance and popularity during that period (HTCTM, 2000).

Its unique historical background and its distinct natural resources made Harbin a famous tourist destination in China, and it was selected as China's best Tourist City together with other 53 cities in China's first accreditation of this kind. The Songhua River, the second longest river in Heilongjiang Province (2,309 kilometres long), flows through the city and adds beauty as well as facilitating one of most popular tourist activities in summer, the Songhua River cruise. Every winter, Harbin's Ice and Snow Festival draws over a million visitors from home and abroad. Harbin also has China's best ski resort-Yabuli about 200 kilometres east of the city, where the Third Asian Winter Games was held. For the above reasons, Harbin's tourism has developed very fast with an annual growth rate of almost 10% in the last three years (HTB, 2001). In the year 2000, the city received 155,000 international visitors and 9 million domestic tourists, who bought in US$ 5.8 million and RMB¥ 4 billion (around US$ 500 million) tourism income respectively (HTB, 2001).

Data collection

The main aim of this research is to identify the aspects of their lives residents think have been influenced by tourism development and the degree of each influence. Hypothesis has also been made that significant differences would be found among the residents between age groups with regard to their general and specific perceptions towards tourism development's impacts in Harbin.

A face-to-face questionnaire survey was conducted in Harbin between May and June 2002. 290 residents over 18 years of age were contacted. Of these, 232 responded, and the response rate was 80%. The high response rate was helped by the adoption of a face-to-face household survey method. This method was not only useful to limit the probability of respondents' misunderstanding of questionnaire questions through direct communication, but also helpful to achieve a relatively balanced number of respondents from each age group by the control of the researcher.

A preliminary list of measurement items was developed through a review of the relevant literatures regarding tourism impacts and people perceived quality of life (Ap, 1992; Pizam, 1978; Tomljenovic and Faulkner, 2000). Modifications were made to suit the Harbin context. For example, questions were added in to test government's influence (see Table 1 for specific factors included in the questionnaire). The original questionnaire was designed in English. In order to minimize the language and translation biases and mismatches, the questionnaire was translated and revised by three bi-lingual (English and Chinese) speakers. The instrument was then pilot tested using a small sample of twenty Harbin residents. The final questionnaires containing 47 questions (with 36 perceptual statements) were hand-delivered individually to random adults within selected residential areas, close to Harbin's most popular tourist attractions including "Zhaolin Park", "Zhongyang Street", "Stalin Park", and "St. Sophia Church".

Table 1 Major factors covered in the questionnaire

Area		Example
• General background		i.e. Gender, age, length of residency, distance from respondents' home to the nearest tourist attraction, subjective definition of "tourist", the degree of encountering with tourists, personal economic reliance on tourism, and income level.
• Residential perceptions towards	Economic impacts	e.g. Employment opportunities, cost of living, etc.
	Socio-cultural impacts	e.g. cultural/citizenship identity, entertainment/ recreation opportunity, quality of public services, and crime, etc.
	Environmental impacts	e.g. litter, noise, damage to/improvement of natural / city environment, etc.
	Tourism policy-making	e.g. willingness for participating in tourism policy making

The survey questionnaire was mainly composed of structured questions. This method is good for achieving straightforward opinions from a wide range of people (Horn and Simmons, 2002) and gives a clear idea of residents' perceptions of tourism. It is also convenient for comparison between different subgroups' opinions (i.e. different age and income groups). However, one open-ended question was also used in seeking out broader and/or more specific residential concerns about Harbin tourism.

Thus, the questionnaire used contained three parts:

1. questions concerned with demographic background and the involvement of respondents in tourism, including gender, age, and length of residency, income level, employment history and so on;
2. a battery of 36 statements referring to both positive and negative economic, social, and environmental impacts of tourism development in Harbin. Respondents were asked to indicate the degree of their agreement or disagreement on a five point Likert-

type scale (where a score of 1 represents "strongly disagree" and a score of 5, "strongly disagree"). "0" has been used to represent "Don't know" to avoid the "filter effect" (Hall, 2001);

3. one open-ended question that residents were asked to state whatever they thought about current local tourism development.

Study Results

In General

The Statistical Package for the Social Sciences (SPSS) 12.0 was used as the basic software to analyse and interpret collected quantitative data for this study. Answers for the open-ended question were grouped manually by the researcher. The valid sample (232 residents) of the research was made up of roughly half female (112) and half male respondents (120). The mean age of the sample was 44 years ranging from 20 to 83 years old. Over half of respondents had monthly income over RMB1200 (56.9%). Over half of the respondents lived at their current address more than five years. The findings in general showed a favourable impression of residents towards tourism. Over two-thirds of households did not want to see restrictions on future local tourism development. When asked if the local authorities were making efforts to encourage tourism development, 93% agreed. Yet it was also interesting to notice that 24% of respondents stated that they believed tourism advantaged the community only because that government said so. Besides, the length of residency and income level did not seem to affect the strength of positive views held among residents in general.

85% of people agreed that tourism increased employment opportunities in the society, but only 66% of respondents believed tourism brought remarkable economic benefits to Harbin. Respondents were evenly divided in responding to the statement of "tourism economic benefits are overrated", with 35% agreeing and 34% disagreeing. 70% of people agreed that tourism contributed to the greater choices in local shops. It was felt that tourism has not caused increases in the cost of living as residents felt that other factors (e.g. business environment and urbanization), not tourism, were more influential in increasing the cost of living. One-fifth (20%) households considered tourism caused traffic congestion, while more than half (56%) of respondents didn't agree. The environmental degradation, widely identified in such research, has not been regarded as the result of tourism development in Harbin. Contradictorily, over 70% of respondents believed "tourism contributes to environmental conservation", which may be because of Harbin's industrial city background.

Residents in Harbin regarded tourists as very different from themselves, but instead of negative feelings towards them, they expressed predominantly positive opinions of tourists. Not surprisingly, almost all the respondents thought foreigners were tourists. Over 30% of respondents didn't include "day-trippers" as tourists. These opinions certainly had influenced their judgements of overcrowding, traffic congestion, and cultural impacts caused by tourists.

The majority of residents (80%) were of the opinion that tourism did not affect their own lifestyles. Neither the majority (75%) thought tourism undermined the local culture. Contradictorily, four-fifths of respondents had the feeling that tourists enriched Harbin's culture. Over 86% of residents agreed that "tourism make Harbin become more interesting and exciting". 77% respondents expressed their willingness to see more tourists. And exactly half of the total respondents declared that they liked international visitors more than domestic tourists because of their "politer" behaviour.

An optional open-ended question was used in the survey questionnaire asking respondents to give free comments on Harbin tourism development, with a view to suggesting explanations for a variety of perceived dimensions of tourism impacts on Harbin by local residents. Answers to this question provided about 120 written comments, which have certainly given researchers a more comprehensive understanding of local attitudes. Overwhelming positive views toward Harbin tourism development again were found here, but citizens also pointed out several unsatisfying aspects and existing problems regarding current tourism development in Harbin, concerning issues like: seasonality, tourism product development, and tourism education. In most comments, in addition to some similar expressions about the benefits which tourism has brought to Harbin, residents voiced an urgent need of improving service quality in tourism-related industries to meet higher-standard requirements from both international and domestic tourists. Though all respondents expressed their support for future Harbin tourism development, some would prefer themselves to be excused from the planning process and concerned about the insufficiency of their tourism-related knowledge. This view was strongly held by older residents.

Comparisons between Different Residential Groups

The second objective of this study was to investigate to what extent residents' perceptions towards local tourism development varied between different interest groups. Further comparisons have also been conducted. Variables like, age, income and employment link have been chosen as some of the main criteria to classify different residential groups.

Adult respondents were divided into four age groups, with the youngest group containing residents between 18 and 29, followed by people aged 30-49, 50-59 and 60 and over respectively. After comparison, the linkage between age and residents' perceptions towards general tourism development in Harbin was not clearly represented (i.e. the differences were not statistically significant), since the overwhelmingly supportive opinions were held by residents across all age groups, and older residents were found to share supportive attitudes towards overall tourism development as strong as other groups. However, relatively mixed perceptions were found regarding specific tourism-related issues among different age groups (as indicated in Table 2). Though the differences were limited, some of the results are worth being mentioned here to assist local tourism planning.

Table 2 Comparison of Harbin residents' perceptions towards tourism development between age groups

Statement	Mean				
	By Age Groups				
	a. 18-29 N=69	b.30-49 N=37	c. 50-59 N=47	d. 60+ N=79	Overall N=232
Some of the positive statements					
Tourism makes Harbin more interesting and exciting	4.26	4.22	4.32	3.99	4.17
Harbin residents have greater choices in shops	3.87	4.11	3.98	3.70	3.87
Improves neighbourhood	3.41	3.86	3.83	3.66	3.65
Creates employment opportunities	4.22	4.22	4.21	3.94	4.12
Lots of economic benefits	3.51	3.81	3.68	3.77	3.68
Contributes to natural preservation	3.39	3.41	3.19	3.38	3.35
Improves police/emergency services	3.13	3.35	3.38	3.30	3.28
Improves medical services	3.12	3.22	3.34	3.03	3.15
Tourists enrich the local culture	4.10	4.11	4.13	3.95	4.06
Tourism makes me proud to be Harbin citizen	3.80	3.89	4.06	3.87	3.89
Tourism development advantages Harbin's development	4.12	4.43	4.11	4.10	4.16
More tourists should be encouraged	4.38	4.68	4.36	4.28	4.39
Some of the negative statements					
Tourists increase litter on our streets	2.74	2.84	2.81	3.13	2.90
Recreational areas are overcrowded	3.10	2.95	2.91	3.10	3.04
Causes traffic congestion	2.68	2.35	2.47	2.57	2.55
Noisier neighbourhood	2.42	2.65	2.74	2.56	2.57
Causes crime/social problems	2.70	2.59	2.55	2.82	2.69
Damages natural environment	2.71	2.86	2.64	2.84	2.76
Excessive concerns about economic gains	2.67_b	3.32_a	3.06	2.92	2.94
Not enough police to cope with tourism related crimes	2.90	2.81	2.70	2.90	2.84
Hospitals can not cope	3.01	2.86	3.17	2.99	3.01
Increases costs of living	2.51	2.57	2.72	2.61	2.59
Servicing international tourists undermines local culture	1.81	2.30	1.94	2.16	2.03
Tourists intrude my life style	1.91	2.27	2.13	2.09	2.07
Economic contributions of tourism are overrated	2.78	2.81	2.96	3.23	2.97
I don't care Harbin's tourism development	1.80	1.81	1.91	*2.77*	2.16
Some of the multi-attitude statements					
I like international tourists more than domestic ones	3.51	3.70	3.30	3.37	3.45
I believe tourism benefits Harbin only because the government says so	2.23_d	2.46	2.70	2.85_a	2.57

Notes:
1) Means were based on a 5-point Likert-type scale, where 1= strongly disagree; 2= disagree; 3= either agree or disagree (neutral); 4= agree; 5= strongly agree
2) Subscripts indicate that this mean is significantly different from the corresponding mean in the indicated cluster based on Bonferroni post hoc testing (where p≤.05); bolded and italic numbers indicate means that are significantly higher than other three clusters based on Bonferroni post hoc testing (where p≤.05); underlined numbers indicate means that are significantly lower than the other three clusters based on Bonferroni post hoc testing (where p≤.05).

The results showed that compared with the other three age groups, the older residents (60 and over) were the least likely to pay special attention to Harbin's tourism development, although they seemed to share similar supportive attitudes toward local tourism development like others (see Table 2), which is slightly surprising considering that this age group may be particularly vulnerable to adverse impacts of tourism due to "the aging process" (Morgan and Kunkel, 1998). Furthermore, this group's perceptions of tourism were reported likely being influenced by the government's propaganda. This may be explained by the historical built-up 'trust' relationship between people and the Chinese government, which the older generation had experienced during the early stage of the PRC's development. Compared with the middle-aged groups, younger residents in Harbin seemed to be more concerned with the social impact brought about by the local tourism development, which made them hold stronger beliefs that present social values have become more materialistic partially because of tourism development (see Table 2).

It has always been assumed that people with higher income are more likely to benefit more from tourism development. Although it is not necessarily the case, the findings in this research seemed to support that income level does influence Harbin residents' perceptions on tourism (see Table 3). For example, the lower income group (monthly income less then RMB 800) included in this research has less stronger feeling about tourism's positive influence either on their life or on the local culture compared with the higher income group. Also, they are less worried about the capacity of the local police in coping with tourism-related crime. This may be due to the fact that people in this group are less likely to become the targets for burglary.

Table 3 Different income levels' influence on residents' perceptions toward Harbin's tourism

Statement	Mean		t-value	Sig.
	Below RMB 800* ≈18% respondents	RMB 800 & over* ≈82% respondents		(p≤05)
Tourism makes Harbin more interesting and exciting	3.78	4.26	3.142	.002
Not enough police to cope with tourism related crimes	2.41	2.94	2.553	.011
Tourists enrich the local culture	3.78	4.12	2.213	.028

*Note: Income level here refers to the respondent's monthly income range

One of the few relatively consistent findings in the area of residents' perception of tourism is that residents who derive financial benefit from the industry tend to hold more positive opinions of it (e.g. Ap 1992). The result in this research seemed have supported this assumption to a certain extent (see Table 3), although the design of this research has not been able to clarify whether such positive tendencies are explainable by the social exchange theory, which assumes that people in such a position may trade off negative impacts against pecuniary gains. Either way, respondents in this research who themselves, or those having relatives currently working in tourism-related industries, tended to possess more positive attitudes towards Harbin's tourism development than those who are not. Understandably, those who have employment links with the industry have stronger beliefs about the economic benefits of tourism development, especially in terms of creating employment opportunities. Unsurprisingly, this may also help to explain why they have sung higher praise for the tourism industry and given more attention to its development (as shown in Table 4).

Table 4 Current employment link with the tourism industry and its influence on respondents' perceptions on the local tourism's development impact

Statement	Mean		t-value	Sig.
	The respondent /his relative(s) is/are currently working in the tourism related industries			
	Yes ≈40% respondents	No ≈60% respondents		(p≤05)
Tourism makes Harbin more interesting and exciting	4.33	4.07	2.058	.041
Tourism creates employment opportunities	4.28	4.01	2.141	.033
Lots of economic benefits	3.85	3.57	1.999	.047
Tourism makes me proud to be Harbin citizen	4.05	3.79	1.983	.049
I don't care Harbin's tourism development	1.85	2.36	-3.301	.001

Discussion of Findings

Tourism is generally considered as having lifted the quality of life of local residents in Harbin, though only to a moderate degree. This positive opinion may change over time with further tourism development, as a higher influx of tourists could create more friction. As most respondents could not distinguish domestic tourists from unknown locals, some common problems occurred in urban areas, like traffic congestion and rising prices, although these have not been regarded as the side-effects of tourism development. Neither have the local residents perceived any intrusion to the local culture because of tourism development. This may be attributed to the fact that Harbin itself is a "fusion" of many cultures with its local community composed of more than 40 local ethnic groups. Therefore, perhaps, further research would be helpful to reveal whether responses to the factors examined in this research remain static or change over time in responding to the increase in tourism activities.

Few respondents perceived that tourism development has influenced the quality of health care or other social services in Harbin. This may be a reflection that residents were not quite satisfied with the speed in improvements of local public medical and police services. But further analysis of the answers to the open-ended question suggested that this result might also due to the unawareness of respondents about the "spin-offs" effects which tourism may have on social services. A lack of knowledge of 'tourism' in general, together with limited public access to the local tourism development information, may also explain the fact that a noticeable number of respondents chose "don't know" to certain questions.

Public leisure gardens in China are not so common as in most developed countries. Construction of gardens has been heavily limited by local economic conditions. This shortage is serious in urban areas since land can be "expensive" there. In open comments, older residents expressed their need for more green fields and public gardens around residential districts. As currently more than 9% of Harbin's population is over 60 and another 9% are aged between 50 and 59, such need should be given attention in order to create a "happier" host community. Also, as senior citizens were more reluctant to be involved in tourism policy-making, there is a challenge for local planners about how to reflect the needs of this "silent group" in their tourism development plans.

4. Concluding Remarks

This research is taken in response to the calls for timely tourism impact research in China and in urban scenarios. While a 'one-shot' study, this research provides valuable information for establishing baseline data of tourism impacts in Harbin through residents' point of view. Through the analysis of tendencies within different interest groups, especially by focusing on their age and income features, it provides an insight into the structure of community reactions to tourism, which enables more effectively targeted remedial or development actions aiming at increasing tourism benefits to the host community. However, the contribution of this research is better viewed as a wake-up call for more well designed tourism social impact research in China. As experienced in many tourism developing countries, the negative impacts of tourism can always be overlooked under its "glorious" cover of economic benefits. In the long-term, an ongoing assessment and continuously evaluation of tourism impacts on a given tourist destination and its community with plural theoretical approaches is desirable to cope with the diversity in reality. Most importantly, there is a necessity to improve the cooperation between academic researchers and tourism planners in order to transfer relevant research findings into the subsequent phrases of tourism planning.

References

Ahmed, S. (1986). Understanding residents' reaction to tourism marketing strategies. Journal of Travel Research 25:13-18

Allen, L.R., P. T. Long, R. R. Perdue and S. Kieselbach (1988). The Impact of Tourism Development on Residents' Perceptions of Community Life. Journal of Travel Research, 27(1), 16-21.

Ap, J and J.L. Crompton (1993). Residents' Strategies for Responding to Tourism Impacts. Journal of Travel Research, 32 (1), 47-50.

Ap, J. (1992). Residents' Perceptions of Tourism Impacts. Annals of Tourism Research, 19, 665-690.

Ap, J., and J. L. Crompton (1998). Developing and Testing a Tourism Impact Scale. Journal of Travel Research, 37(2), 120-130.

Ashworth, G. J. (1989). Urban Tourism: An Imbalance in Attention, in C.P. Cooper (eds.), Progress in Tourism, Recreation and Hospitality Management , Belhaven, London.

Bastias-Perez, P. and T. Var (1995). Perceived Impacts of Tourism by Residents-Research Notes and Reports. Annals of Tourism Research, 22 (1), 208-209.

Belisle, J. and D. Hoy (1980). The Perceived Impact of Tourism by Residents: A Case Study in Santa Marta. Annals of Tourism Research, 7, 83-99.

Brayley, R., P.S. Sheldonand and T. Var (1990). Perceived Influence of Tourism on Social Issues. Annals of Tourism Research, 17, 285-289.

Brunt, P. and P. Courtney (1999). Host Perceptions of Socio-Cultural Impacts. Annals of Tourism Research, 26 (3), 493-515.

Butler, R. W. (1980). The Concept of a Tourism Area Cycle of Evolution: Implications for the Management of Resources. Canadian Geographer, 24, 5-12.

CNTA. 2000-2003. The Yearbook of China Tourism Statistics, China National Tourism Administration, Beijing.

Davis, D., J. Allen and R.M. Cosenza (1988). Segmenting Local Residents by Their Attitudes Interests and Opinions toward Tourism. Journal of Travel Research, 27 (2), 2-8.

Fredline, E and B. Faulkner (2000). Host Community Reactions-A Cluster Analysis. Annals of Tourism Research, 27 (3), 763-784.

Gilbert, D. and M. Clark (1997). An Exploratory Examination of Urban Tourism Impact with Reference to Residents Attitudes in the Cities of Canterbury and Guildford. Cities, 14 (6), 343-352.

Hall, C. M. (1994). Tourism and Politics, Policy, Power and Place, John Wiley: Chichester:

Hall, T.E. (2001). Opinion Filter in Recreation Research: the Effect of Including "No Opinion" and "Not Notice" Response Categories in Questionnaires. Tourism Analysis, 6, 1-15.

Horn, C. and D. Simmons (2002). Community Adaptation to Tourism: Comparisons between Rotorua and Kaikoura, New Zealand. Tourism Management, 23, 133-143.

HTB (2001). The Tenth Five-year Plan of the Tourism Development of Harbin City, Harbin Tourism Bureau, Harbin.

HTCTM (2000). Harbin Tourist & Commercial Traffic Map, Harbin Cartographic Publishing House, Harbin.

Joppe, M. (1996). Sustainable Community Tourism Development Revisited. Tourism Management, 17, 475-479.

Lankford, S.V. and D. R. Howard (1994). Developing a Tourism Impact Attitude Scale. Annals of Tourism Research, 21, 121-139.

LeBlanc, G. (1992). Factors Affecting Customer Evaluations of Service Quality in Travel Agencies: An Investigation of Customer Perspectives. Journal of Travel Research, 30, 10-16.

Lickorish, L.J. (1991). Developing Tourism Destinations-Policies and Perspectives, Longman, Essex.

Long, P., R. Perdue and L. Allen (1990). Rural Resident Tourism Perceptions and Attitudes by Community Level of Tourism. Journal of Travel Research, 28 (3), 32- 44.

Mason, P. and J. Cheyne (2000). Residents' Attitudes to Proposed Tourism Development. Annals of Tourism Research, 27 (2), 391-411.

Morgan, L. and Kunkel, S. (1998). Aging-the Social Context, Pine Forge Press, London.

Pearce, P. L. (1994). Tourist-Resident Impacts: Examples, Explanations and Emerging Solutions, in W. Theobald (eds.), Global Tourism: the Next Decade, , Butterworth Heinemann, Oxford

Pearce, P. L.; G. Moscardo and G. F. Ross. (1996). Tourism Community Relationships, Pergamon Press Ltd, London.

Perdue, R.; P. Long and L. Allen (1990). Resident Support for Tourism Development. Annals of Tourism Research, 17 (4), 586-599.

Pizam, A. (1978). Tourism Impact: the Social Cost to Destination Community as Perceived by Its Residents. Journal of Travel Research, 16, 8-12.

Rothman, R. (1978). Residents and Transients: Community Reaction to Seasonal Visitors. Journal of Travel Research, 16, 8-13.

Singh, S. (1997). Developing Human Resources for the Tourism Industry with Reference to India. Tourism Management, 18 (5), 299-306.

Smith, V. 1978. Host and Guests: the Anthropology of Tourism, Blackwell, Oxford.

Snaith, T and A. Haley (1999). Residents' Opinions of Tourism Development in the Historic City of York, England. Tourism Management, 20: 595-603.

Teo, P. (1994). Managing Socio-Cultural Impacts: the Case of Singapore. Tourism Management, 15 (2), 126-136.

Tomljenovic, R. and B. Faulkner (2000). Tourism and Older Residents in a Sunbelt Resort. Annals of Tourism Research, 27(1), 93-114.

Wahab, S. and J J. Pigram (1997). Tourism, Development and Growth: the Challenge of Sustainability, Routledge, London..

Weaver, D. and L. J. Lawton (2004). Visitor Attitudes toward Tourism Development and Product Integration in an Australian Urban-rural Fringe. Journal of Travel Research, 42, 286-296.

Zhao, X.L. and X. Y. Li. (1999). Guide to Heilongjiang China, Heilongjiang People's Publishing House, Harbin, China.

The Social Impacts of Tourism in a Beijing Hutong — A Case of Environmental Change

Chris Ryan[*]

University of Waikato Management School, New Zealand

Huimin Gu

Beijing International Studies University, China

Abstract:

The paper reports the results of a qualitative study that separately interviewed over 40 residents and over 40 business people in Shi Cha Hai hutong. It identifies four major groups of impacts being noted as arising from the development of tourism, namely changes in physical appearance of the hutong, increased noise, increased congestion and issues of safety and public order. It relates these changes to a growth of migrant entrepreneurs and the specific growth of the pedicab business. The data permit the development of a hutong destination life cycle framework of analysis that modifies the Butlerian life cycle by the addition of a further axis and a discussion of a continuum of localization, globalization and glocalisation.

1. Introduction

The purpose of this paper is to examine attitudes towards tourism expressed by residents of a Beijing hutong. The structure of the paper is to first describe the context of the study with reference to a) the location of the research and b) the literature pertaining to destination life cycles and community involvement in tourism. Second, the research process and findings will be described and finally, within a discussion of the results it will be suggested that the findings permit a new conceptualization of the tourist destination. It also needs to be stated that this paper is part of a wider research project and will briefly include for comparative purposes, data emanating from interviews with business personnel within the hutong. This has been included in the belief that it

---

* Corresponding author

Chris Ryan, Professor of Tourism at the University of Waikato and editor of Tourism Management. Email: caryan@waikato.ac.nz.

Huimin Gu, Professor and Deputy Dean of the School of Tourism Management, Beijing International Studies University. Email: guhuimin@bisu.edu.cn.

contributes to the development of the conceptualization suggested in the final part of the paper. This last is thought important because several have criticized the current state of tourism research in China. For example, Wu, Guo, Song, and Deng (2005, p. 19) state that 'China's tourism research work has achieved a lot during the last 20 years. However, a gap still exists compared with the international level, including severe confusion of many basic tourism concepts, a lag in the constitution of conceptual systems, the relatively narrow eyeshot, simplex research methods, the lack of theoretical backgrounds in most researches and the lack of systemization of theoretical research' - a sentiment which has also been expressed by other Chinese researchers (e.g. Y. H. Liu, Ma, & Zhu, 2005). It is hoped this paper will, in part, address these perceived deficiencies.

Shi Cha Hai Hutong

Anecdotally it is stated that there are as many hutong in Beijing, China, as there are hairs on a cow. Alternatively, it is sometimes stated there are 3,000 famous hutong in Beijing, and 3,000 not so famous (Rowswell, 2006). It may be said that Shi Cha Hai represents not only one of the former, but also a heritage that is beginning to disappear under the new sky line of high rise office blocks and apartments that are characterizing the 'new' Beijing. The hutong are the areas of small alley ways that connect primarily one and two storey households centered on small courtyards. In the poorer areas each side of the courtyard would be occupied by a separate family, whereas wealthier families could occupy one house that possessed a myriad of rooms themselves forming squares around small, private gardens. In age, many of these houses can date back several centuries and be within the possession of one family for generations. Some hutong like Shi Cha Hai, may now be primarily residential, but others on the outskirts of Beijing near the international airport may be the location of small industrial businesses.

Shi Cha Hai is located within Xicheng District in the northwest of the downtown area of Beijing comprising West Changan Street, Exhibition Road, Finance Road, Yuetan, Desheng and Shichahai. In 2005 the district's population was 831,000. Xicheng District is the one of the most developed in Beijing, and its tertiary (service) industry accounts for 89% of its economic activity. In recent years, finance, advertising, tourism and real estate have become emergent industries of note (Beijing Statistical Information Net, 2007). Property prices have risen faster in this area than in other parts of Beijing and stood 7.9 percent higher in June 2006 than in 2004 (北京市西城区统计信息网, 2007).

As China is still oriented toward a planned economy the government remains heavily involved in the planning process. The municipal government focuses more on general planning, while its tourism bodies, including the Beijing Tourism Administration, focus on tourism planning. In 2005, the government started a programme of infrastructure construction following the rapid development of tourism in this area. Remedying dilapidated houses in Shi Cha Hai is one of more important parts of this plan. In 2006 there were 20 blocks under construction. The plan incorporates specific conservation objectives – for example in 2006 a special concern was a project for protecting

Smoke-bag Slanting Street. In addition, road repair and upgrading is included. An island on Shi Cha Hai lake is also under construction and a new viewing spot will be built by May 2007 (中国 什刹海网站, 2006). Additionally, each year the municipal government holds the Shi Cha Hai Tourism Culture Festival for promoting and marketing Shi Cha Hai, which also has its own websites, some of which were funded by governmental funds. How to balance the development and conservation of hutong is an issue of concern to the government. For example the Beijing municipal government will be building new quadrangle hotels with traditional Beijing Architecture style to replace the current dirty inns in Dazhalan area (Beijing Tourism Administration , 2006; China. org.cn, 2006; 中国什刹海网站, 2006).

As a potential tourist attraction, Shi Cha Hai possesses specific heritage attributes partly due to its location to the north of the Forbidden Palace. Its former occupants included officials and members of the Royal Family, and thus some of the homes are quite ornate even whilst the external walls and doorways will only hint at their interiors through the marking of lions or a given number of bosses on a door lintel to note the status of the family. Currently Shi Cha Hai is an area in transition. It is still possible to wend through lanes that are either muddy or dusty dependent upon season, but elsewhere new paving and roads mark the ways, and between May and October during the daylight hours the paved alleys are busy with the pedicab drivers taking tourists through the maze of streets.

Figure 1 Interior courtyard of former upper social class hutong courtyard

Picture courtesy of Chris Ryan

According to the residents interviewed for this study, the development of tourism began approximately in 1997. However, Wang (1997) argues that tourism development began in 1994 with the formation of the Beijing Hutong Tour Agency by Xü Yong, a photographer familiar with the area. Today 17 licensed pedicab companies exist competing fiercely for the tourist dollar, and a new bar and restaurant area has developed. In 2005 the Beijing City administration nominated 25 areas as outstanding heritage and being of historical interest, and Shi Cha Hai was the largest of these.

2. Literature Review

The issue of resident attitudes toward tourism has long been recognised by the academic tourism literature. For example, Doxey's Irridex (Irritation Index) dates from 1975 while Butler's Destination Life Cycle theory (1980) has obvious implications for the quality of life offered to residents in holiday destinations. In 1978 Ritchie and Zins identified eight areas in which tourism might have an impact; which areas included economic, social and environmental impacts. Early studies that adopted a quantitative approach upon which this study is premised included the work of Belisle and Hoy (1980), Brougham and Butler (1981), J. C. Liu and Var (1986), Davis, Allen and Cosenza, (1988), Allen, Long, Perdue and Kieselbach (1988), and Long, Perdue and Allen (1990).

Variables that emerge from such studies include overcrowding, changing retail patterns, house prices and home affordability, environmental degradation, employment creation, opportunities for artistic creativity and understandings of planning policies. Studies from New Zealand, such as that of Lawson, Williams, Young and Cossens (1998) have offered researchers an opportunity for a temporal comparison with previous studies. Selected locations illustrated places with different roles and levels of involvement with the tourism industry, and permitted longitudinal study. The results from Auckland, Christchurch and Rotorua showed how residents of larger cities with developed infrastructure and wide economic bases were more moderate in their views of tourism, and were generally neither critical nor enthusiastic about the industry, while smaller locations experiencing rapid tourism development showed more signs of social stress, at least in the early stages of the destination life cycle.

Initially research of this nature was motivated by a wish to both identify variables thought to be important in shaping resident attitudes, and to assess the strength of beliefs attributed to these items. Subsequent to this researchers sought to identify determinants of beliefs and attitude formation and model the relationships. Mason and Cheyne (2000) found that direct economic dependence on the tourism industry was the single most important factor affecting views, and that some residents were tolerant of increased tourist arrivals due to the lack of alternatives that could generate economic growth. Capenerhurst (1994) argued many of the studies that highlight the fears of community members towards tourism development are based on a premise that communities fear 'losing control' of their environment; a premise, however, that he describes as a romantic notion. Nonetheless Capenerhurst (p. 152) went on to say 'if community members feel their identity to be threatened by this industry they will develop attitudes which are at best unfavourable.' He also argued that smaller destinations are likely to react more strongly to such development as it will be a lot more visible.

Ryan, Scotland and Montgomery (1998) found a number of factors seemed to affect resident perceptions. These included the amount of time a person had been resident in the region, whether they were employed in the tourism industry and how much they knew about tourism. They concluded that respondents in a location that is in the early stages of the destination life cycle tend to express high levels of altruism about tourism, that is, it is seen as a benefit to the region because of the thought that it created jobs for other people, even if respondents were unable to identify any personal benefit. However, as development continues and thereby more directly affects people, such altruism may become subject to more questioning, and attitudes tend to harden either for or against as personal core values come more to the fore.

Ryan and Cooper (2004) summarised findings from the literature thus:

The perceived level of tourism development
1. Residents of places with a longer history of tourism development are more aware of both the positive and negative impacts of tourism (J. C. Liu, Sheldon, & Var, 1987).
2. The Guest/host ratio has importance – the lower the ratio the more the social impacts of tourism will be diluted (Lawson et al., 1998).
3. There is a curvilinear relationship between perceptions of negative impacts and development of tourism, though not as strong as a relationship between perceptions of negative impacts and population growth (Allen et al., 1988). In short, tourism may be 'blamed' for some aspects that perhaps should be more correctly attributed to population growth.
4. Stage of the destination life cycle (Lawson et al., 1998).
5. Type of tourism encountered within the community (Murphy, 1985).

Economic Dependency on Tourism (from the perspective of those who have been or currently are employed in the tourism industry).
1. There is a positive relationship between employment in, and support for tourism (Glasson, 1994).
2. Those who were more dependent on tourism were more positive about tourism (Lankford & Howard, 1994).
3. Personal benefits of tourism were the best predictors of perceptions of positive impacts (Prentice, 1993).
4. Host's control over decision making – levels of support for tourism decreases as non-resident control over development increases (Lawson et al., 1998).

Respondent Demographics
1. Older residents were less positive about tourism (Brougham & Butler, 1981).
2. Perceived cultural or psychic distance between host and guest – the greater the cultural differences between residents and visitors, the larger were the social impacts (Thyne & Lawson, 2001).

Community Attachment
1. People who had lived longer in a community were more positive about some types of tourists (Brougham & Butler, 1981).

2. A greater attachment to a community was associated with higher ratings of both positive and negative impacts of tourism (McCool & Martin, 1994).

More recent literature has sought to model relationships between these variables. For example Gursoy, Jurowski and Uysal (2002) found, among other items, no inverse relationship existed between perceived community attachment and costs of tourism and no direct relationship between perceived community attachment and perceived benefits derived from tourism. On the other hand, of importance were the state of the local economy, resident utilisation of tourist resources, eco-centric values and perceived costs and benefits of tourism.

Lindberg, Dellaert and Rassing (1999) used logit modelling in a study premised on social exchange theory to conclude that residents are fully aware that benefits offered by tourism are associated with costs, but that some residents tended to concentrate upon one sub-set of options that, arguably, reflect a set of values. Williams and Lawson (2001), and Fredline and Faulkner (2000) are among a number of studies that utilise cluster analysis based on attitudinal data to argue that shared opinions and attitudes may be one of the better predictors of resident responses to tourism development.

It has been noted that Butler's destination life cycle theory (1980, 2006a, 2006b) is one of the better known concepts in the tourism literature, and traces the development of a destination through the stages of exploration, involvement, consolidation, stagnation and thence potential rejuvenation or decline. Each stage has various implications for land use patterns (Russo, 2006; Young, 1983) and for the nature of business enterprise (Ryan, 1991). Equally, it has been long suggested that associated with each stage are different types of tourists (Cohen, 1972) and also different patterns of resident responses (Doxey, 1975). Because of the significant impacts that tourism can have on environments and communities, there has long been a call for community participation in tourism planning (Getz, 1982, 1993; Jamal & Getz, 1999; Murphy, 1985). Such calls have, in many western societies, elicited practical responses as described, for example, by Getz and Jamal (1994) in the case of Canmore, Alberta, and through various legislations that require, under given conditions, public participation in the planning process (e.g. New Zealand's Resource Management Act, 1991). However, with reference to the planning procedures of the People's Republic of China, Wall (2005) noted that calls for public participation in tourism planning were inappropriate given the legislative, political and social structures of that country, and a more pertinent approach would be planning processes that permitted public participation in benefit rather than process. Evidence for the pertinence of this observation arose within this study whereby some residents made comments indicating that development was effectively a government decision which people had to accept. For example, a 49 year old female, resident all her life in the hutong, stated 'It's the government's decision to develop Hutong tourism. Common people have no opportunities to express our ideas. Some may benefit from it, but others may not. My family belongs to the former. My house was leased out and used as a bar. Now the rental has taken up one third of my family income.' Others expressed an indifference based upon resignation, such as the view of a 31 year old male resident in

Shi Cha Hai for 6 years, who when asked if he would leave the hutong, answered 'I do not care. Do you have any chance if the government asks you to move out?' Such attitudes are not wholly explained by a political regime based upon the Communist uprising of the 1940s, but are also related to a deeper cultural perspective based on the role of hierarchies and acceptances of status and life chances derived from Confucian and Buddhist teachings.

Associated with this are the views of Galston and Baehler (1995, p. 27) who argue that the defining element of any development should be that of equity stating that 'growth strategies that unfairly impact on the least advantaged members of the community cannot be justified and should not be implemented.' They identify three principles of equity. The first of 'no harm' states that any development should not harm the least advantaged. The second of 'maximim' should seek to benefit the least advantaged while the third principle of equalisation should seek eventually to establish parity between the least and most advantaged. Their wider debate relates to the roles of efficiency and equity, but the perspectives expressed are consistent with Wall's (2005) premise that within China participation in benefit and not necessarily process might be the way forward within the current socio-political environment.

3. The Research Process

As previously noted the research has the objective of ascertaining the perceptions of residents as to the changes being created within the hutong by tourism. The research is predicated on a constructionist paradigm whereby the researcher seeks rich descriptive data from which attitudinal dimensions might be 'constructed'. Such 'paradigmatic dialogues' (Guba, 1990) are consistent with precepts of personal construct theory (Allport, 1955, 1961, 1968; Kelly, 1955) and require a minimum of 20 respondents to elicit common dimensions to an attitude. Given that potential differences might exist between key groups based upon gender and period of residential duration, it was decided to double this number of interviews, and eventually 43 interviews were conducted. Respondents were selected through a combination of 'snowballing' and initial contact and thus the research is subject to the limitations applicable to such approaches, namely the ability to generalise is limited. However, the purpose of such research is to obtain insights that can lead to conceptual propositions that in turn can be subjected to further testing through other research methods.

The key issue for research of this type is the nature of the interpretation, and a balance needs to be struck between (a) letting the voice of the respondents be heard, (b) the danger that researchers attribute structures to respondents that are not actually present, (c) interpretations are individualistic and loose credibility and (c) data remains that of isolated voices and unrelated to commonalities of experience that can inform wider debate. Consideration was given to these issues. All the interviews were based on a semi-structured, open-ended questionnaire. This was used as a guide as the process was conversational (conducted in Mandarin) and thus not every interview followed the same sequence, but for the most part all interviews covered the same topics. These were based on initially establishing residency and duration of that residency, and then the extent to which changes in the hutong been identified, what where those changes and an evaluation of the degree to which they were positive or negative. The data were recorded and supported by notes made on laptops. The analysis was then undertaken by breaking down the conversations into responses to given questions and noted in Word and Excel files. This permitted categorical analysis, and the use of the program 'CatPac'. This last mentioned computer program is based on principles of artificial neural networks and aids textual analysis by creating dendograms of word relationships, word counts and perceptual maps based upon various statistical routines where the raw data are word locations. Like many such programs it is an aid by structuring the researcher's analysis and requiring the researcher to develop commonalities of meaning. The first stages are to standardize the text by creating rules whereby positive and negative statements, singulars and plurals, tenses of verbs and categories of adjectives are reduced to commonalities. One potential drawback is that the actual 'keywords' that emerge may not actually be those of the original respondents although the finalized text might be said to represent the underlying dimensions. It might be compared to the process of factor analysis where an underlying dimension summarises a series of separate items. Its structuring of the text is, however, consistent with personal construct theory in that it generates dimensions of shared meanings common to the text originally generated by the respondents. Finally, it should be noted that the data reported below is based upon the total sample in that initial analysis did not confirm dimensions of textual constructs specific to gender or duration of residency. Additionally, the paper reverts back to the original text as illustrative of the dimensions revealed by the analysis rather than using the output of the program as undertaken by other researchers such as, for example, Lockyer (2003) who used the dendograms in his analysis of hotel quality.

As noted sampling was based on snowballing, but the study took care to ensure that a wide range of individuals were engaged. The characteristics of the respondents included the following. The mean age was 42 years and 5 months, but the ages ranged from a 12 year old school boy to an 81 year old lady. Of the total, two-thirds had been born in the hutong. Of those born in the hutong, the mean period of residence was 40 years and 6 months, while for those now living but not born in the hutong, the average length of residency was 19 years and 3 months. Of the sample 26 were females, 25 were males, 1 was a married couple interviewed together, and one was a family group.

It became quickly evident that by and large, residents were not involved in the tourism industry within the hutong, and so a further process of interviews took place with those involved in tourism enterprise in Shi Cha Hai. This second sample comprised 47 interviews, and the methods of data collection and interpretation were similar to that used for the collection of responses from residents. The nature of the businesses included 8 bar owners and managers, 3 boat operators, 2 female cake makers, 12 pedicab operators/owners/employees, 8 restaurant managers/owners plus 15 others engaged in various retail operations including clothes, candy floss, china and pottery, and groceries. Of the sample just 9 were native to Beijing, and the sample revealed high levels of inward migration to start or work for businesses already existing in the hutong. The provinces from which the respondents had come were Inner Mongolia, Gansu, Hebei, Jiangsu, Shangdong, Shanxi, and Sichuan. For the purposes of this paper the emphasis is upon the perceptions of the residents, but a brief comparison with those of the business people will be made for purposes of confirmation and analytical development.

4. Research Findings

The Residents

The research findings are indicated by Figure 2, which is premised upon residents' observations of change in the hutong. Indeed, all but two of the respondents confirmed that change had taken place, and that these changes had commenced about 1998 but had been more noticeable since 2003. In short, the discussion within the paper follows a construction 'imposed' by the researchers upon residents' perceptions in order to sustain an order of categorisation. The four categories are: appearance of the hutong, noise, congestion and public safety and order. It should be noted that these categories are not wholly independent and relationships exist between them. To illustrate the themes text from the interviews is included and in some instances the quotations go beyond the immediate category to illustrate the linkages between the themes. The text is deliberately retained to give voice to the respondents and permit them to retain an 'independence' from the constructs devised by the authors. The perspective adopted in the following sections is that the role of the researcher is to facilitate the voice of respondents as much as it is to interpret those voices.

Figure 2 Main perceived changes in Shi Cha Hai

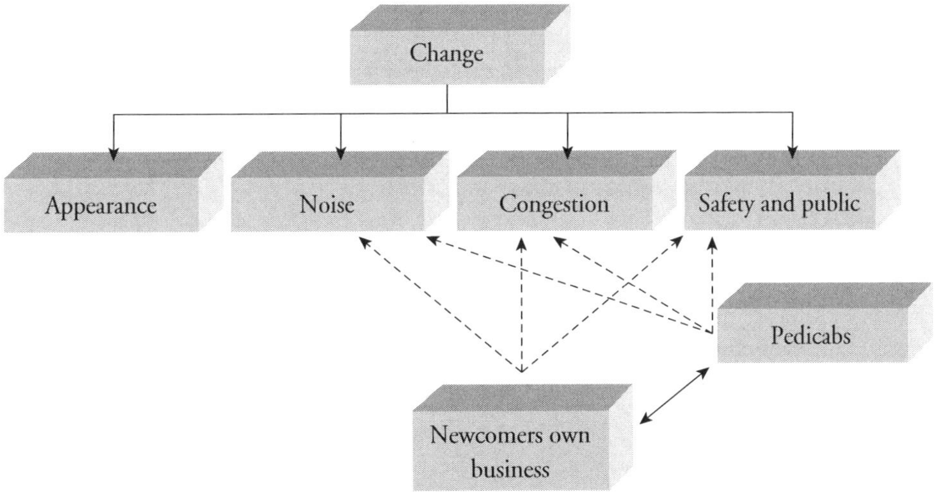

Appearance

The most noticeable difference for many of the residents has been the improvement on the road system within the hutong with previously unpaved and unsealed roads being paved and concreted over. However, some of these road improvements have not apparently come without some costs because one resident referred to some homes being demolished to create wider road ways while another noted that there were disturbances and noise during the actual construction period, and that sometimes once laid roads were then again torn up and re-laid, presumably because of a need for drainage systems and the like. Certainly improvements in sanitation were also noted, and indeed any visitor to the hutong can see the investment made in public toilets and showers as shown in Figure 3.

Figure 3 Government investment in hutong public toilets and showers

Picture courtesy of Chris Ryan

Such improvements have been due to public investment but some improvements have been paid for by private owners such as the external appearance of houses. Examples of quotations here include:

Male – 70 years old, has resided in the hutong for 60 years.

Q: Has the hutong changed a lot?
A: Yes, a lot. Take an example, the road is much better.
Q: Compared to the past?
A: It was too decrepit in the past. But now everything is modernized.
Q: Do you like the changes?
A: Of course.

Male – 40 years old, has lived in the hutong for 12 years

> Q: Do you think there are any changes in hutong after tourism development?
> A: In the past, the road was muddy. But now all the roads have been paved with bricks…
> Q: What about the living environment now, especially after tourism development?
> A: It became better. There are many investments by the government…
> Q: What are the investments used for?
> A: For public facilities, such as street lamps and public toilets.

However, while such benefits were easily identified some respondents made reference to negative environmental impacts arising from tourism. Two made reference to the waters in the lake becoming more polluted because of engine oil from the boats that were using the lake, while the bars also encroached on road ways by placing tables and chairs outside their premises, which in the eyes of this informant added to the confusion and congestion of the roads. This raises the related issue of noise.

Noise

Of the respondents 17 made unprompted specific references to noise. There was a consensus among these respondents that the hutong was noisier than had once been the case, and for this three specific reasons existed. First, there was the growth in the number of bars and restaurants and their trading hours being much longer during the main tourist season of May to October. Second, there was an increase in general traffic and third, for a minority, associated with this traffic there was the issue of the pedicabs which sometimes associated with shouting and disputes. Examples of the text on these issues include the following:

50 year-old male – resident since birth

> … with the development of tourism, it takes on various changes including some beneficial ones and some disadvantageous ones. For example, on one hand, it has brought remarkable improvement to the basic facilities and there are much more business opportunities than ever before. However, on the other hand, it has been becoming noisy, which has affected people's normal life to a certain extent.

Over 50 years of age, male

> … it affects our daily lives and gives birth to noise, crowded traffic and bad environment…

Over 50 years of age, female

Yes. There are more outsiders than before, and the bars make a lot of noise in the evening...

A contributory factor to the noise is the growing traffic congestion, which is discussed below.

Congestion

The alley ways and roads of the hutong are narrow. They were historically related to pedestrian traffic but over the last century are being used by cyclists and rickshaws. However, in more recent decades increasing residential wealth and tourist born traffic has seen car borne traffic increase significantly, and the narrow wall lined roads mean that the sound echoes around the walls. Another contributory factor has been taxi borne traffic to restaurants, bars and hotels. However, the most nominated user that drew criticism was the growing numbers of pedicabs, or cycle driven rickshaws. Almost half of the respondents made unprompted references to these, and overwhelmingly the comments were negative in tone. For example:

30 year-old female – recent resident

Certainly it is (getting noisier). As you know, the buses can't get into the hutong, so you can only take local pedicabs to get in, which are out of control and noisy. However, they come by only during daytime and never break into local houses; this makes things not so bad...

50 year-old male – born in the hutong and lifelong resident

It changes a lot, the hutong used to be very quiet before tourism developed... say last 3-4 years, more and more tourists visit here and there are nearly 1,000 pedicabs, which threatens our daily safety. The operators from other provinces often quarrel and fight with each other, as well as cheating foreigners. What's more, they usually misguide tourists and mess the traffic up. They even break into local people's houses. We feel unsafe and the modern building ruined the traditional landscape here. Actually, the landscape changes a lot, which was very beautiful before...

It has to be added that for some respondents there was a recognition that the pedicabs are an important aspect of local tourism and thus two main suggestions emanated from this minority. These were a) that there should be proper guide training – one respondent said they often fabricated the history of the hutong for tourists, and b) there should be better organisation of the pedicab operators. This latter comment is consistent with the views expressed by many of the operators themselves as indicated below.

Public safety and order

As indicated by the above respondent, concerns about public safety and order appear to be broadly centred upon petty theft, litter, congestion, leading to potential annoyance and danger to pedestrians, noise as indicated above, and the apparent lack of control over the numbers and actions of pedicab riders. As will be seen below, by and large the residents do not see the tourists themselves as a direct source of problems in terms of their own behaviours. Rather, indirectly tourism is held to account for these other developments, although again it must be noted that a minority (two respondents) did hold to the view that some of these issues were a reflection of a growing affluence within the hutong itself. On the other hand an increased police presence was also noted. In the group discussion, among the views expressed were shown as follows:

Q: What is your opinion about hutong tourism?

A: It brings so many problems. We would like it if we could return to past ways.

Q: What are the problems?

A (1): The relevant administrations do not care about us. For example, our inhabitants have no parking spaces…

A (2): The environment and public security has become worse.

A (3): Hutong tourism is a very important program. Yet not much success is achieved even though much money is invested in it. Even some relevant management departments are creating some buildings illegally…

While on the whole there is faith in the management and administrative processes pertinent to the hutong, for a small minority there was a distrust of those processes. It might be due to the fact that the interviews were taking place during a high profile corruption case in Shanghai that might have prompted such responses. In the case of one respondent the question about government role was met by a sarcastic retort that we would have to ask them about that! While noting this undercurrent, it needs to be emphasised that generally there was little criticism per se of the systems of control – rather there was a wish that those systems performed better in meeting local residents' concerns of the nature outlined above. As observed by Wall (2005) residents generally accepted that they would have no direct role in any planning process, but did expect that plans should take their concerns into consideration. Of course, it is obvious that the planning authorities may not aware of those concerns unless there is some mode of communication between different stakeholders.

Comparison with Hutong Business People's Views

As noted above, comparative data were derived from interviews with those doing business in the hutong. Broadly speaking, these businessmen also concurred with a view that tourism had commenced in about 1998 but there was a strong view that this had grown significantly since 2003 and the end of the SARS crisis. Strangely, given its high profile, neither residents nor business people made much reference to the forthcoming 2008 Olympic Games as a spur for tourism development. There was also agreement between many of the business people and the residents that the current state of tourism was 'disorderly' and this was specifically true of, but not confined to the pedicab business. Competition was described as intense, and market conditions as 'chaotic'. Opinion was divided as to how to address this problem. The majority called for a better implementation of licensing conditions, while a sizeable minority thought the nature of the market place was competition and that it was through competition that the situation would be resolved.

It was interesting that many of the business people recognised that tourism could impede upon the daily life of hutong residents. They also made reference to the improved physical conditions of the hutong and its infrastructure, and to the issues of congestion, noise and public order. It is suggested that there was a strong congruence of views between the two groups in terms of generating categories of impacts, but the emphasis as to the importance of these categories differed. For the business people market conditions tended to be uppermost on their mind, and the social costs to residents were secondary; while market conditions were hardly mentioned from a business perspective by the residents, the social costs and benefits and the ways in which they impacted upon local life were important.

Intervening Factors in Attitude Formation

Taking both the views of business people and residents together, two intervening variables were readily identified that could moderate residents' views and impact on the tolerance they exercised with reference to the development of tourism. The first related to seasonal and daily patterns of business. With reference to seasonality, business people pointed out that due to climatic conditions and the nature of Beijing's winters, strong seasonal variations in income existed. The peak season was between May and October and, by implication, the negative impacts of noise, congestion and rushing pedicabs would be mitigated for many months of the year through a diminution of business. With reference to daily patterns of business, pedicabs were not permitted to operate within certain parts of the hutong before 11.00 am, and most ceased after about 5.00 pm. Equally, the noisy impact of the bars was primarily noted during the hours of darkness.

The second variable was that of location. The hutong is not homogenous in terms of current patterns of improvement, and large areas can still be found with unmade roads. These are not generally visited by tourists and the pedicabs also tend not to operate in these areas. They therefore remain quieter and more traditional in life style, and this was reflected in some residents' comments that, where they lived, they did not suffer from the noise created by the bars and restaurants. Similarly some business people fell back on the well known mantra that success in business was dependent upon location, and that their location meant they did not access the major flows of tourists and thus a significant amount of their business was dependent upon local residents. A third variable that reduced contact between residents and tourists was that of price structures. Residents were asked whether they used the facilities that had developed as a result of tourism. Generally the answers were in the negative, the main reason being that the prices were thought to be too high. It should be noted that this factor operated in two ways. For some the prices were considered so high as not to be affordable, while in other cases, while affordable, residents saw no reason to pay for services that they could obtain elsewhere more reasonably.

5. Discussion

It was originally noted that a qualitative approach was adopted for this study to permit conceptualisations to be developed that would address an apparent deficiency in Chinese tourism research while also aiding future research (Wu et al., 2005). The findings were reported within a framework developed from an analysis of semi-structured conversational text: that is perceptions were based on themes of changes in appearance, increased levels of noise, increased congestion, and issues of safety and congestion, while it was recognised that new business opportunities exist. It is suggested that a hutong destination life cycle can be identified, as indicated in Figure 4. The core of the diagram is the conventional Butlerian life cycle of numbers of tourists growing over time whereby the destination proceeds through stages of exploration, involvement, consolidation, stagnation and then either decline or rejuvenation. Associated with these stages are not only changes in land use but also sources of capital funding. In the initial stages tourism is conventionally thought to be based within a local domestic framework, and then as tourism grows, and capital requirements also grow, there is a need to utilise external sources of finance and also external marketing 'capital' such as distribution channels external to the destination. Past studies of rejuvenation also seem to suggest that the destination public sector in co-operation with local and external private sector capital is required to redevelop the destination (Baum, 2006; Cooper, 2006). This is shown below the core diagram as a new horizontal axis.

Figure 4 Modified Destination Life Cycle

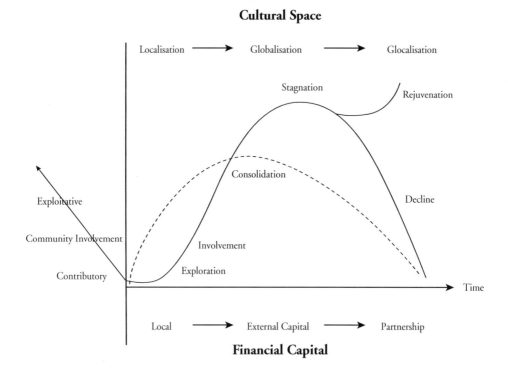

Notes: The solid curve shows the conventional relationship between visitor numbers and time

The dotted curve shows the relationship between community involvement and time – hus at the exploration stage community involvement is high and contributes to tourism development, then over time it becomes less and external forces then 'exploit' local community assets, until such time as glocalisation requires again a positive involvement of local communities create destination uniqueness based on local history, culture and peoples.

The hutong is demonstrating this process as the Beijing Municipal and Tourism Administration is upgrading infrastructure and co-operating with the private sector in the development of small quadrangle hotels consistent with the architectural heritage of the area. What further complicates the issue is a growth of incomes from industries other than tourism, where, within the wider district, the emergence of the service sector as a major employer is increasing incomes, and the desirability of residence in the hutong. A process of 'gentrification' is occurring as has happened in other large cities – e.g. the Barnsbury area of London, or in villages like Deya in Mallorca. Tourism is part of, and a contributor to this process, and creates a mix of residence populations as the affluent enter areas once occupied by lower income groups. The area thus demonstrates aspects of rejuvenation of infrastructure and construction at an early stage of the tourism cycle.

Another aspect of contemporary tourism that follows from this capital movement is a move from the local and its history and culture toward the more global – as external capital is attracted the destination comes to assume some of the features of a more global economy as it moves into a more mass market orientation. Again, as the destination in due course may wish to achieve rejuvenation, it has to rediscover and utilise its history and heritage more proactively to develop points of difference from other global destinations, and thus a process of 'glocalisation' may be said to occur where the local is incorporated with the global to reach global markets. This process toward globalisation is illustrated in both small and larger ways by the nature of the improvements being made. For example the hutong is being opened to vehicles through road widening and surface enhancements. The changed appearance and congregation of small service outlets at cross roads is consistent with town planning adopted in western cities as part of street furniture and 'beautification' programmes. However, the presence of a strong central planning regime ensures that outlets are locally managed and Chinese owned, and thus, to use a problematic phraseology, a cultural 'authenticity' is sustained. The international visitor is thus presented with a physical environment with which familiar parallels can be drawn even whilst being reassured that travel has indeed brought them somewhere new.

It now becomes possible to add a third axis, which is the quality of life axis with reference to residents' perspectives and support for tourism development. In the exploration and early involvement stages residents may support or be tolerant of tourism for the perceived benefits it brings, but as it increasingly takes on the global and the residents see a loss of place identity, then it might be argued they also perceive a diminution of quality of life as they trade a past life style for one characterised as being less traditional, more global and more stressed by tourist numbers. Processes of glocalisation, however, recreate a participatory role of local residents and potential improvements in quality of life. Consequently, as noted, strong local planning mechanisms that retain as their priority the involvement of local people mitigates some of the worse excesses of gloablisation and movements of external capital into a tourist zone, and reinforces the rapid emergence of a glocalisation stage. Figure 4, as a conceptualisation of possible change, is thus already problematical as the glocalisation stage in a place like Shi Cha Hai hutong is pushed into an earlier appearance as a mitigating and not recovery stage; and thereby arguably aiding the longer term sustainability of the tourism product.

The case of Shi Cha Hai hutong and the views being expressed in 2006 by its residents represents an interesting case of social impact that can be contextualised within the social, physical and economic changes envisaged by the Butler life cycle. From one perspective it might be said to be moving into an early consolidation phase prior to the Olympic Games. It is certainly being identified as a destination in its own right within Beijing as evidenced by entries in guide books such as *The Lonely Planet, The Rough Guide* and *Chikyuno-arukikata* and through the promotional policies of governmental authorities. Equally it can be said that a process of globalisation is beginning to occur in the sense of residents possessing a sense of change that involves a loss of traditional life styles without necessarily being able to fully participate in the new as these are seen as intrusions rather than enrichments of life. On the other hand the presence of strong planning regimes ensures that a Chinese character is sustained; a process also reinforced by home ownership changes.

Of course, there are many caveats to this scenario. Like Butler's original concept, the successive stages are not wholly automatic, and nor does the theory clearly postulate the turning points of the various stages. Indeed, it can be claimed that appropriate destination site management might mean some stages are never reached. However, thus far, on the basis of the evidence presented in this paper, the scenario represented in Figure 3 represents a model that extends the literature.

Of course, therein lays a limitation of the research, as the data are limited and thus arguably insufficient to support the generalisation being made. However, while the data are time, place and respondent specific, the in-depth detail characteristic of these types of data permit model building to be tested in subsequent research. Such research, like good planning, requires monitoring of changes, and thus currently it is proposed that future research will be undertaken using a combination of larger sample sizes to permit statistical testing and qualitative work to monitor changes prior to and after the Olympic Games. Perhaps in this way Wall's (2005) and Jurowski, Daniels and Peninngton-Gray's (2006) conceptualisation of increased equity through participation in tourism benefits may be aided.

Acknowledgement:

This paper is part of the result of the project sponsored by the Beijing Municipal Government funding of "21 Century Beijing Creative Group". We are also very grateful to Li Huimin, Qi Fangli, Lin Wei, Li Bing, Wan Lili, Zhou Huanhuan, the graduate students in School of Tourism Management, Beijing International Studies University for their help in doing the survey and data input. A travel grant form the University of Waikato Management School is also acknowledged.

References

Allen, R. L., Long, P. T., Perdue, R. R., & Kieselbach, S. (1988). The impact of tourism development on residents' perceptions of community life. *Journal of Travel Research, 27*(1), 16-21.

Allport, G. (1955). *Becoming: Basic considerations for a psychology of personality.* New Haven: Yale University Press.

Allport, G. (1961). *Pattern and growth in personality.* New York: Holt, Rinehart and Winston.

Allport, G. (1968). *The person in psychology; Selected Essays.* Boston: Beacon Press.

Baum, T. (2006). Revisiting the TALC: Is there an off-ramp. In R. W. Butler (Ed.), *The tourism area life cycle: Vol. 2. Conceptual and theoretical issues* (pp. 219-230). Clevedon: Channel View Publications.

Beijing Tourism Administration. (2006). Retrieved October 14, 2006, from www.bjta.gov.cn

Beijing Statistical Information Net. (2007). Beijing Municipal Bureau of Statistics. Retrieved May 1, 2007, from www.bjstats.gov.cn

Belisle, J., & Hoy, D. (1980). The perceived impact of tourism by residents: A case study in Santa Maria, Columbia. *Annals of Tourism Research, 7*(1), 83-99.

Brougham, J. E., & Butler, R. W. (1981). A segmentation analysis of resident attitudes to the social impact of tourism. *Annals of Tourism Research, 8*(4), 569-590.

Butler, R. (1980). The concept of tourist area cycle of evolution: Implications for the management of resources. *Canadian Geographer, 24*, 5-12.

Butler, R. (Ed.). (2006a). *The tourism area life cycle: Vol. 2. Conceptual and theoretical issues*. Clevedon: Channel View Press.

Butler, R. (Ed.). (2006b). *The tourism area life cycle: Vol. 1. Applications and modifications*. Clevedon: Channel View Press.

Capenerhurst, J. (1994). Community tourism. In L. Haywood (Ed.), *Community leisure and recreation: Theory and practice* (pp. 144-171). Oxford, UK: Butterworth Heinemann.

China.org.cn. (2006). Retrieved November 27, 2006, from http://big5.china.com.cn/news

Cohen, E. (1972). Toward a sociology of international tourism. *Social Research, 39*(1), 164-182.

Cooper, C. (2006). The anatomy of the rejuvenation stage of the TALC. In R. W. Butler (Ed.), *The tourism area life cycle: Vol. 2. Conceptual and theoretical issues* (pp. 183-200). Clevedon: Channel View Publications.

Davis, D., Allen, J., & Cosenza, R. M. (1988). Segmenting local residents by their attitudes, interests, and opinions toward tourism. *Journal of Travel Research, 27*(2), 2-8.

Doxey, G. V. (1975). A causation theory of visitor-resident irritants: Methodology and research inferences. *Proceedings of the 6th Annual Conference of the Travel Research Association, San Diego CA*, 195-198.

Fredline, E., & Faulkner, B. (2000). Host community reactions: A cluster analysis. *Annals of Tourism Research, 27*(3), 764-785.

Galston, W.A., & Baehler, K. J. (1995). *Rural development in the United States: Connecting theory, practice, and possibilities*. Washington DC: Island Press.

Getz, D. (1982). A rationale and methodology for assessing capacity to absorb tourism. *Ontario Geography, 19*, 92-102.

Getz, D. (1993). Impacts of tourism on residents' leisure: Concepts and a longitudinal case study of Spey Valley, Scotland. *Journal of Tourism Studies, 4*(2), 33-44.

Getz, D., & Jamal, T. (1994). The environment-community symbiosis: A case for collaborative tourism planning. *Journal of Sustainable Tourism, 2*(3), 152-173.

Glasson, J. (1994). Oxford: A heritage city under pressure: Visitors, impacts and management responses. *Tourism Management, 15*(2), 137-144.

Guba, E. G. (Ed.). (1990). *The paradigm dialog*. Newbury Park: Sage.

Gursoy, D., Jurowski, C., & Uysal, M. (2002). Resident attitudes: A structural modelling approach. *Annals of Tourism Research, 29*(1), 79-105.

Jamal, T., & Getz, D. (1999). Community-based round tables for tourism-related conflicts: The dialectics of consensus and process structures. *Journal of Sustainable Tourism, 7*(3/4), 290-313.

Jurowski, C., Daniels, M. J., & Peninngton-Gray, L. (2006). The distribution of tourism benefits. In G. Jennings & N. P. Nickerson (Eds.), *Quality tourism experiences* (pp. 192-207). Oxford: Elsevier Butterworth-Heinemann.

Kelly, G. (1955). *Psychology of personal constructs*. London: Routledge.

Lankford, S. V., & Howard, D. R. (1994). Developing a tourism impact attitude scale. *Annals of Tourism Research, 21*(1), 121-139.

Lawson, R. W., Williams, J., Young, T., & Cossens, J. (1998). A comparison of residents' attitudes towards tourism in 10 New Zealand destinations. *Tourism Management, 19*(3), 247-256.

Lindberg, K., Dellaert, B. G. C., & Rassing, C. R. (1999). Resident tradeoffs: A choice modeling approach. *Annals of Tourism Research, 26*(3), 554-569.

Liu, J. C., & Var, T. (1986). Resident attitudes toward tourism impacts in Hawaii. *Annals of Tourism Research, 13*(2), 193-214.

Liu, J. C., Sheldon, P. J., & Var, T. (1987). Resident perception of the environmental impacts of tourism. *Annals of Tourism Research, 14*(1), 17-37.

Liu, Y. H., Ma, L., & Zhu, H. (2005). Viewing differences between Chinese and Foreign tourism research and their trends by comparing articles published in Tourism Tribune and Annals of Tourism Research. *Chinese Tourism Research Annual (English Edition), 1*, 362-370.

Lockyer, T. (2003). Hotel cleanliness-how to guests view it? Let's get specific: A New Zealand case study. *International Journal of Hospitality Management, 22*(3), 297-305.

Long, P. T., Perdue, R. R., & Allen, L. (1990). Rural resident tourist perceptions and attitudes by community level of tourism. *Journal of Travel Research, 28*(3), 3-9.

Mason, P., & Cheyne, J. (2000). Residents' attitudes to proposed tourism development. *Annals of Tourism Research, 27*(2), 391-411.

McCool, S. F., & Martin, S. R. (1994). Community attachment and attitudes toward tourism development. *Journal of Travel Research, 32*(3), 29-34.

Murphy, P. E. (1985). *Tourism: A community Approach*. New York: Methuen.

New Zealand Ministry for the Environment. (1991). *Ministry for the Environment New Zealand*. Retrieved June 20, 2007, from www.mfe.govt.nz/laws/rma

Prentice, R. (1993). Community-driven tourism planning and residents' preferences. *Tourism Management, 14*(3), 218-227.

Ritchie, J. R., & Zins, M. (1978). Culture as a determinant of the attractiveness of a tourist region. *Annals of Tourism Research, 5*, 252-270.

Rowswell, M. (Producer). (2006, November 14). *Learn to speak Chinese* [Television broadcast]. New Zealand: CCTV-9.

Russo, A. P. (2006). A re-foundation of the TALC for heritage cities. In R.W. Butler (Ed.), *The tourism area life cycle: Vol. 1. Applications and modifications* (pp. 139-161). Clevedon: Channel View Publications.

Ryan, C. (1991). *Recreational tourism*. London: Routledge.

Ryan, C., & Cooper, C. (2004). Residents' perceptions of tourism development: The case of Raglan, New Zealand. *Tourism Review International, 8*(1), 1-17.

Ryan, C., Scotland, A., & Montgomery, D. (1998). Resident attitudes to tourism development: A comparative study between the Rangitikei, New Zealand and Bakewell, United Kingdom. *Progress in Tourism and Hospitality Research, 4*(2), 115-130.

Thyne, M., & Lawson, R. (2001). The design of a traditional social distance scale to be used in the context of tourism. In P. M. Tidwell & T. E. Muller (Eds.), *Asia Pacific - Advances in consumer research: Vol. IV.* (pp. 102-107). Valdosta, GA: Association for Consumer Research.

Wall, G. (2005, July). *Tourism planning in the People's Republic of China*. Paper presented at the International Academy for the study of Tourism Conference, Beijing, China.

Wang, N. (1997). Vernacular house as an attraction: Illustration from hutong tourism in Beijing. *Tourism Management, 18*(8), 573-580.

Williams, J., & Lawson, R. (2001). Community issues and resident opinions of tourism. *Annals of Tourism Research, 28*(2), 269-290.

Wu, B. H., Guo, Y. J., Song, Z. Q., & Deng, L. H. (2005). Fourteen years' tourism research in China: Literature review on papers references published in the Journal of Tourism Tribune. *Chinese Tourism Research Annual (English Edition), 1*, 10-22.

Young, B. (1983). Touristisation of traditional Maltese fishing-farming villages. *Tourism Management, 12* (1), 35-41.

北京市西城区统计信息网。(2007)。<u>北京市西城区统计局</u>。2007年5月1日，取自：www.xc.bjstats.
gov.cn

中国什刹海网站。(2006)。2006 年 11 月 27 日，取自：www.bjsch.net

A Study of Inbound Business Tourists' Shopping Behavior and Influencing Factors—A Case Study of the Canton Fair in Guangzhou

境外商务游客购物行为特征及其影响因素研究 —以广交会境外采购商为例

QIUJU LUO
XIANGYU LU

Shopping facilities play an important role in the marketing and development of tourism destinations, and business tourists are an important and distinctive group of shoppers. Analysis of the shopping behavior of business tourists can contribute to enhancing the image of a destination, the promotion of retail sales, and the overall development of tourism. Canton Fair, which is the largest trade fair in China, contributes significantly to the development and promotion of shopping facilities in the city of Guangzhou. This study examines the shopping behavior of business tourists at the Canton Fair, and the factors influencing their behavior, based on a questionnaire survey and in-depth interviews. During the 105th Canton Fair in April 2009, 402 questionnaires were administered and 24 in-depth interviews were conducted. The results of the case study show that (a) business tourists behave differently from sightseeing tourists; (b) business travelers' shopping behavior is influenced by their sociodemographic characteristics, such as gender, age, cultural background, country of origin, and income level; and (c) the major factors that affect shopping behavior are the overall image and retail environment of the destination, the business tourists' association with and experience of the destination, and their personal tastes. The implications for merchants are also discussed.

购物作为一种旅游吸引物，能与其他吸引物相互补充、相互促进，是旅游目的地营销的重要组成部分。分析不同背景商务游客的购物行为特征及其影响因素可以改善目的地形象，促进旅游消费，进而促进目的地旅游发展。广交会有中国第一展之称，对广州的旅游购物消费带动大，且具有稳定性和持续性。本文以参加广交会的境外采购商(典型的商务游客)为研究对象，通过402份问卷和 24人的深入访谈，对其购物行为特征及影响因素进行分析。研究发现：(1)境外商务游客在购物花费、商品偏好、购物时间偏好、交通方式、购物目的上不同于一般游客。(2)不同性别、文化背景（客源地）、经历和收入的游客表现出不同的购物行为。(3)目的地整体形象、目的地购物环境、个体背景及购物经历和个体偏好四个层面的因素通过三条复杂的作用机制影响境外商务游客购物消费行为。

Qiuju Luo is Associate Professor of the School of Tourism Management at Sun Yat-sen University, Guangzhou, China (E-mail: bettyluoqiuju@126.com).
Xiangyu Lu is a master's student of the School of Tourism Management at Sun Yat-sen University, Guangzhou, China (E-mail: 395867868@qq.com).

Introduction

Business tourism began to develop in the 1980s. At the end of the 1990s, the Asia–Pacific region, following similar changes in North America and Europe, began to develop as an important business tourism market. In China, the number of inbound business tourists reached 5.23 million in 2009, accounting for 23.9% of the total number of inbound tourists. In 2000, the average expenditure of inbound tourists was RMB 930.6, whereas inbound business tourists spent RMB 1,067.8 on average. In the same year, the average expenditure of domestic tourists was RMB 426.6, whereas domestic business tourists spent an average of RMB 1,422 (Dai, 2002). These figures indicate that the business tourism market has great potential for growth, considering the high levels of expenditure of business tourists, compared to general tourists, as well as the scale of the business tourism market.

Business tourism can promote the economic development of a destination. Individually, business tourists contribute to the revenues of tourism enterprises and to that of the destination as a whole. At the same time, business tourism can attract investment, create jobs, and promote the development of infrastructure, hospitality services, entertainment, and cultural activities (P. Hu, 2008). Business tourism can also lead to the development of new tourism-related products and structures and can balance the discrepancy between peak- and low-season incomes, because business tourism is seldom affected by the climate or tourism seasons (Wu, 2005).

Shopping is an important element of tourism (W. M. Choi, Chan, & Wu, 1999; Timothy & Butler, 1995). It is one of the most pervasive leisure activities for tourists and can have significant economic, psychological, and social benefits (W. M. Choi et al.; Snepenger, Murphy, O'Connell, & Gregg, 2003). However, shopping is not only a must-do activity for tourists (Cohen, 1995), it is also a destination attraction (Timothy & Butler) that is frequently combined with other attractions (Mak, Tsang, & Cheung, 1999). For some tourists, shopping carries a higher priority than sightseeing, recreation, or any other holiday activities (Reisinger & Waryszak, 1996). Timothy and Butler noted that shopping can be the primary purpose of travel for tourists. They argued that the desire and necessity for shopping can even motivate a tourist to travel.

Tourism shopping, as a form of non-basic consumption, greatly contributes to the economy of a destination and generates employment for the host community. Previous research has shown that shopping expenditures account for approximately one third of the total tourism spending (Kim & Littrell, 2001; Wong & Law, 2003). Shopping is also an important element in destination marketing (Verbeke, 1988). Shopping creates an inviting environment and acts as an incentive to travel, develops an attractive tourist product, and is a source of pleasure and excitement. Big retail stores and shopping complexes have become indispensable facilities in modern tourism destinations (Turner & Reisinger, 2001).

Guangzhou, the capital of Guangdong province in China, is a typical business tourism destination and is well known as a "shopper's paradise." The city is host to the biannual Canton Fair, which has been a comprehensive trade fair for importers and exporters since 1957. With the longest history among trade fairs in China, the Canton Fair has been popular for its high quality of goods, large scale, and good business turnover. The fair attracts exhibitors and business visitors from all around the world, with the total number of visitors thus reaching as far as 4.7 million.

This study investigates the behavior of international business tourists to the Canton Fair. These business tourists tend to visit Guangzhou repeatedly, thereby contributing significantly to Guangzhou's tourism industry and to the city's economy.

An investigation of the shopping behavior of business travelers, as well as the factors influencing that behavior, is potentially of great importance because the findings will enable the local government to strategically plan and effectively market Guangzhou's tourism shopping facilities. Such knowledge can help enhance the destination image, improve the shopping environment, increase the revenue from tourism shopping, and, ultimately, promote business tourism to the destination. Retail enterprises can also benefit from a better understanding of business travelers' shopping behaviors by enabling them to better meet their needs in terms of product development, pricing, and marketing. This will, in turn, further enhance the destination image, stimulate tourism shopping expenditure, and optimize the structure of tourism consumption.

This article is based on a case study of the shopping behavior of a sample of international business tourists attending Canton Fair. The article tries to answer three research questions: (a) What are the shopping characteristics of business tourists, and how do they differ from those of leisure tourists? (b) Do business tourists with different personal characteristics and from different regions behave differently? (c) What are the main factors influencing business tourists' shopping behaviors, and in what ways do those factors influence those behaviors?

Literature Review

After the 1980s, the focus of international tourism shopping research gradually turned from the object (e.g., the specific commodity, the shopping mall) to the subject (the shopper; Chen & Huang, 2007; Wang & Su, 2008). However, Ma (2006) reviewed the domestic literature on tourism shopping in China and found that domestic research on tourism shopping continued to focus on commodities, industries, and markets. Given the relative youth of the Chinese domestic tourism market, these different research approaches suggest that, when tourism shopping in a particular destination is in its early stages of development, studies tend to focus on the impact of tourism shopping on the destination, the authenticity of the facilities, and the planning of tourism shopping areas. On the other hand, once tourism shopping has become established, the focus of research turns to the psychology, behavior, perception, satisfaction, and market segmentation of tourism shoppers. Accordingly, as the overseas industry developed, research shifted from evaluating the supply side to studying the demand side of the tourism shopping market.

Research on the demand side of tourism shopping mainly focuses on factors relating to the tourism shopper, including market segmentation, shopping motives and influences, and shopping characteristics. The classification of tourism shoppers in terms of market segmentation is based on factors such as the types of tourism activity, attributes of individual shoppers, and types of commodities purchased (Wang & Su, 2008). Although there are limitations to this form of classification, such as its tendency to ignore cultural differences (Swarbrooke & Horner, 2004), it can reveal the needs and behaviors of consumers in specific niche markets, which is helpful for establishing tourism enterprises, individual commodities, and sales and marketing structures (Kent, Shock, & Snow, 1983). Lesser and Hughes (1986) classified tourists' interests in shopping as either shopping enthusiastic or shopping unenthusiastic. Littrell, Baizerman, and Rita (1994) classified tourists according to their tourism activity preferences, such as local culture and history tourists, urban entertainment tourists, and nature and outdoors tourists. Moscardo (2004) divided tourism shoppers into categories of serious-minded shoppers, unnecessary shoppers, handicraft shoppers, and nonshoppers. Geuens, Vantomme, and Brengman (2004) divided airport shoppers into mood shoppers, shopping lovers, and apathetic shoppers. Josiam, Kinley, and Kim (2005) segmented tourists into high-involved shoppers, mid-involved shoppers, and low-involved shoppers. B. Hu and Yu (2007) divided tourists into categories of shopping enthusiasts, shopping lovers, and indifferent shoppers. Oh, Cheng, and Lehto (2004) classified tourists according to their commodity preferences as cultural product shoppers, antique shoppers, gourmet shoppers, craft shoppers, and garment shoppers. Yu and Littrell (2003) classified tourists as either product orientated or process orientated, based on their shopping motives. Though research on the classification of tourism shoppers is thorough and comprehensive, there are no universal classifications capable of including all kinds of tourism shoppers (Wang & Su).

Different kinds of tourism shoppers behave differently, a result of their different motives and different influencing factors. For instance, the motives of ethnic-products shoppers, symbolic-marker shoppers, and generic-handcrafts shoppers obviously vary because they are influenced by specific tourism experiences (Kim & Littrell, 2001). Possible tourism shopping motives include buying discounted or duty-free products (Carmichael & Smith, 2004; Matteo & Matteo, 1996; Timothy, 1995), buying souvenirs related to the tourism experience (Turner & Reisinger, 2001), or buying on impulse (Carmichael & Smith). Shopping for entertainment or as a leisure activity is a distinct shopping motive from shopping out of necessity (Timothy & Butler, 1995). Dholakia (1999) proposed that tourism shoppers make their purchases based on practical motives, entertainment motives, and household and social motives. Geuens et al. (2004) further classified shopping motives as experience motives, social motives, and functional motives. Though Moscardo (2004) proposed expressive motives (leisure, escape, social relations, identity) and instrumental motives (travel related, social and cultural needs, experiencing local culture) for tourism shopping, he also indicated that these two types of motives can be affected by the cultural background, sense of social responsibility, values, and type of tourism shoppers, which consequently affects their shopping behavior. Kim and Littrell (2001) and Rosenbaum and Spears (2005) also explored the factors affecting shopping motives, with the latter indicating that cultural background is the main factor leading to shopping-type diversity.

Research on the characteristics of tourism shoppers has mainly focused on shopping expenditure, commodities preference, and shopping space–time characteristics. T. M. Choi, Liu, Pang, and Chow (2008) analyzed tourists' shopping behaviors in terms of categories such as shopping expenditure, commodity type, shopping destination, brand preference, and decision-making type. In addition, they explored influencing factors such as the type of product, environment, service, and sales policies. Gee, Makens, and Choy (1997) found that shopping is always either the first or the last thing conducted by tourists. Conversely, Dellaert, Borgers, and Timmermans (1995) indicated that there are no shopping-time preferences for tourists. Kemperman, Borgers, and Timmermans (2009) explored tourist shopping route choices and developed a tourist shopping behavior model. The results indicated that tourists' route choices are affected by factors such as merchandise supply, accessibility, the specific motivation for the shopping trip, familiarity with the destination, and whether or not the shopping route was planned in advance. Snepenger et al. (2003) explored the similarities and differences between tourist-heavy users and tourist-light users in terms of shopping expenditure, shopping space–time characteristics, and shopping preferences. Yuksel (2004) also analyzed the differences between domestic tourists and international tourists in terms of shopping preferences and experience.

Tourists' shopping behaviors are largely affected by factors such as age, gender, cultural background, tourism type, and tourism purpose. Lehto, Cai, and O'Leary (2004) indicated that tourism purpose, tourism type, and the age and gender of tourists are the main factors affecting shopping expenditure and the choice of commodities purchased. Oh et al. (2004) also indicated that age, gender, and tourism type are related to tourists' shopping behaviors and verified the importance of different factors for different types of shopping behavior. Male tourists are more interested in collectable commodities than female tourists (Liang & Hao, 2005), who prefer souvenirs (Xie & Bao, 2006) as well as food and garments (Liang & Hao). Suh and Leo (2005) indicated that Europeans and Americans prefer culture-centered commodities, whereas Japanese tourists prefer price-advantaged commodities. Keown (1989) pointed out that international tourists' shopping tendencies and preferences depend on the types of products available, the levels of import duties on foreign goods, the levels of tax on domestic goods, the presence of duty-free stores, the value of specific goods abroad compared to their value in tourists' home countries, and stores' retail strategies. Chang, Yang, and Yu (2006) stated that the interaction between salespeople and tourists affects tourists' motives and levels of satisfaction and that service-oriented selling behavior can stimulate tourists' shopping desires better than profit-oriented selling behavior. Furthermore, the shopping environment significantly affects the emotions of shopping tourists, which consequently affects their shopping behaviors and shopping value perceptions (Yuksel, 2007). Turley and Milliman (2000) also stated that the shopping environment can greatly affect shoppers' attitudes and behaviors. A disorderly shopping environment will lower customer satisfaction (Bitner, 1990). A crowded shopping environment will change the way the customer acts on information, which also consequently affects customer satisfaction (Eroglu & Machleit, 1990). A comfortable shopping environment can increase shopping expenditure (Chebat & Michon, 2003), whereas customers' evaluations of the quality and value of merchandise decline with the decline in the comfort of the atmosphere of the shopping environment, leading to a decline in customers' willingness to shop (Babin, Chebat, & Michon, 2004). Yuksel and Fisun (2007) also stated that tourists' perceptions of a destination's safety and security, regardless of whether or not they are accurate, strongly affect their emotions, loyalty, and sense of satisfaction as shoppers in that destination.

The foregoing studies have made great contributions to the research on tourism shopping behavior. However, they mainly focus on shopping expenditure, commodity preferences, and space–time characteristics and ignore factors such as shopping times and frequency, transportation options, and choices about shopping companions. In addition, the existing studies seldom distinguish between business tourists and sightseeing tourists and mainly focus solely on sightseeing tourists or study all tourists as a whole.

Business tourists vary from general sightseeing tourists in terms of tourism type and tourism purpose. The foregoing literature review shows that tourism type and tourism purpose affect tourists' shopping motives and shopping behaviors. Therefore, as this article demonstrates, business tourists also vary from general sightseeing tourists in terms of shopping behavior. The literature review above also indicates that tourists of different genders, ages, and cultural backgrounds behave differently when shopping. Accordingly, this article analyzes shopping behavior differences among business tourists of different genders, ages, and cultural backgrounds (countries of origin), as well as educational backgrounds and income levels. Previous research examined factors influencing shopping behavior and shopping motives from the macroscopic (e.g., destination type, destination image), mesospheric (e.g., shopping mall environment, sales policies, sales behavior), and microcosmic (e.g., sociodemographics, tourism experience) perspectives. However, these studies neither considered the three aspects simultaneously nor analyzed the relationships between them. This article analyzes the factors influencing business tourism shopping behavior at the macroscopic, mesospheric, and microcosmic levels.

Methodology and Sampling

The research object of this article is the typical international business tourist at the biannual Canton Fair in Guangzhou. Business tourists visit the Canton Fair to make purchases for their companies or organizations and they frequently choose to shop for themselves outside the exhibition center during their stay. In this case, tourism shopping excludes purchases for business purposes and refers to the economic and/or cultural behavior involved in the tourists' purchases of physical commodities (Shi, 2004). Accordingly, this article examines the personal shopping behaviors of business tourists at the Canton Fair outside the exhibition center, rather than their business purchases inside the exhibition center.

A questionnaire survey and in-depth interviews were used in this study. The main target sample was a group of international visitors engaged in shopping activities outside the exhibition center. However, because salespeople in retail locations in Guangzhou also know a great deal about the shopping behavior of international visitors to the Canton Fair, they were also included in the interview sample.

The study was carried out in three phases.

- Phase I (conducted during the 104th Canton Fair, from October 15 to 20, 2008) was an exploratory phase, which consisted of observations and general interviews with business tourists and salespeople, with the aim of identifying the tourists' general shopping behaviors and accumulating general information for the formal survey.
- In phase II (conducted during the 104th Canton Fair, from October 21 to November 6, 2008) a pilot survey was conducted. Modifications were made to the survey based on the 20 pilot questionnaires returned (15 male respondents, 5 female respondents). Because duty-free shopping is limited in Guangzhou, the respondents seldom chose to shop at duty-free stores, so this category was deleted. The pilot questionnaire indicated that visitors to the Canton Fair shopped far more often in evening than during the day, so shopping time choices were added. In addition, several of the respondents indicated that they rented a car when shopping or hired a tour guide, so these two choices were also added.
- In phase III (conducted during the 105th Canton Fair, from April 15 to May 7, 2009), the questionnaire survey and in-depth interviews were formally conducted, in preparation for the data analysis.

The questionnaires for the Canton Fair visitors were divided into two parts. Part 1 was designed to acquire general shopping data and Part 2 collected demographic data. The design of the questionnaires was based on the literature review and the preliminary interviews conducted in Phase I. According to the results of the research in Phase I, business tourists' shopping behaviors varied in terms of shopping time, frequency, type, pattern, and payment type. There may also have been some relationship between shopping behavior and sociodemographic factors, such as country of origin, gender, education, income, and age. Accordingly, specific demographic and shopping-related questions were included in the final questionnaire (see Appendix).

Random sampling was adopted to select the target survey respondents in the exhibition center and at shopping sites (various categories of retail stores located in two major shopping areas in Guangzhou: Beijing Road and the Tianhe business district). The research team members were evenly distributed across different exhibition halls and shopping sites and selected respondents randomly. When a target respondent was selected, he or she was asked whether he or she was a business tourist to ensure that he or she belonged to the target group. Four hundred and forty questionnaires were distributed by the team of research assistants, with 402 valid questionnaires returned, to yield a valid rate of 91.36%. The demographics of the respondents varied in terms of age, gender, marital status, education level, and ethnic background (see Table 1). The sampling is valid, because gender and country-of-origin percentages in the sample are consistent with those in the larger population of Canton Fair visitors.

Interviews were conducted with business tourists at the exhibition center and tourists and salespeople at the various shopping sites to explore the factors affecting their shopping behaviors. In the case of the tourists, those who expressed interest in sharing their experiences and opinions about shopping were selected for the in-depth interviews. The interviews were conducted simultaneously with the questionnaire survey. The interview questions were primarily related to specific responses the interviewees had given on the questionnaire. For example, why are you only staying in Guangzhou for 3 days? Why do you not plan to do any shopping? Why will you do much/little shopping? Why do you shop during the day/evening? Why do you shop alone/with friends/with relatives? Why do you prefer certain forms of transportation? Why do you prefer certain commodities? (The business tourists' shopping experiences and decision-making processes were also explored to determine and analyze influencing factors.) The decision to interview specific salespeople primarily depended on the location and category of the stores in which they worked. The interview questions focused on the salespeople's perceptions of tourists' shopping behaviors and influencing factors. For example, at what time of the day do business tourists shop the most? What kinds of commodities do they choose to buy? What features of those commodities are most important to them? What are the differences in expenditure between international tourists and general tourists?

Eighteen interviews were conducted with tourists and six with salespeople. The demographics of the tourist interviewees varied in terms of gender, age, cultural background, professional position, and income (see Table 2). The SPSS V16.0 (SPSS China Inc.) statistical software package was used to analyze the data.

Findings

The main objective of this study is to explore the shopping behavior of business tourists and the factors affecting their shopping behaviors. The research findings can be used to improve the image of the destination and promote tourism shopping consumption and the development of tourism. First, the general shopping behavior characteristics of the sample are analyzed according to duration of stay, shopping time, shopping frequency, shopping duration, marital status, transportation choice, commodity type, shopping purpose, shopping expenditure, and payment method. Then, the relationships between sociodemographic characteristics and shopping behavior are analyzed. However, not all sociodemographic characteristics affect shopping behavior, so only the

Table 1. Questionnaire Survey Sample.

Gender							
	Male			Female			
Percentage(%)	80.7			19.3			
Region	Asia	Europe	Oceania	America	Africa		
Percentage(%)	52.9	12.0	3.4	16.1	15.6		
Education	Below high school	High school	College/university	Master's/PhD			
Percentage(%)	4.2	16.2	57.6	21.9			
Age	Under 20	20–29	30–39	40–49	50–59	Over 59	
Percentage(%)	0.8	26.4	32.6	22.2	13.6	4.4	
Marital status	Single	Married	Other				
Percentage(%)	33.8	63.9	2.3				
Position	Self-employed	Senior manager	Middle manager	Lower manager	Staff		
Percentage(%)	10.1	51.1	26.6	5.6	6.6		
Monthly income (RMB)	Under 1,000	1,001–2,500	2,501–4,000	4,001–6,000	6,001–8,000	8,001–10,000	10,001–20,000	Over 20,000
Percentage(%)	6.8	23.2	16.7	14.5	7.9	7.9	8.7	14.2

Table 2. Interview Sample.

No.	Nationality	Gender	Age	Position	Monthly income	Date
1	India	Male	36	Staff member	Under US$ 500	2009.4.17
2	Indonesia	Female	45	Senior manager	US$2,500–4,000	2009.4.17
3	Australia	Male	Unknown	Senior manager	Unknown	2009.4.18
4	USA	Male	38	Senior manager	Over US$20,000	2009.4.18
5	Australia	Female	28	Middle manager	US$4,000–6,000	2009.4.19
6	Colombia	Male	42	Middle manager	US$6,000–8,000	2009.4.19
7	South Africa	Male	40	Lower manager	US$1,000–2,000	2009.4.25
8	Germany	Male	48	Senior manager	US$10,000–20,000	2009.4.25
9	Morocco	Male	25	Staff member	Under US$1,000	2009.4.26
10	Nigeria	Male	45	Middle manager	Under US$1,000	2009.4.26
11	New Zealand	Male	36	Self-employed	US$8,000–10,000	2009.4.27
12	Czech	Male	38	Senior manager	US$10,000–20,000	2009.4.28
13	Mexico	Male	49	Self-employed	Over US$ 20,000	2009.4.28
14	Malaysia	Male	52	Middle manager	US$4,000–6,000	2009.4.28
15	China	Female	Unknown	Salesman, digital store at Tianhe		2009.5.1
16	Iran	Male	60	Self-employed	US$6,000–8,000	2009.5.1
17	China	Female	Unknown	Salesperson, clothing store on Beijing Road		2009.5.2
18	Algeria	Male	45	Senior manager	US$10,000–20,000	2009.5.2
19	Tanzania	Male	28	Middle manager	US$6,000–8,000	2009.5.3
20	China	Female	Unknown	Salesperson, Yishion Agency on Beijing Road		2009.5.3
21	China	Female	Unknown	Salesperson, Tee Mall on Beijing Road		2009.5.4
22	Thailand	Male	50	Senior manager	US$10,000–20,000	2009.5.4
23	China	Male	Unknown	Salesperson, PC store at Tianhe		2009.5.4
24	China	Female	Unknown	Salesperson, silk store on Beijing Road		2009.5.5

sociodemographic characteristics and shopping behavior characteristics that are significantly related to one another are analyzed. Finally, the factors affecting business tourists' shopping behavior are analyzed from the perspectives of the holistic image and the shopping environment of the destination and the personal background, experience, and preferences of the tourist.

General Shopping Behavior Characteristics

The general shopping behavior characteristics of the international business tourist shoppers visiting Canton Fair according to the statistical data (see Table 3) are as follows.

The revisit rate of international business tourists attending the Canton Fair is high. However, the average duration of their stay in Guangzhou is comparatively short. Though most (76.0%) international business tourists have visited Guangzhou more than once, some (7.1%) have visited Guangzhou more than 10 times. Consequently, the average number of visits was 5.32. Almost half (49.5%) of the sample stay in Guangzhou for fewer than 5 days, and the average duration of their stay in Guangzhou was only 8.38 days, which is significantly shorter than that of general inbound tourists. General inbound tourists stay in China for 13.34 days on average, with 73.3% staying in China for more than 15 days (Zhao, 2005). The duration of visits of business and general international tourists to China tend to differ for the following reasons. First, international business tourists, especially those attending trade fairs and events, travel mainly to conduct business negotiations. Because the locations for exhibitions tend to remain the same over time and business participants generally attend the exhibitions repeatedly, their revisit rate is quite high. Second, unlike general sightseeing tourists, business tourists have specific business to conduct and often do not have time to extend their stay for leisure purposes. Third, business tourists are more likely to travel to more destinations within China over a short period of time than general tourists, which would also lead to them staying in Guangzhou for shorter times than general tourists.

Business tourists attending the Canton Fair shop at the infrequent rate of once every 3.32 days. They also spend relatively little time at shopping locations, with 45.8% spending 1–2 hours for a shopping trip. Over half of the sample (59.8%) reported going shopping only one to three times during their stay in Guangzhou. One possible explanation for this relative lack of interest in shopping is that there is no urgency for business tourists to visit specific shopping sites in Guangzhou during a single trip, because they are likely to return to the Canton Fair in the future. The attractiveness of shopping may also decline as the frequency of visits increases.

Though general tourists have no specific shopping time preferences (Dellaert et al., 1995), business tourists prefer to shop in the evenings. The majority of Canton Fair visitors shop after 6:00 p.m. (71.6%), especially between 6:00 and 9:00 p.m. (54%), which may be related to the exhibition schedules, because business at the fair is conducted during the day, as well as personal preference (many respondents indicated a general preference for nighttime shopping).

Most (75.5%) visitors to the Canton Fair shop with their relatives, friends, or colleagues. They mainly go to shopping destinations by taxi (66.6%), on foot (28.6%), or by metro (25.3%); only a few (9.2%) take a bus. In general, international business tourists visit large cities, where light rail and subway transportation tend to be widely available and efficient. In addition, unlike general tourists traveling by chartered bus who tend to shop in

Table 3. Shopping Behavior.

Visits	1 Time	2–4 Times	5–7 Times	8–10 Times	Over 10 Times
Percentage	24.0	35.8	16.3	16.8	7.1
Stay duration	1–5 Day(s)	6–10 Days	10–15 Days	15–20 Days	Over 20 days
Percentage	49.5	28.4	9.9	4.3	7.9
Shopping frequency	0	1–3 Times	4–6 Times	7–9 Times	Over 9 times
Percentage	0	59.8	22.9	5.7	5.9
Frequency	0–1 Days/times	1–3 Days/times	3–5 Days/times	5–7 Days/times	>7 Days/times
Percentage	9.2	47.2	23.1	10.5	9.0
Duration	0–1 Hours	1–2 Hours	2–3 Hours	3–4 Hours	4–12 Hours
Percentage	0.8	45.8	24.6	14.1	14.7
Shopping time	Before 12:00	12:01–15:00	15:01–18:00	18:01–21:00	After 21:00
Percentage	11.4	14.9	17.8	54	17.6

Shopping companions	Alone	With relatives	With colleagues	With friends	With tour guide	Others
Percentage	16.8	12.1	20.6	42.8	6.2	1.5
Transportation method	On foot	By Metro	By taxi	By rental car	By bus	Other
Percentage	28.6	25.3	66.6	5.1	9.2	1.3

Travel time	Under 10 min	10–20 Min	21–30 Min	Over 30 Min
Percentage	7	50.4	32	10.6

Commodity	Household	Cosmetic	Electrical	Clothing	Native crafts	Art works	Jewelry	Watch	Cases/bags	Souvenirs	Other
Percentage	15	11.7	44.2	62.2	12.7	10.9	7	17.1	20.5	30.8	6.2

Purpose of purchases	Personal use	Gift for relatives	Gift for friends	Remembrance	Other
Percentage	59.3	57	47.2	11.1	3.6
Expenditure	Under RMB 500	RMB 500–2,500	RMB 2,501–5,000	RMB 5,001–10,000	Over RMB 10,000
Percentage	7.3	45.1	24.3	23	10.3

Payment method	RMB	US$	Credit card	Other
Percentage	65.6	18.3	15.0	1.1

large groups, business tourists tend to shop only with a few relatives or friends and so are apt to take the metro or a taxi. Those who shop at stores near their hotels prefer to travel on foot. Those surveyed did not spend much time commuting to their shopping destinations, with 22.84 minutes being the average for a one-way trip. Most (82.4%) spend 10–30 minutes on one single journey, with 50.4% commuting for 10–20 minutes. Hectic schedules and convenient transportation were cited as the main reasons for the short trips.

Though international business tourists tend to purchase various kinds of merchandise, their purchases mostly concentrate on clothing, electronics, and souvenirs. Clothing purchases are most common (62.2%), followed by electronics (44.2%) and souvenirs (30.8%), which is consistent with previous research. Zhao (2005) pointed out that inbound tourists prefer to buy handcrafts, clothing, artwork, and jewelry. Wu (2005) also indicated that foreign tourists prefer artwork and clothing. However, overseas business tourists visiting Guangzhou also purchase electronics, which may be related to the fact that Guangdong province is a major production base for clothing and electronics, making these items popular with foreign tourists for their price advantages. Visitors to the Canton Fair generally purchase items for themselves or as gifts. Of those surveyed, 59.3% shopped for themselves, 57% purchased gifts for relatives, and 47.2% purchased gifts for friends. In contrast with previous research, only 11.1% of those surveyed shopped for souvenirs with the intention of remembering the tourism location. Similar to general tourists, most international business tourists have practical and social motives for shopping, but unlike general tourists they do not shop with the intention of remembering the destination because they will likely visit the same destination many times. The shopping expenditure of international business tourists at the Canton Fair is high (RMB 4,717.55), compared with that of general sightseeing and on-holiday tourists. Most of those surveyed (65.6%) paid in RMB when shopping, followed by U.S. dollars (18.3%) and credit cards (15.0%).

Sociodemographic Characteristics and Shopping Behavior

This article analyzes the relationship between sociodemographic characteristics and shopping behavior among international business tourists to the Canton Fair. Independent-sample t-tests and one-way analysis of variance (ANOVA) were used to analyze the relationships between the ratio variables (stay duration, shopping time, shopping frequency, shopping duration, and commute time) and personal characteristics of business shoppers. Multiple-response cross-tabulation analysis and cross-tabulation analysis were used to analyze the relationships between nominal variables (shopping time, transportation method, accompanying party, commodity type, shopping purpose, and payment method) and personal characteristics. The results show that there were significant relationships between gender and duration of stay, commute time, commodities preference, the decision to shop alone or with relatives or friends, as well as between country of origin and stay duration, shopping expenditure, and commodities preference. The following discussion only refers to the significant relationships mentioned above.

Independent-sample t-tests were used to find out whether there are significant differences between male and female business tourists in terms of duration of stay in Guangzhou and commute time to shopping destinations. The findings according to the statistical data (see Table 4) are as follows.

The average duration of stay for males and females was 7.99 days and 10.18 days, respectively. The value of F was 8.496, with a significance of 0.004, which does not meet the homogeneity of variance hypothesis. The corresponding t-statistic was −2.051, with

Table 4. Duration and Commute Time Comparisons (Gender).

Indicator	Male	Female	F	Sig.	T	Sig.
Duration	7.99	10.18	8.496	0.004	−2.051	0.043
Commute time	23.55	19.60	2.972	0.086	2.292	0.022

a significance of 0.043, which indicates that the average duration of stay for females was significantly longer than that for males.

The average commute times to shopping destinations for males and females were 23.55 and 19.60 minutes, respectively. The value of F was 2.972, with a significance of 0.086, which meets the homogeneity of variance hypothesis. The corresponding t-statistic was 2.292, with a significance of 0.022, which indicates that the average transportation time to shopping destinations for females was significantly shorter than that for males. Although female tourists tend to enjoy shopping more than male tourists (Michalkó, 2006; Oh et al., 2004; Xie & Bao, 2006), it is comparatively more difficult for female tourists to accept long shopping commute times because of differences in physical characteristics.

Multiple response cross-tabulation analysis was used to analyze the relationship between gender and shopping commodity preferences. The findings (see Table 5) are as follows.

The shopping commodity preferences of males were generally consistent with those of females, with both sexes preferring clothing, electronics, and souvenirs. However, the degree to which they are interested in these commodities varies. The percentages of cosmetics, jewelry, suitcases and bags, clothing, and electronics chosen by males and females were 7.7 vs. 29.6%, 5.2 vs. 14.1%, 17.4 vs. 33.8%, 60.3 vs. 70.4%, and 48.4 vs. 70.4%, respectively, which indicates that females prefer to purchase cosmetics, jewelry, suitcases and bags, and clothing, whereas males prefer to purchase electronics. This is also consistent with previous research. Liang and Hao (2005) found that female tourists prefer to buy clothing and food. Michalkó (2006) indicated that female tourists prefer female-style commodities like clothing, shoes, suitcases and bags, and jewelry. Oh et al. (2004) also stated that female tourists are almost twice more likely than males to buy clothing, shoes, and jewelry, whereas males prefer to buy electronic products.

Cross-tabulation analysis was used to analyze the relationships between gender and choices of shopping companion. The findings according to the statistical data (see Table 6) are as follows.

Males and females both tend to shop with relatives and friends, but they vary slightly in their preferences. The percentages of male and female business tourists shopping alone, shopping with relatives, and shopping with colleagues were 18.8 vs. 7.0%, 10.2 vs. 21.1%, and 19.4 vs. 26.8%, respectively, which indicates that females are more likely to shop with someone else, whereas males are more likely to shop alone. Tourism involves leaving a familiar home environment for a relatively strange place, where the visitor may feel unsafe. The perception of insecurity can affect the choice of shopping companions for tourists. Generally, females have a stronger perception of insecurity than males. Neil (2001) indicated that female tourists are more easily aware of risk at night and that male tourists are less likely than female tourists to sense risk in public areas. To overcome perceived risk, female tourists tend to shop with companions to avoid traveling alone. Female tourists also tend to follow suggestions from friends,

Table 5. Relationships Between Gender and Commodities.

		Household	Cosmetics	Electronics	Clothing	Crafts	Artwork	Jewelry	Watches	Suitcases	Souvenirs	Other	Total
Gender													
Female	Count	10	21	19	50	8	7	10	11	24	25	4	71
	% Within gender	14.1	29.6	26.8	70.4	11.3	9.9	14.1	15.5	33.8	35.2	5.6	
Male	Count	48	24	150	188	41	35	16	53	54	93	20	312
	% Within gender	15.4	7.7	48.1	60.3	13.1	11.2	5.1	17.0	17.3	29.8	6.4	
Total	Count	58	45	169	238	49	42	26	64	78	118	24	383

Commodity[a]

Note. Percentages and totals are based on the numbers of respondents.

Table 6. Relationship Between Gender and Choice of Shopping Companion.

				Companion				
		Alone	Relative	Colleague	Friends	Tour Guide	Other	Total
Gender								
Female	Count	5	15	19	27	4	1	71
	% Within gender	7.0	21.1	26.8	38.0	5.6	1.4	100.0
Male	Count	59	32	61	137	20	5	314
	% Within gender	18.8	10.2	19.4	43.6	6.4	1.6	100.0
Total	Count	64	47	80	164	24	6	385
	% Within gender	16.6	12.2	20.8	42.6	6.2	1.6	100.0

relatives, and tour guides when they shop (Michalkó, 2006), which may also contribute to female tourists' greater tendency to shop with a companion.

One-way ANOVA was used to determine whether the duration of stay in Guangzhou and the shopping expenditure during the stay were significantly different for business tourists traveling from different countries and regions. The findings according to the statistical data (see Table 7) are as follows.

The duration of stay in Guangzhou during the Canton Fair for those surveyed traveling from Asia, Europe, Oceania, America, and Africa was 6.74, 8.72, 10, 10.81, and 10.24 days, respectively, with corresponding shopping expenditures of RMB 4,492.35, RMB 3,254.61, RMB 2,408.89, RMB 3,050.38, and RMB 8,322.20. According to Levene's homogeneity of variance test, the significances of F for both duration of stay and expenditure were less than 0.05, indicating that the data do not meet the homogeneity of variance hypothesis. The Welch test was then applied and the corresponding significances of F were 0.001 and 0.019, respectively, which indicates that the average stay durations and shopping expenditures of those surveyed traveling from different regions were significantly different at a level of 0.05. Next, Tamhane's T2 post hoc multiple comparisons was applied to compare the detailed difference. The significances of the difference in duration between Asia and America and between Asia and Africa and the difference in expenditure between Africa and Oceania were 0.003, 0.011, and 0.054, respectively, which indicates that the duration of stay in Guangzhou for Asian business tourists to the Canton Fair was significantly shorter than that of American and African business tourists, and the shopping expenditure of African tourists was significantly higher than that of tourists from Oceania. Because the travel distances and travel costs for Asian tourists were comparatively lower, they had comparatively better accessibility. Moreover, because they had more opportunities to visit Guangzhou, their willingness to stay was comparatively lower. Although the levels of economic development and average incomes in Africa are lower than those on other continents, recognition of the "made in China" label, price advantages, and the extensive choice of merchandise may stimulate the shopping interests and desires of African

Table 7. Trip Duration and Expenditure Comparisons (by Country of Origin).

	Asia	Europe	Oceania	America	Africa	F (Levene)	Sig.	F (Welch)	Sig.
Duration	6.74	8.72	10.00	10.81	10.24	8.391	0.000	5.684	0.001
Expenditure	4,492.35	3,254.61	2,408.89	3,050.38	8,322.20	4.987	0.001	3.211	0.019

Tamhane's T2

	(I) Area	(J) Area	Mean Difference	Std. Error	Sig.	95% Confidence Interval	
						Lower Bound	Upper Bound
Duration	Asia	America	−4.069*	1.086	0.003	−7.19	−0.95
		Africa	−3.500*	1.036	0.011	−6.48	−0.52
Expenditure	Africa	Oceania	−5,913.311	2,049.393	0.054	−11,882.06	55.44

*The mean difference is significant at the 0.05 level.

business tourists at the Canton Fair, causing the shopping expenditure of African tourists to be higher than that of other tourists.

Multiple response cross-tabulation analysis was used to analyze the relationships between business tourists' countries or regions of origin and their commodity preferences. The findings according to the statistical data (see Table 8) are as follows.

The shopping commodity preferences of business tourists from different regions were largely consistent. Across groups, those surveyed preferred clothing, electronics, and souvenirs, though there were some noteworthy variations. The percentages of respondents from Africa who indicated a preference for electronics, respondents from Oceania who indicated a preference for clothing, and respondents from Europe who indicated a preference for souvenirs were 61.4, 92.3, and 46.7%, respectively, and the percentage for each group was significantly higher than the percentages of other respondents who indicated preferences for these categories. The data indicate that African business tourists are most likely to purchase electronics, business tourists from Oceania are most likely to purchase clothing, and European tourists are most likely to purchase souvenirs. Suh and Leo (2005) indicated that people from different areas have different commodity preferences. For instance, European and American tourists prefer culture-centered commodities, whereas Japanese tourists prefer commodities based on price advantage. The results of this study are consistent with these findings.

Factors and Mechanism

Previous research has analyzed the influences on tourism shopping in terms of the external environmental factors and international intellectual and emotional factors that can affect tourists' shopping behavior to varying degrees. External factors include tourism type, commodity availability, the relative value of commodities, shopping atmosphere or environment, and sales policies (Chang et al., 2006; Keown, 1989; Lehto et al., 2004; Moscardo, 2004; Turley & Milliman, 2000; Yuksel, 2007), whereas internal factors include age, gender, cultural background, personal values, travel purpose, shopping risk perception, and personal experience (Kim & Littrell, 2001; Lehto et al., 2004; Liang & Hao, 2005; Suh & Leo, 2005; Xie & Bao, 2006; Yuksel & Fisun, 2007). Existing research on internal influences is thorough and covers almost all aspects of the relevant factors. However, existing research on external influencing factors mainly focuses on stores or commodities, ignoring the holistic tourism image of the destination and the holistic shopping environments. Influencing factors like the ones outlined above can explain most tourism shopping behavior. However, it is important to consider that even tourists of the same gender, professional position, income, and nationality may have different shopping behaviors that can be explained by personal preferences. The external environment and an individual's personal characteristics and experiences can affect their personal preferences to some extent. However, these factors cannot explain all of the variations in the shopping behavior of individuals. The introduction of an individual preference variable can contribute to a more complete analysis of the influencing factors and their mechanisms. In addition, the existing studies only take single influencing factors as their study object and these studies neither conduct a comprehensive analysis nor explore the relationships among all of the factors and mechanisms. This article analyzes influencing factors and mechanisms in terms of the holistic image of the destination and the shopping environments

Table 8. Relationships Between Country of Origin and Commodity Preference.

Region		Household	Cosmetics	Electronics	Clothing	Crafts	Artwork	Jewelry	Watches	Suitcases	Souvenirs	Other	Total
Asia	Count	37	17	83	116	21	23	12	29	32	48	13	195
	% Within area	19.0	8.7	42.6	59.5	10.8	11.8	6.2	14.9	16.4	24.6	6.7	
Europe	Count	6	7	18	27	9	7	2	5	11	21	1	45
	% Within area	13.3	15.6	40.0	60.0	20.0	15.6	4.4	11.1	24.4	46.7	2.2	
Oceania	Count	3	4	3	12	0	0	2	3	6	2	1	13
	% Within area	23.1	30.8	23.1	92.3	.0	.0	15.4	23.1	46.2	15.4	7.7	
America	Count	3	10	28	40	9	5	8	15	13	25	5	57
	% Within area	5.3	17.5	49.1	70.2	15.8	8.8	14.0	26.3	22.8	43.9	8.8	
Africa	Count	6	5	35	35	6	7	2	12	15	16	3	57
	% Within area	10.5	8.8	61.4	61.4	10.5	12.3	3.5	21.1	26.3	28.1	5.3	
Total	Count	55	55	43	167	230	45	42	26	64	77	112	23

Note. Percentages and totals are based on the numbers of respondents.

and the personal characteristics, experiences, and preferences of business tourists based on the interview responses and the literature review.

China now serves as a "world factory" in terms of manufacturing (Li, 2003). Products made in China are exported to countries all over the world, and knowledge of this can have an impact on shopping psychologies and shopping behavior all over the world. Moreover, Chinese clothes and electronic products are renowned abroad for their high quality or low price or both. Guangzhou is one of the most important industrial bases producing electronic consumer products, as well as clothing and silk textiles. Furthermore, Guangzhou is widely known for its highly developed and extensive retail sector, making it, in addition to being a world factory, a "shopper's paradise." Each of these points is reflected in comments made by interview subjects in this study:

> Products made in China are pretty good. Many products in my home are made in China. They are not only cheap, but also with high quality. Every time I come to Guangzhou, I spend one or two days on shopping, mainly to get some electronic products and clothes. Here is the producing place, so the price is lower than that in India. Interviewee 1 (Indian, male, employee), April 17, 2009
>
> Chinese silk is quite famous. The silk in my country is imported from China. That's why every time I come to Guangzhou I will get some silk. The silk here has more styles and the prices are lower. Interviewee 2 (Indonesian, female, senior manager), April 17, 2009
>
> Each year the Canton Fair attracts lots of foreigners who shop. . . . They like Chinese clothes made of silk. Usually they buy a lot each time, and it seems that they don't care much about the money. Interviewee 24 (Chinese, female, salesperson in a silk shop), May 5, 2009

Although products made in China are competitive in price, the quality and the style are not consistently satisfactory to customers, which can have an impact on the desires and motivations of shoppers from overseas.

> I used to bring many electronic products back home, because they are cheap. But usually they went wrong after I used them a few times, and they were not guaranteed to stay in good condition. Now I don't buy any electronic products in Guangzhou anymore. Interviewee 6 (Colombian, male, middle manager), April 19, 2009
>
> I buy some clothes but just a few, not very much. I come to Guangzhou often, and every time I go shopping the things are almost the same, nothing special. Interviewee 11 (New Zealander, male, self-employed), April 27, 2009

What's more, Guangzhou often falls under the shadow of nearby Hong Kong, which has more of an international identity as a shopping destination in terms of the range of products available, the holistic shopping environment, and the quality of service offered.

> Guangzhou is not so international. For example, the international flights are just a few. Every time I come to Guangzhou I need to transfer in Hong

Kong. ... I had never heard of Guangzhou before I came to the Canton Fair. I don't know much about the city so usually I don't go shopping here. Most of the time I go shopping in Hong Kong—the products, the service, and the environment are better. Interviewee 4 (American, male, senior manager), April 18, 2009

In other words, though China's reputation as a major manufacturing and export country has an impact on overseas visitors, Chinese products can be less attractive to overseas visitors than products from other countries because of their lower quality or limited variation in style. What is more, Guangzhou has less of an international identity than other cities in Asia, which has an impact on visitors' shopping desires and motivations.

On the other hand, the economy in Guangzhou is well developed and the public transportation is convenient, which has led to the recent dynamic development of Guangzhou's shopping industry. Because of the various shopping centers, the different levels and styles of products, and competitive prices, many consumers indeed view Guangzhou as a shopping paradise.

I like shopping here, quite convenient and there are different kinds of shops and commodities. I can get whatever I want here. Interviewee 5 (Australian, female, senior manager), April 19, 2009

The shopping locations in Guangzhou are relatively concentrated. Beijing Road and Tee Mall are well known to overseas visitors. The commodities sold on Beijing Road mainly include clothes, bags, silk, watches, and souvenirs, all at very competitive prices, whereas the commodities available in Tee Mall are mainly electronics and high-end goods. Both locations are easily accessible by metro. In addition, the convenience stores and several wholesale markets specializing in bags, clothing, stationery, and gifts, distributed in different parts of Guangzhou, can facilitate the shopping activities of international business tourists.

Mostly I buy clothes; I like to shop in Beijing Road. There are quite a lot of shops and the styles of the clothes there vary greatly. The prices are comparatively low and the transportation is convenient. I can directly get there by metro. Interviewee 2 (Indonesian, female, senior manager), April 17, 2009

Usually I go shopping in Tee Mall because there are lots of electronic products with different styles and levels. What's more, it's so convenient that it just takes a few minutes from the hotel to there by metro. Interviewee 7 (South African, male, supervisor), April 17, 2009

I don't go shopping often; usually I just go to the stores near the hotel to get some daily stuff. There are lots of stores near the hotel and the things are complete, transportation is convenient and just takes several minutes to go. Interviewee 3 (Australian, male, senior manager), April 18, 2009

However, Guangzhou's shopping environment has its shortcomings. The use of English is low in Guangzhou, and this language barrier can be a significant obstacle for tourist shoppers. International shoppers have difficulty communicating with taxi drivers, passersby, and staff in shops, and the street signs in Guangzhou are almost entirely in Chinese. All of these factors can hinder international visitors' shopping activities and even have a negative impact on their shopping experiences and satisfaction.

> The biggest problem is the language. The staff in the shop can't speak English. ... I don't go shopping without special need. Interviewee 18 (Algerian, male, senior manager), May 2, 2009
>
> Shopping in Guangzhou is okay. The goods are with a wide range of selection and the environment in the shop is good, however the road signs are all in Chinese and people here can't speak English. It's easy to get lost. ... Usually I don't go shopping on my own. Interviewee 1 (Thailand, male, senior manager), May 4, 2009
>
> There are lots of foreigners here to do some shopping. ... The biggest problem is the language. [We cannot] speak English, so we can just use our body language to bargain. As to customer's needs and basic information of the products, basically we cannot identify and deliver. The staff here usually cannot speak English. Interviewee 17 (Chinese, female, staff in a shop), April 19, 2009

In summary, the shopping environment in Guangzhou has many advantages, such as a wide variety of shops, concentrated shopping locations, a wide range of products, and convenient public transportation. However, the language barrier is a significant disadvantage that can enormously affect visitors' experiences and behavior.

Personal Background and Shopping Experience

The research findings in this study indicate that differences in income level and personal experience have a significant impact on tourism shopping behavior.

Income level has a significant influence on consumption behavior, especially in terms of the choices of shops and products, expenditure, perception of the shopping environment, and choice of transportation. Visitors with lower incomes tend to focus more on the products, rather than the shopping environment, and prefer relatively cheaper products and mid- or low-level shops. They do not care much about brand recognition and/or quality of service, and they tend to go shopping by metro because it is more economical. In general, the expenditure of visitors with lower incomes is lower. On the other hand, visitors with higher incomes place strong emphasis on the shopping environment and are not so sensitive to price. They think highly of particular brands, are discerning in terms of the quality of the products they buy, and have a higher demand for service. In general, the shopping expenditure of visitors with higher incomes is higher.

> Generally, I get clothes in Beijing Road because the clothes there differ greatly in styles; the prices are also competitive. The environment is so-so, but it is not that important. The quality and the price are more important. ... usually I go there by metro, convenient and cheap. Interviewee 2 (Indonesian, female, senior manager), April 17, 2009
>
> Usually I do the shopping in Tee Mall to get some electronic products. They are at low prices. .... Although the quality cannot be as good as that of other brands, the price is lower. Interviewee 1 (Indian, male, employee), April 17, 2009

> Usually I go shopping in Hong Kong and I did some shopping in Guangzhou a few times. I feel that the shopping environment in Guangzhou is inferior to that in Hong Kong. The products here are at a lower level. The price is lower but I believe that the brands, the quality, and the services are much more vital. Interviewee 4 (American, male, senior manager), April 18, 2009

Interviewees 1 and 2 had monthly incomes of under US$500, whereas interviewee 4 earned more than US$20,000 per month. Their behaviors were significantly different, especially in terms of their choices of shops, products, and shopping values.

Personal experience can also heavily influence shopping behavior. Those who have had a pleasant initial shopping experience in a particular environment tend to repeat previous shopping behavior, whereas those who have had unpleasant shopping experiences tend to change their shopping behavior patterns. The latter are likely to reduce their frequency of shopping in that environment or even avoid shopping there at all.

> I had quite a good time shopping here in Guangzhou several times. The quality, the prices, and the service are good. I believe I will go shopping every time I come here. Interviewee 5 (Australian, female, middle manager), April 19, 2009
>
> Last time I took a taxi to shop in Beijing Road. I was caught in a traffic jam and it took me nearly 2 hours to get there. I will never go shopping in Guangzhou by taxi. Metro is more convenient and can avoid traffic jams. Interviewee 13 (Mexican, male, self-employed), April 28, 2009
>
> I went shopping last time just by myself and got lost. Nobody spoke English and it took me a long time to get back to the hotel. Never will I go shopping again in Guangzhou. Or I will never go shopping just by myself again. Interviewee 22 (Thai, male, senior manager), May 4, 2009
>
> I used to buy many electronic products in Guangzhou but they went wrong just after I used them a few times. And I got some fake products several times. I won't buy electronic products any more in Guangzhou. Even if I go shopping, I will just go to high-level shops. The prices are higher but the quality is guaranteed: no fake products are sold and I will not be deceived. Interviewee 14 (Malaysian, male, middle manager), April 28, 2009

To sum up, personal characteristics and shopping experiences clearly influence shopping patterns. Visitors of various ages, genders, income levels, cultural backgrounds, and shopping experience possess significantly different shopping behavior.

Personal Preference

Even individuals from the same country, with similar professional positions, gender, and income levels vary in terms of their personal preferences, which can lead to different shopping behaviors. The in-depth interviews conducted during this study suggest that shopping behaviors are influenced by preferences for shopping type and destination, the distance required to reach the shopping destination, shopping time, products, brands, and choice of shopping companion.

Preferences in relation to shopping type and destination, shopping frequency, and shopping duration have major influences on shopping behavior. For some business tourists, access to shopping opportunities is one of the major reasons for making the trip. They shop more frequently and spend more time shopping than other categories of tourism shoppers. Furthermore, business tourists are willing to commute greater distances to shop. On the other hand, some business tourists do not enjoy shopping, so they shop less often and for shorter periods. These business tourists also commute shorter distances to shopping destinations than their more enthusiastic colleagues.

> I don't feel like shopping. Every time I just spend half an hour to shop and hang around in the convenient shops near the hotel. After the Canton Fair, I am so tired that I just want to rest in the hotel. Interviewee 3 (Australian, male, senior manager), April 18, 2009
>
> I love shopping. It's such an amazing thing. I go shopping whenever I am available. . . . Between the periods of the Canton Fair, I would spend the whole day shopping. . . . Shopping is one of the main reasons I come here. Interviewee 5 (Australian, female, middle manager), April 19, 2009

Time and distance preferences are often reflected in tourism shoppers' decisions about shopping times, shopping durations, and transport distances.

> I usually go shopping in the daytime. In the daytime I feel more energetic and safer. . . . Shopping is one of my main reasons to come here. I don't care where to shop, wherever I can get what I want I am willing to spend one hour to get there. If time permits, I would go shopping for a whole day. Interviewee 16 (Iran, male, self-employed), May 1, 2009
>
> I like shopping at night. In the evening the shopping atmosphere is better. I don't like cars. That's why I choose to shop near the hotel and usually it won't take more than 20 minutes by car . . . one or two hours is enough for me to go shopping and I head back to the hotel once I get what I want. Interviewee 12 (Czech, male, senior manager), April 28, 2009

Commodity and brand preferences are reflected in tourism shoppers' choices of products, shops, prices, and brands.

> Generally I will buy some clothes, whether they are brands or not. If I like the style I will get it. Interviewee 5 (Australian, female, middle manager), April 19, 2009
>
> In Guangzhou I buy some electronic products, comparatively cheaper. I usually choose the independent shops in Tee Mall. I don't care whether they are brands or not. If they work well and are competitive in price, that's okay to me. Interviewee 7 (South African, male, employee), April 25, 2009
>
> No matter what products, only if they are delicate and creative I would get them. But they must be in good quality. That's why I go to high-level shops or brand shops for shopping. Interviewee 19 (Tanzanian, male, middle manager), May 3, 2009

Some visitors prefer shopping on their own, some prefer shopping with their friends or relatives, and others like to be accompanied by a tourist guide.

I feel like shopping by myself. I am free to go to any shop and to decide when to go and when to be back. Interviewee 7 (South African, male, employee), April 25, 2009

Usually I go shopping with my relatives or my friends. Accompanied by others, you can get some suggestions and you can chat with them while shopping. You won't be so lonely. Interviewee 5 (Australian, female, middle manager), April 19, 2009

Usually I go shopping with the tourist guide. First I will not get lost; second, the guide can give me some shopping tips. Interviewee 22 (Thai, male, senior manager), May 4, 2009

The Mechanisms of Shopping Behavior

By analyzing three layers of factors, we can sum up the following mechanisms of business tourists' shopping behaviors.

1. The external holistic environment of the tourism destination can affect the holistic image of shopping at the destination and the commodities available. The holistic image of shopping at the destination will either stimulate or discourage tourists' shopping desires, and the commodities available at the destination will directly affect tourists' shopping tendencies and preferences (Keown, 1989). As a world factory, China exports products to countries all over the world, and this has resulted in high international recognition of the made in China label and its implications. Furthermore, price advantage, which is one motive of tourist shopping (Carmichael & Smith, 2004; Matteo & Matteo, 1996; Timothy, 1995), can stimulate tourists' shopping desires. However, inferior quality and lack of innovation can also discourage tourists' shopping desires. Because Guangzhou is a light industrial base and a center for electronics manufacturing, the region can determine the range of products to sell to tourists to some extent, which may affect tourism shoppers' preferences for clothing and electronics in Guangzhou. This may also be the reason why tourists visiting Guangzhou have greater preferences for electronics than tourists visiting other destinations in China.

2. The local environment of the destination, including the transport facilities, the language situation, and the holistic shopping environment, can affect tourists' shopping experiences and consequently contribute to their shopping preferences or their tendency to avoid shopping. Terrible traffic will cause an unpleasant shopping experience, resulting in future avoidance of shopping in the destination or a change in the mode of transportation selected. The opposite is also true, because hassle-free transportation can contribute to a pleasant shopping experience and consequently strengthen tourist shoppers' confidence in that mode of transportation at the destination. Language barriers can also result in unpleasant shopping experiences, leading tourists to avoid shopping in the same destination or to choose to shop with a tour guide in the future. In addition, the overall environment of the shopping location can affect tourists' shopping behaviors and shopping value perceptions by affecting tourists' shopping emotions (Yuksel, 2007).

3. Tourists' age, gender, income, and cultural background can lead to various personal preferences and can have further effects on their shopping patterns. For instance, females prefer cosmetics, jewelry, suitcases and bags, and shoes, whereas males prefer electronics. Males prefer shopping alone, whereas females prefer shopping with relatives and friends. African tourists prefer electrical products, tourists from Oceania

prefer clothing, and European tourists prefer souvenirs. Tourists with higher income levels prefer branded commodities and emphasize the shopping environment and commodity quality, whereas tourists with lower income levels emphasize the price.

Each mechanism outlined above influences consumers' shopping behavior. The relationships between the mechanisms are shown in Figure 1.

Conclusion and Discussion

Summary and Suggestions

The main conclusions of this article are as follows.

1. The shopping behaviors of international business tourists differ from general tourists in terms of shopping expenditures, commodity preferences, shopping time preferences, transportation methods, and shopping purposes. Business tourists' expenditures on shopping average RMB 4717.55, which is much higher than that of general tourists. Business tourists tend to shop at night, whereas general tourists have no specific shopping-time preferences. Like general tourists, business tourists shop mainly to purchase items for themselves and for gifts. However, the tendency to purchase souvenirs for remembrance purposes is much lower among business tourists than among general tourists. Business tourists prefer to take taxis or the metro to go shopping, rather than tour buses. In terms of commodity preferences, business tourists prefer clothing and electronics. In this study, business tourists' preference for electronics is related at least partially to Guangzhou's position as a producer of electronic goods, so the question of whether preferences for such commodities are affected by the type of tourism (business or sightseeing) requires further study. Because this study found no differences between business tourists and general tourists in terms of shopping times, shopping frequency, choice of shopping companion, commute time, and payment method, and because there is no relevant literature about the effect of these factors on differences between business tourists and general tourists, these factors are not compared or discussed here.
2. Gender, cultural background (country of origin), personal experience, and income level significantly affect business tourists' shopping behaviors, whereas the relationships between age, education, professional position, and shopping behavior are not significant. Females prefer cosmetics, jewelry, suitcases and bags, and shoes, whereas males prefer electronics. Males prefer shopping alone, whereas females prefer shopping with relatives or friends. African tourists prefer electronics, tourists from Oceania prefer clothing, and European tourists prefer souvenirs. Tourists with higher incomes prefer branded commodities and emphasize the shopping environment and commodity quality, whereas tourists with lower income place emphasis on price.
3. The holistic image and shopping environment of the destination, and individuals' background, shopping experience, and personal preferences have significant effects on business tourists' shopping behavior according to the following three interrelated mechanisms: (a) China's manufacturing image and Guangzhou's position as a light industrial base and electronics-producing base promote overseas tourists' shopping expenditures and also partially determine the type of commodities purchased; (b) the shopping environment in Guangzhou affects visitors' shopping experiences, which consequently influences their shopping patterns; and (c) tourists' gender, income,

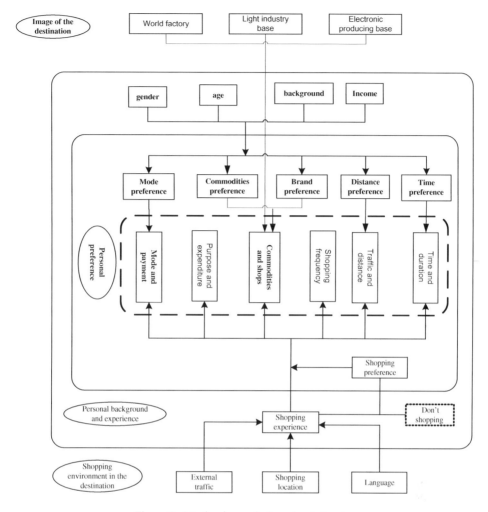

Figure 1. Mechanisms of shopping behaviors.

and cultural background can contribute to various personal preferences and can have further effects on their shopping patterns.

Marketing based on tourists' established shopping behaviors could be conducted at the government and merchant levels to improve the attractiveness of Guangzhou as a business tourism destination and to promote development of the tourism industry in Guangzhou.

For the Government

1. Boost the internationalization of Guangzhou. Improve the road sign system by adding English road signs. Enhance English skills training for taxi drivers to help create a friendly and safe shopping environment for overseas tourists and thereby stimulate their shopping desires.

2. Enhance supervision of the quality of commodities offerred and work to avoid fake and inferior commodities. These improvements can increase tourists' satisfaction and their likelihood of returning.

3. Enhance the planning and marketing of shopping areas to improve the recognition and the accessibility of "shopping in Guangzhou." It is essential to integrate the various types of shops that sell clothes, electronics, and gifts. In addition, marketing needs to target tourists and the infrastructure needs to be improved to provide rest and entertainment areas within shopping areas, thereby improving tourists' shopping experiences and extending the duration of their shopping trips, which will ultimately increase shopping expenditures.

For Merchants

1. Increase promotional activities that target tourists and enhance marketing, with the aim of improving potential visitors' recognition of shopping in Guangzhou and increase their shopping desires and motivations. Organize shuttle bus services to the shops from the convention center and hotels to increase accessibility.

2. Emphasize the importance of English skills training to salespeople to help overcome language barriers.

3. Base marketing campaigns on the innovation and superior quality of commodities rather than on low prices and discounts. Such high-end campaigns are more likely to enhance the attractiveness of particular commodities to business tourists and to increase tourists' desires to return.

4. Conduct niche marketing aimed at target customers. The market can be divided into clothes, electronics, and gift markets, etc., according to the type of commodity provided. The market can also be divided into high-, mid-, and low-level categories. In addition, these different market segments need to be organized according to different local suppliers and tailored to the promotion activities. Shop closing times should also be postponed during the Canton Fair, because many overseas visitors prefer to shop at night.

Limitations

The research object of this article is international business tourists attending the Canton Fair. The article analyzes shopping behavior differences among business tourists with different backgrounds, which is helpful to gain a better understanding of the shopping behavior of business tourists. The factors affecting business tourists' shopping behaviors and the related mechanisms are also analyzed. However, there are still a number of shortcomings to this article and questions that require further discussion.

1. This article only studies international business tourists attending the Canton Fair. Whether such tourists are in fact representative of the broader group of business tourists internationally and whether they behave similarly to general business tourists still need to be studied.

2. Because of language obstacles, the sample studied only included those business tourists who could speak English. Whether this sample is representative of all business tourists regardless of language preference or ability still needs to be addressed. In addition, the answers of some respondents with limited English may

have been affected by their inability to fully understand the questionnaire, which may have led to biased conclusions.

3. Recent changes in the numbers of visitors to and the countries of origin represented at the Canton Fair due to the world financial crisis may have an impact on patterns of shopping behavior among international business tourists in Guangzhou.

References

Babin, B. J., Chebat, J., & Michon, R. (2004). Perceived appropriateness and its effect on quality, affect and behavior. *Journal of Retailing and Consumer Services, 11*(5), 287–298.

Bitner, M. J. (1990). Evaluating service encounters: The effects of physical surroundings and employee responses. *Journal of Marketing, 54*(2), 69–82.

Carmichael, B. A., & Smith, W. W. (2004). Canadian domestic travel behavior: A market segmentation study of rural shoppers. *Journal of Vacation Marketing, 10*(4), 333–347.

Chang, J., Yang, B. T., & Yu, C. G. (2006). The moderating effect of salespersons' selling behavior on shopping motivation and satisfaction: Taiwan tourists in China. *Tourism Management, 27*, 934–942.

Chebat, J., & Michon, R. (2003). Impact of ambient odors on mall shoppers' emotions, cognition, and spending: A test of competitive causal theories. *Journal of Business Research, 56*(7), 529–539.

Chen, G., & Huang, Y. (2007). A summary of overseas studies on tourism shopping—An analysis based on ATR and TM. *Tourism Tribune, 22*(12), 88–92.

Choi, T. M., Liu, S. C., Pang, K. M., & Chow, P. S. (2008). Shopping behaviors of individual tourists from the Chinese Mainland to Hong Kong. *Tourism Management, 29*(4), 811–820.

Choi, W. M., Chan, A., & Wu, J. (1999). A qualitative and quantitative assessment of Hong Kong's image as a tourist destination. *Tourism Management, 20*(3), 361–365.

Cohen, E. (1995). Touristic craft ribbon development in Thailand. *Tourism Management, 16*(3), 225–235.

Dai, B. (2002, June 30). The development of Chinese business tourism. *International Commercial Daily*, p. 16.

Dellaert, B., Borgers, A., & Timmermans, H. (1995). A day in the city: Using conjoint choice experiments to model urban tourists' choice of activity packages. *Tourism Management, 16*(5), 347–353.

Dholakia, P. R. (1999). Going shopping: Key determinants of shopping behaviors and motivations. *International Journal of Retail and Distribution Management, 27*(4), 154–165.

Eroglu, S. A., & Machleit, K. A. (1990). An empirical examination of retail crowding: Antecedents and consequences. *Journal of Retailing, 66*(2), 201–221.

Gee, C. Y., Makens, J. C., & Choy, D. J. L. (Eds.). (1997). *The travel industry*. New York, NY: Van Nostrand Reinhold.

Geuens, M., Vantomme, D., & Brengman, M. (2004). Developing a typology of airport shoppers. *Tourism Management, 25*(5), 615–622.

Hu, B., & Yu, H. (2007). Segmentation by craft selection criteria and shopping involvement. *Tourism Management, 28*(4), 1079–1092.

Hu, P. (2008). An empirical research on tourist satisfaction at business tourism destinations: A case study of Xujiahui district in Shanghai. *Tourism Science, 22*(1), 29–33.

Josiam, B. M., Kinley, T. R., & Kim, Y. K. (2005). Involvement and the tourist shopper: Using the involvement construct to segment the American tourist shopper at the mall. *Journal of Vacation Marketing, 11*(2), 135–154.

Kemperman, A. D. A. M., Borgers, A. W. J., & Timmermans, H. J. P. (2009). Tourist shopping behavior in a historic downtown area. *Tourism Management, 30*(2), 208–218.

Kent, W. E., Shock, P. J., & Snow, R. E. (1983). Shopping: Tourism's unsung hero. *Journal of Travel Research, 21*(4), 2–4.

Keown, C. F. (1989). A model of tourists' to buy: Case of Japanese visitors to Hawaii. *Journal of Travel Research*, *27*(3), 31–34.

Kim, S., & Littrell, M. A. (2001). Souvenir buying intentions for self versus others. *Annals of Tourism Research*, *28*(3), 638–657.

Lehto, X. Y., Cai, L. A., & O'Leary, J. T. (2004). Tourist shopping preferences and expenditure behaviors: The case of the Taiwanese outbound market. *Journal of vacation Marketing*, *10*(4), 320–332.

Lesser, J. A., & Hughes, M. A. (1986). Towards a typology of shoppers. *Business Horizons*, *29*(6), 56–62.

Li, L. (2003). *The challenge of becoming the world factory*. Retrieved from http://www.people.com.cn/GB/paper81/9347/866471.html

Liang, X., & Hao, S. (2005). An analysis of the differences of domestic tourists demand for tourism commodities—Taking Xi'an tourism commodity market as an example. *Tourism Tribune*, *20*(4), 51–55.

Littrell, M. A., Baizerman, S. K., & Rita, G. S. (1994). Souvenirs and tourism styles. *Journal of Travel Research*, *33*(1), 3–11.

Ma, J. (2006). A summary of domestic research on tourism shopping. *Journal of Beijing Second Foreign Language Institute*, *9*, 9–14.

Mak, B. L., Tsang, N. K., & Cheung, I. C. (1999). Taiwanese tourists' shopping preference. *Journal of Vacation Marketing*, *5*(2), 190–198.

Matteo, L. D., & Matteo, R. D. (1996). An analysis of Canadian cross-border travel. *Annals of Tourism Research*, *23*(1), 103–122.

Michalkó, G. (2006). Typically female features in Hungarian shopping tourism. *Migration and Ethnic Themes*, *22*, 79–93.

Moscardo, G. (2004). Shopping as a destination attraction: An empirical examination of the role of shopping in tourists' destination choice and experience. *Journal of Vacation Marketing*, *10*(4), 294–307.

Neil, C. (2001). An exploratory study of gendered differences in young tourists' perception of danger within London. *Tourism Management*, *22*(5), 565–570.

Oh, J. Y., Cheng, C. K., & Lehto, X. Y. (2004). Predictors of tourists' shopping behavior: Examination of socio-demographic characteristics and trip typologies. *Journal of Vacation Marketing*, *10*(4), 308–319.

Reisinger, Y., & Waryszak, R. (1996). Catering to Japanese tourists: What service do they expect from food and drinking establishments Australia? *Journal of Restaurant and Foodservice Marketing*, *1*(3/4), 53–71.

Rosenbaum, M. S., & Spears, D. L. (2005). Who buys that? Who does that? Analysis of cross-cultural consumption behaviors among tourists in Hawaii. *Journal of Vacation Marketing*, *11*(3), 235–247.

Shi, M. (2004). A theoretical research on tourism shopping. *Tourism Tribune*, *19*(1), 32–36.

Snepenger, D. J., Murphy, L., O'Connell, R., & Gregg, E. (2003). Tourists and residents use of a shopping space. *Annals of Tourism Research*, *30*(3), 567–580.

Suh, Y. K., & Leo, M. A. (2005). Preferences and trip expenditures: A conjoint analysis of visitors to Seoul, Korea. *Tourism Management*, *26*(3), 325–333.

Swarbrooke, J., & Horner, S. (2004). *A study of tourism consumers' behavior*. Beijing, China: Electronic Industry Press.

Timothy, D. J. (1995). Political boundaries and tourism: Borders as tourist attractions. *Tourism Management*, *16*(7), 525–532.

Timothy, D. J., & Butler, R. W. (1995). Cross-border shopping: A North American perspective. *Annals of Tourism Research*, *22*(1), 16–34.

Turley, L. W., & Milliman, R. E. (2000). Atmospheric effects on shopping behavior: A review of the experimental evidence. *Journal of Business Research*, *49*, 193–211.

Turner, L. W., & Reisinger, Y. (2001). Shopping satisfaction for domestic tourists. *Journal of Retailing and Consumer Services*, *8*(1), 15–27.

Verbeke, J. M. (1988). Leisure, recreation and tourism in inner cities: Explorative case studies. *Netherlands Geographical Studies*, *58*, 109–111.

Wang, R., & Su, Q. (2008). A summary of overseas research on the tourist shopper typology. *Journal of Beijing Second Foreign Language Institute*, *5*, 36–42.

Wong, J., & Law, R. (2003). Differences in shopping satisfaction levels: A study of tourists in Hong Kong. *Tourism Management*, *24*(4), 401–410.

Wu, B. (2005). *A study on the travel behavior mode of inbound business tourists*. Shanxi, China: Shanxi Normal University.

Xie, H., & Bao, J. (2006). A study of gender differences in tourist behavior. *Tourism Tribune*, *21*(1), 44–49.

Yu, H., & Littrell, M. A. (2003). Product and process orientations to tourism shopping. *Journal of Travel Research*, *42*(2), 140–150.

Yuksel, A. (2004). Shopping experience evaluation: A case of domestic and international visitors. *Tourism Management*, *25*(6), 751–759.

Yuksel, A. (2007). Tourist shopping habitat: Effects on emotions, shopping value and behaviors. *Tourism Management*, *28*(1), 58–69.

Yuksel, A., & Fisun, Y. R. (2007). Shopping risk perceptions: Effects on tourists' emotions, satisfaction and expressed loyalty intentions. *Tourism Management*, *28*(3), 703–713.

Zhao, X. (2005). *A study of tourism behavior of inbound tourists in Kunming*. Shanxi, China: Shangxi Normal University.

Appendix
Visitor's Shopping Behavior Questionnaire

Dear Sir/Madam,

Welcome to Guangzhou! I am a senior student from Sun Yat-Sen University and I am conducting a survey on the foreign visitor's shopping behavior for my graduation thesis. I sincerely hope you could spend a few minutes completing the following questions. All information collected will be used **for academic purposes only**. Thank you for your kind participation!

Part A. General Information. Please "√" the option which is the closest to your response or fill in the blanks. All information collected will be used **For Statistical Purposes** only.

---

1. Country: _____
2. Gender: ☐ Female ☐ Male
3. Age: _____
4. Marital status: ☐ Single ☐ Married ☐ Other _____
5. Education Level:
   ☐ Under high school ☐ High school ☐ College/University level ☐ Master's/PhD level
6. Your position at your company:
   ☐ Senior management ☐ Middle management ☐ Supervisor ☐ Staff ☐ Self-employed
7. Your average monthly income level is _____

   ☐ Below $1,000 ☐ $1,001–2,500 ☐ $2,501–4,000 ☐ $4,001–6,000
   ☐ $6,001–8,000 ☐ $8,001–10,000 ☐ $10,001–20,000 ☐ Over $20,000

Part B. General Question. The information collected will be used for statistical purposes only. Please "√" the option which is the closest to your response or fill in the blanks.

1. How many times have you attended Canton Fair (including this time)? _____ Time(s).
2. How long will you stay in Guangzhou this time? _____ Day(s).
3. How many times will you do shopping in Guangzhou during this stay? About _____ Time(s).
4. When will you do shopping in Guangzhou? (You may "√" more than one)
   ☐ Before 12:00 ☐ 12:01–15:00 ☐ 15:01–18:00 ☐ 18:01–21:00 ☐ After 21:00
5. How long will you spend for one shopping trip? About _____ hour(s).
6. When shopping in Guangzhou, your favorite store type is _____. (You may tick more than one)
   ☐ Fashion chain store ☐ Individual shop in shopping mall ☐ Individual shop on street
   ☐ Hypermarket ☐ Department store ☐ Other (please specify) _____
7. When shopping in Guangzhou, _____ will go with you as a companion.
   ☐ Nobody ☐ Relatives ☐ Colleagues ☐ Friends ☐ Tour guide ☐ Other (please specify) _____
8. You will go shopping _____ (You may "√" more than one)
   ☐ On foot ☐ By metro ☐ By taxi ☐ By car rented ☐ By bus ☐ Other (please specify) _____
9. How long will it take to come from your hotel to the shopping store? About _____ minutes.
10. What kind of merchandise you may buy from shopping mall, store, etc. (outside the exhibition center) in Guangzhou? (You may "√" more than one)
    ☐ Household appliance ☐ Cosmetics ☐ Electronic products ☐ Clothes/shoes
    ☐ Native products ☐ Artworks/antiques ☐ Jewel ☐ Watch ☐ Suitcases & bags
    ☐ Souvenirs ☐ Other (please specify) _____
11. You buy these merchandise above in Guangzhou for _____ (You may "√" more than one)
    ☐ Self-use ☐ Gift for relatives ☐ Gift for friends
    ☐ Memorial purpose ☐ Other (please specify) _____
12. How much do you pay for shopping in Guangzhou (from shopping mall, store rather than the exhibition center) About _____ (RMB, US$, EUR, HKD, GBP, etc.)
13. Which is your major payment method?
    ☐ RMB currency ☐ U.S. currency ☐ Credit card ☐ Other (please specify)
    _____

Thanks Again!

Visitor and Resident Images of Qingdao, China, as a Tourism Destination

游客与居民对中国青岛市作为旅游目的地的形象感知

SHAOJUN JI
GEOFFREY WALL

This article compares the images of Qingdao, China, as perceived by visitors and residents and examines whether these images are affected by information sources, age, education, and place attachment. The data were collected using a self-administered survey of 578 visitors and 337 residents of Qingdao throughout June and July of 2009. The image construct was conceptualized into two dimensions: cognitive and affective. It was found that the images perceived by visitors and residents converged primarily on cognitive images and less so on affective images. The results of a Mann-Whitney U test reveal that the main differences between the images held by visitors and residents are in 10 cognitive images (seafood, cultural attraction, highway system, traffic congestion, airline schedules, local people, beaches, weather, scenery, and hygiene and cleanliness) and in two affective images (arousing–sleepy and exciting–gloomy). Spearman's rank correlation test revealed that there is a weak positive correlation between place attachment and the images of Qingdao perceived by both visitors and residents. Age, education, and information sources are only partially correlated with visitor and resident images, with weak correlations.

本文旨在比较游客与居民对中国青岛市作为旅游目的地的形象感知,并同时检验这些感知形象是否受信息源、年龄、教育程度与地方依附感四个因素的影响。研究数据来源于2009年6月与7月对578名青岛游客与337名居民所作的问卷调查。对感知形象的分析包括两个方面:认知形象与情感形象。*Mann-Whitney U*检验结果表明游客与居民在认知形象方面相似点较多。然而,两组群体在10个认知形象属性与 2个情感形象属性方面存在明显差异。此外,*Spearman's Rank Correlation Test* 证明了地方依附感与游客以及居民的感知形象之间存在较弱的正相关性,而信息源、年龄与教育程度只对这两个群体的部分感知形象具有较弱的影响。

Shaojun Ji is a Ph.D. student in the Department of Geography and Environmental Management at University of Waterloo, N2L 3G1, Canada (E-mail: s2ji@uwaterloo.ca).

Geoffrey Wall is Professor of the Department of Geography and Environmental Management at University of Waterloo, N2L 3G1, Canada (E-mail: gwall@uwaterloo.ca).

Introduction

Because the role of tourism in stimulating economic development is recognized by governments of many countries (Sinclair, 1998), tourism destinations have proliferated worldwide in the past few decades. This has resulted in intensified competition among destinations for visitors (Page & Connell, 2006). In response, marketers have put great effort into developing effective marketing strategies to enhance the competitiveness of their places. A primary strategy adopted by municipal governments in many countries is to promote an appealing destination image to inform the potential consumers about the destination. The underlying rationale is that individuals' images of a destination have a significant influence on their travel choices (Page & Connell; Tasci & Gartner, 2007). If an individual has a strong and positive image about a destination, he or she is more likely to consider and choose this destination when making travel decisions (Andreu, Bigne, & Cooper, 2000). Consequently, adequately understanding the destination images that potential consumers hold is critical for a successful place marketing (Baloglu & McCleary, 1999).

Academic effort on studying destination image started in the early 1970s (Castro, Armario, & Ruiz, 2007) with a wide range of research areas being covered on this subject, including conceptualization, components and dimensions, formation processes, assessment, positioning strategies and management policies, influence of image, image differences between different groups, and image change over time (S. D. Pike, 2002; Selby, 2004; Zou, 2007). These studies have focused mainly on the images perceived by visitors to the destination, whereas the images held by local residents on the destination where they reside have been largely neglected (Schroeder, 1996). This disregard impedes a comprehensive understanding of perceived images because residents are equally potential consumers of the destination as long as they are involved in tourism activities and use recreational facilities within their home communities (Cowley, Spurr, Robins, & Woodside, 2004). Additionally, residents' images of their home destination can influence potential visitors' images of that place as an information source (word-of-mouth; Gunn, 1997; Schroeder). Furthermore, residents themselves are an image element (Echtner & Ritchie, 1991). Consequently, their attitudes toward tourists can affect tourists' perceptions of a certain destination (Gallarza, Saura, & Garcia, 2002). For these reasons, studying the images of both visitors and residents provides insight into the identification of the perceived strengths and weaknesses of the attributes of the destination, thereby helping it improve tourism products and services provided (J. S. Chen & Uysal, 2002).

Another important and frequently discussed topic in image studies centers on factors influencing image formation. According to Goodall (1990), understanding factors that influence image formation helps marketers determine their target markets and assures that they promote an image that is tailored to a particular market segment. A review of the literature indicates that sociodemographic characteristics (e.g., age, education) and information sources are key factors, among others, that affect the perceptions of both visitors and residents of the destination, although which factors have an impact on the perceived image formation vary case by case. In this regard, knowing the particular influential factors associated with a destination is critical for its successful marketing practice.

In addition to the aforementioned factors, place attachment, a significant predictor of tourism and leisure behaviors (Bricker & Kerstetter, 2000; Hammitt, Backlund, & Bixler, 2006), is proposed to be closely related to or the basis for forming individuals' images about the destination (Carter, Dyer, & Sharma, 2007; Govers & Go, 2005; Molenaar, 1996, 2002; Ramshaw & Hinch, 2006). However, whether place attachment affects perceived image has remained unclear. Given its increasingly important role in the managerial paradigm of urban renewal and development (Williams & Vaske, 2003), an empirical study on its influence on the perceived image can benefit the destination market practice and add to the literature.

The purposes of this study are to examine the images that visitors and local residents have of Qingdao, China, and to determine whether these images are influenced by information sources, certain sociodemographic characteristics (age and education), and place attachment. The research questions are as follows: (a) What are the differences in the perceived images of visitors and residents of Qingdao? (b) What are the similarities in the perceived images of visitors and residents of Qingdao? (c) What factors (i.e., information sources, age, education, and place attachment) are related to the images of current visitors regarding Qingdao? (d) What factors (i.e., information sources, age, education, and place attachment) are related to the images of residents regarding Qingdao?

Components of Destination Image

What comprises destination image has been of great interest to image researchers, and a number of components have been proposed to conceptualize and measure the image concept (Kwek & Lee, 2007). Of all of the components raised, the cognitive and affective ones have been widely accepted by researchers across different disciplines (e.g., Baloglu, 1997; Baloglu & Brinberg, 1997; Chon, 1991; Hosany, Ekinci, & Uysal, 2006; Kim & Yoon, 2003; Lin, Morais, Kerstetter, & Hou, 2007; Naoi, 2003; Stern & Krakover, 1993; Vogt & Andereck, 2003; Walmsley & Young, 1998; Zhang, Li, & Chen, 2006). According to Baloglu and McCleary (1999), *cognitive image* refers to individuals' evaluations of the quality of a destination's attributes. These attributes could be weather, landscape, transportation, food, recreational facilities, or attitudes of local people. The affective component is individuals' evaluation of the emotional quality of the destination. Individuals' feelings, such as being relaxed, happy, sleepy, or gloomy, belong to this affective image group. Although the cognitive and affective images are distinct, they are interrelated with each other; the formation of the affective image depends on the cognitive image and is as a function of it (Anand, Holbrook, & Stephens, 1988; Baloglu & McCleary; Gartner, 1993; Stern & Krakover).

Though accepting of this cognitive–affective dimension, a number of researchers have further developed the image concept by adding other components. One group of these researchers has proposed that an overall image is formed after the cognitive and affective evaluation of the destination attributes (Baloglu & McCleary, 1999; Kneesel, Baloglu, & Millar, 2010; Lin et al., 2007; Rezende-Parker, Morrison, & Ismail, 2003; Sonmez & Sirakaya, 2002; Stepchenkova & Morrison, 2008). They found that the cognitive image can directly impact the overall image and/or indirectly influence it through the affective image. Another group of researchers has conceptualized destination image as three notably different but interrelated components: cognitive, affective, and conative (Gartner, 1993; Manstead, 1996; S. Pike & Ryan, 2004). The conative image, as Gartner (1993) defined it, is a behavioral component associated with decision making. It is the result of assessment during the cognitive and affective phases as well as a transition from the cognitive and affective images to a decision about whether the proposed destination is worth visiting. Tasci, Gartner, and Cavusgil (2007) clarified the relationship among the cognitive, affective, overall, and conative images. They claimed that with cognitive and affective images interacting with each other, the holistic/overall image is constructed, leading to the formation of the conative image that, in turn, results in the process of decision making.

These research efforts on conceptualizing destination image provide valuable insights into understanding the complex process of image formation. However, some concepts raised have been less than clear. For example, the overall image is conceptualized as resulting from the cognitive or affective images or a combination of them; it is unknown whether this image can readily be derived from the summation of individual image attributes. For this reason, this study only examined the cognitive and affective dimensions that are widely accepted by researchers. Additionally, this study focused on the image formation structure rather than behavioral intentions; therefore, the conative image was also excluded from this research.

Factors Influencing Image Formation

Place Attachment

Place attachment refers to the cognitive and emotional bonding between individuals and places. It has two components: place identity and place dependence (Hammitt et al., 2006). According to Proshansky (1978), place identity is

> those dimensions of the self that define the individual's personal identity in relation with the physical environment by means of a complex pattern of conscious and unconscious ideas, beliefs, preferences, feelings, values, goals and behavioral tendency and skills relevant to this environment. (p. 155)

In this regard, a place is not only a resource for fulfilling individuals' behavioral or experiential goals but it also is an essential part of oneself, leading to a strong emotional attachment to the place. Such a place could be a park for year-round family gatherings or be seen as a heritage site that generates abstract and symbolic meanings (Williams, Patterson, Roggenbuck, & Watson, 1992). Place dependence refers to the functional attachment to a place due to its ability to provide desired experiences (Stokols & Shumaker, 1981). It emphasizes the value of a particular place, sometimes when compared to similar settings, in providing the amenities necessary for satisfying the needs of individuals based on the setting's specificity, functionality, satisfaction, and "goodness" for hiking, diving, etc. (Kyle, Graefe, Manning, & Bacon, 2003). A few researchers have found that this functional place attachment is positively and moderately correlated with place identity (Kyle et al., 2003; Kyle, Graefe, Manning, & Bacon, 2004; Vaske & Kobrin, 2001; Williams, Anderson, McDonald, & Patterson, 1995; Williams & Vaske, 2003). Moore and Graefe (1994) also found that place dependence may lead to repeat visitation, which, in turn, entails place identity.

Studies on the relationship between destination image and place attachment focus on the influence of the former on the latter. Existing research has similar findings; that is, that the cognitive image positively affects the formation of individuals' attachment (place identity and place dependence) to a place (H. Chen, 2006; Hou, 2007; Lee, 2009; Wu, 2009). H. Chen, for example, discovered that visitors' cognitive images regarding Meinong Town, Taiwan, directly and positively influence their affective images, and these affective images directly and positively influence the place identity and place dependence associated with Meinong. Wu also found that both visitors' cognitive and affective images regarding Sun-Moon Lake National Scenic Area, Taiwan, have a positive effect on forming their place identity and place dependence.

A few studies that focus specifically on the effect of place attachment on destination image have quite diverse results. Kyle et al. (2004) found that respondents' perceptions of setting density are significantly predicted by both place identity and place dependence. Conversely, White, Virden, and van Ripe (2008) showed that neither place identity nor place dependence are significant predictors of respondents' perceptions of recreation conflict. In addition to these empirical studies, Govers and Go (2004) explored the relationship between place identity and perceived image theoretically within a supply–demand framework that involves other elements (tourism experience, projected image, and commercialization). According to those researchers, the projected image is produced based on the destination's commercialized tourism products, which, in turn, are built on place identity. Through marketing efforts, this projected image is transmitted to the demand side and forms the basis for constructing the visitor's perceived images.

Information Sources

Information sources refers to a variety of materials that potential consumers encounter in relation to a destination (Baloglu & McCleary, 1999). In Gunn's (1972) pioneer work, he proposed two image formation levels associated with information sources: organic and induced. The organic image is formed through an accumulation of non-tourism-specific sources obtained from schools, word-of-mouth, or noncommercial newspaper reports, magazine articles, and television programs. It exists prior to access to commercial sources promoted by the destination and can be obtained without having been to the destination. The induced image is derived from promotional materials such as tourist brochures and/ or through actual visitation. Gartner (1993) further developed Gunn's model by adding a third element, autonomous image information agents. These autonomous sources include produced reports, documentaries, movies, or news articles. Gartner illustrated from induced to autonomous to organic images that the degree of destination control on information decreases, whereas the degree of audience credibility increases.

The influence of information sources on cognitive image formation has been reported by a number of researchers (e.g., Baloglu & McCleary, 1999; Burgess, 1978; Gartner, 1993; Holbrook, 1978; Um, 1993; Um & Crompton, 1990; Woodside & Lysonski, 1989). Most of them reported that the variety and type of information sources influence the formation of the cognitive rather than the affective image. However, in a recent study conducted by Li, Pan, Zhang, and Smith (2009), the researchers found that the level and type of information search contribute to both the respondents' cognitive and affective image changes.

Sociodemographic Characteristics

Sociodemographic characteristics have been a common factor integrated into image studies to examine individuals' perceptions of destinations (Beerli & Martin, 2004). Among the variety of sociodemographic characteristics examined, age and education have been considered the major predictors of image (Baloglu & McCleary, 1999). Baloglu and McCleary, for example, studied the perceptions of Turkey, Greece, Italy, and Egypt by Americans who intended to travel to these countries and found that age significantly influenced their cognitive rather than their affective images. Conversely, Walmsley and Jenkins (1993) reported that both age and gender contributed to the affective image perceived by residents of Gosford, Australia. When studying the perceived image of Lanzarote, Spain, by first-time and repeat visitors, Beerli and Martin found that the level of education only had a significant influence on the affective image. Stern and Krakover (1993) discovered that education, age, and gender had an effect on the British travelers' perceptions of Spain.

Study Area

The study area, Qingdao, is located at the east coast of Shandong Peninsula, China, facing Japan, North Korea, and South Korea across the Yellow Sea (Qingdao Shi Qing [QDSQ], 2008). The city has a land area of 1,159 square kilometers and is home to 2.76 million people. Qingdao holds a wealth of natural resources such as the coastline and forests and a considerable historical and cultural heritage resulting from early human civilization and colonial domination. Based on these resources, Qingdao has developed a great number of tourist attractions and has become one of the most popular tourist destinations in China. During the period 1998 to 2007, the average growth rate was 12.99 and 20.97% in the number of domestic tourists and tourist receipts respectively (Qingdao Tourism Administration [QDTA], 2009a). Similarly, the average growth rate of international tourist arrivals and tourist receipts was 19.28 and 23.33%, respectively, during the same period of time. In 2007, the number of domestic tourists reached 32.58 million, which generated US$51.62 billion in terms of tourism revenue. In the same year, Qingdao was ranked eighth of the major Chinese cities in terms of reception of overseas visitors. The foreign tourist arrivals were 1,081,476, and the foreign tourism receipts were US$675 million.

Tourism marketing in Qingdao was put on the agenda by the municipal government in the early 1980s (QDSQ, 2008). Three actions were undertaken since then. First, promotional materials (books, brochures, booklets, posters, billboards, postcards, and videos) concerning the city's landscape, history, architecture, and tourism development were published (QDTA, 2009b). Second, the promotional campaigns at international and national trade fairs and exhibitions were run to promote the city to the outside world. Third, marketing initiatives were implemented through cooperation and joint promotions among businesses in both home and abroad. For example, Qingdao worked together with the cities of Tianjin, Dalian, and Qinhuangdao, creating a travel route Golden Necklace Tour around the Bohai Sea.

The success of winning the bid for the 2008 Olympic Games sailing event provides a good opportunity for Qingdao to present its city image. Since 2002, the Qingdao Olympic Action Plan, emphasizing the theme of "The Sailing Capital" as Qingdao's image, was initiated by the municipality of Qingdao to target the participant countries of the 2008 Olympic Games. Under this plan, the Qingdao municipal government devoted a great deal of manpower and funding (e.g., 30 million yuan each year from 2006 to 2008) to the development and promotion of a positive city image to attract domestic and foreign visitors (QDTA, 2009a). For example, the Qingdao government has sent out promotional groups to more than 20 countries and run 85 marketing campaigns entitled "Meeting at the Olympics, Sailing in Qingdao." After making these efforts, marketers in Qingdao are eager to know whether their image promotions have been successful. In this regard, a case study of Qingdao will provide useful information for its marketing and fill the literature gap as insufficient studies have been done in the Chinese context.

Methods

Measurement

For both visitors and residents, affective images were evaluated using a 5-point semantic-differential scale. Four dimensions (i.e., arousing–sleepy, exciting–gloomy, pleasant–unpleasant, and relaxing–stressful), developed by Baloglu and Brinberg (1997), were adopted in this research. This scale was chosen because it is widely used in image studies; its validity and reliability have been examined in a number of studies and found to be appropriate (Baloglu & McCleary, 1999). Cognitive images were measured through a 5-point Likert-type scale ranging from 1 (*very poor*) to 5 (*very good*). Twenty-six items were developed based on the studies of Beerli and Martin (2004), Echtner and Ritchie (1993), and Mi (2003). Although multiple cognitive attributes were used in these three studies, 26 of the attributes that were adopted were in line with Qingdao's tourism brochures. This scale was chosen because its validity and reliability have been established in the above-mentioned studies. Additionally, the face validity of this scale was confirmed by three professors who have been involved in image studies.

For the evaluation of place attachment, four statements adapted from the work of Hailu, Boxall, and McFarlane (2005) were used to measure its two dimensions (place identity and place dependence) in the visitor questionnaire. These statements include

1. Visiting Qingdao says a lot about who I am.
2. I can identify easily with this destination.
3. I get more satisfaction from visiting Qingdao than from visiting any other destinations.
4. I enjoy doing the types of activities I do in Qingdao more than at any other destinations.

Five statements adapted from the studies of Hwang, Lee, and Chen (2005) and Hailu et al. (2005) were used in the questionnaire for residents to measure place identity and place dependence. These statements include

1. I feel that Qingdao is a part of myself, and I am a part of it.
2. I have many relatives and friends in Qingdao.
3. I will miss Qingdao if I leave the city.
4. I would like to live in Qingdao.
5. I do not want to live in other places except Qingdao.

All of the statements regarding place attachment were measured using a 5-point Likert scale, ranging from 1 (*strongly disagree*) to 5 (*strongly agree*). The scales for measuring visitors' and residents' levels of attachment were chosen based on two criteria: (a) they approximated the purpose of the current research and (b) their validity and reliability have been determined in the above-mentioned studies.

The variety of information sources was measured as the sum of the number of sources that respondents claimed to use, ranging from 1 to 10. These sources were chosen based on the works of Baloglu and McCleary (1999) and Mi (2003). The sources include tourist brochures, mass media advertising campaigns, travel agency staff, the Internet, word-of-mouth (friends, relatives), guidebooks, news, magazines, documentaries and TV programs, and other sources. This scale was adopted because it involved three types of image formation agents that are widely used by image researchers and the nine sources included in this research were appropriate for testing individuals' images of Qingdao.

Another reason for choosing this scale was dependent on how the researcher intended to answer the research questions (group comparison was expected in this study). For respondents' sociodemographic characteristics, respondents' ages (15–24, 25–44, 45–54, and over 55) and educational levels (less than high school, high and professional school, college or university, and postgraduate studies) were included in this research. The scales used to measure age and education were chosen based on how the researcher intended to answer the research questions (group comparison was expected in this study).

Data Collection

Self-administered questionnaires were used to collect data for this research. The survey population consisted of individuals who were over the age of 18 and who passed the three chosen tourist sites (Lanshan Mountain, Zhanqiao Pier, and Qingdao Beer Museum) of Qingdao between June 10 and July 10, 2009. The sampling process included two stages. First, three survey sites were purposely selected from 28 sites recommended on the Qingdao Tourism Bureau's Web site. These three sites were selected because they represent different types of tourist attractions in Qingdao, specifically, natural, cultural and historical, and amusement. The second stage involved interviewing a random sample of individuals who visited the three sites during the survey time period. Every tenth individual who passed by the survey sites between 9 a.m. and 5 p.m. was approached and asked to complete a questionnaire. A total of 990 questionnaires were distributed, 330 at each site. The survey distribution continued until 330 questionnaires were completed at each site. The response rate was 53.7%.

Data Analysis

Survey data were coded and analyzed in three steps, using the Statistical Package for Social Science (SPSS, U.S.) 18. First, descriptive statistics were used to summarize the demographic characteristics of the research sample (i.e., sex, age, and education). Second, a preliminary testing for normality (i.e., Shapiro-Wilks test) was performed. The results indicated that the data used in this research were not normally distributed (the chosen alpha level was 0.05). Consequently, nonparametric statistics were chosen in the subsequent analysis. Third, a Mann-Whitney U test was conducted to identify the image differences and similarities between visitors and residents. This test allows the researcher to determine whether a significant difference exists between two groups' mean ranks using nonnormally distributed data (Diekhoff, 1992). Fourth, Spearman's correlation was computed to determine whether information sources, age, education, and place attachment influenced the images that actual visitors and residents held about Qingdao. The Spearman correlation coefficient analysis allows the researcher to investigate the relationship among variables under investigation using nonnormally distributed data (Diekhoff).

Results

Sociodemographic Characteristics of Participants

The sociodemographic characteristics of respondents can be found in Table 1. The visitor group consisted of 578 individuals, and the resident group consisted of 337 individuals. For both groups, the sex of the participants was almost evenly distributed, with 50.5% male and 49.5% female in the visitor group and 46.6% male and 53.4% female in the

Table 1. Sociodemographic Characteristics of Respondents.

Characteristic	Visitors ($n = 578$)		Residents ($n = 337$)	
Attribute	n	$\%$	n	$\%$
Sex				
Male	292	50.5	157	46.6
Female	286	49.5	180	53.4
Age				
18 to 24 Years old	149	25.8	113	33.5
25 to 44 Years old	303	52.4	114	42.7
45 to 54 Years old	115	19.9	62	18.4
55 and Over	11	1.9	18	5.3
Education				
Less than high school	6	1.0	0	0
High/professional school	109	18.9	107	31.8
College and/or university	414	71.6	225	66.8
Postgraduate	49	8.5	5	1.5

resident group. The age distribution of respondents in the two groups was similar. Individuals under the age of 44 represented the majority of respondents for both groups, 78.2 and 76.2%, respectively. In terms of respondents' educational levels, most respondents in the two groups attended college or graduate school, 71.6 and 66.8%, respectively.

Image Differences and Similarities Between Visitors and Residents

A Mann-Whitney U test was used to compare the images of Qingdao perceived by visitors and residents. As Table 2 shows, no significant differences were found in participants' images of most of the 30 attributes; that is, in 2 affective attributes (pleasant–unpleasant and relaxing–stressful) and in 16 cognitive ones (e.g., accommodation, shopping; $p > .05$). It can also be seen that both visitors and residents have relatively positive images of these 18 image attributes (mean > 3). Conversely, significant differences between the images held by visitors and residents were found in 10 cognitive attributes (e.g., seafood, cultural attraction) and in 2 affective ones (arousing–sleepy and exciting–gloomy; $p < .05$), although the mean scores of these 12 attributes between the two groups did not differ greatly. Of all 12 image attributes, visitors had better images than residents in 2 attributes (cultural attractions and traffic congestion), whereas they had worse images than residents in 10 attributes (e.g., arousing–sleepy, exciting–gloomy).

Influence of Information Sources, Age, Education, and Place Attachment on Visitor Images

Spearman's rho correlations were computed to examine the relationships between visitors' images of Qingdao (4 affective and 26 cognitive image attributes) and several factors (information sources, age, education, and place attachment). The results of the analysis are presented in Table 3. Age was significantly negatively correlated with 4 cognitive image attributes—squares, ethnic attractions, special events, and fashion

Table 2. Comparison of the Perceived Images Between Visitors and Residents.

	Mean			
	Visitor	Resident	Mann-Whitney U	p
Affective image[a]				
Arousing–sleepy	1.66	1.52	86,721.0	.002
Exciting–gloomy	1.75	1.62	88,162.0	.009
Pleasant–unpleasant	1.68	1.58	90,953.5	.065
Relaxing–stressful	1.65	1.60	90,922.5	.063
Cognitive image[b]				
Seafood	4.45	4.62	85,756.0	.002
Accommodation	3.97	3.95	95,610.0	.649
Shopping	3.90	3.82	93,243.0	.616
Cultural attraction	4.09	3.75	84,218.5	.001
Highway system	3.98	4.18	81,527.0	<.001
Traffic congestion	3.35	2.89	66,945.5	<.001
Airline schedules	3.68	3.95	69,242.5	<.001
Transportation cost	3.76	3.76	89,347.0	.540
Public transport	3.97	3.98	85,037.5	.435
Night life	3.72	3.69	83,937.5	.676
Relaxing atmosphere	4.17	4.07	90,627.5	.115
Local people	4.30	4.38	86,837.0	.030
Football games	3.69	3.76	63,471.5	.688
Beaches	4.37	4.64	75,584.0	<.001
Weather	4.25	4.37	88,953.5	.024
Green space	4.29	4.37	91,249.0	.098
Squares	4.25	4.30	92,446.0	.326
Resorts	4.15	4.19	87,316.5	.459
Scenery	4.41	4.52	82,852.0	<.001
Ethnic attractions	4.27	4.25	88,050.0	.531
Golf course	4.07	4.02	54,053.5	.859
Special events	4.29	4.30	84,714.5	.783
Fashion shows	3.88	3.80	53,848.5	.184
Architecture	4.24	4.31	90,293.0	.132
Value for money	3.79	3.72	89,457.0	.110
Hygiene and cleanliness	4.10	4.34	80,626.5	<.001

Notes. [a]1 = *extremely arousing*, 2 = *very arousing*, 3 = *neutral*, 4 = *very sleepy*, 5 = *extremely sleepy*.
[b]1 = *very poor*, 2 = *poor*, 3 = *neutral*, 4 = *good*, 5 = *very good*.

shows ($r_s = -0.110$ to $-0.116, p < .05$) with weak correlations ($r_s < 0.29$; Pallent, 2007). This indicated that the higher the educational level, the less favorable images associated with these 4 attributes. The results also showed that there was no significant correlation between education and any cognitive and affective attributes. Additionally, information sources were found to be significantly and negatively correlated with 9 cognitive attributes; for example, seafood, accommodation, and cultural attraction ($r_s = 0.002$ to $-.162, p < .05$). This indicated that the greater the number of information sources used, the worse the images formed on these 9 attributes.

Table 3. Relationships Between Components of Visitors' Perceived Images and Age, Education, Information Sources, and Place Attachment.

	Age	Education	Information Sources	Attachment 1	Attachment 2	Attachment 3	Attachment 4
Affective image[a]							
Arousing–sleepy	.009	−.031	.016	−.115	−.094	−.203	−.191
	(.825)	(.462)	(.705)	(.007)	(.025)	(<.001)	(<.001)
Exciting–gloomy	−.067	−.002	−.006	−.069	−.063	−.186	−.179
	(.107)	(.968)	(.890)	(.104)	(.132)	(<.001)	(<.001)
Pleasant–unpleasant	−.026	−.041	−.025	−.014	−.093	−.121	−.066
	(.527)	(.325)	(.553)	(.743)	(.026)	(.004)	(.114)
Relaxing–stressful	−.081	−.070	.038	−.094	−.125	−.118	−.139
	(.050)	(.091)	(.365)	(.028)	(.003)	(.005)	(.001)
Cognitive image[b]							
Seafood	.002	−.040	−.162	.208	.176	.257	.294
	(.957)	(.338)	(<.001)	(<.001)	(<.001)	(<.001)	(<.001)
Accommodation	.074	.024	−.121	.106	.117	.164	.225
	(.078)	(.564)	(.004)	(.013)	(.005)	(<.001)	(<.001)
Shopping	−.003	−.061	−.067	.214	.138	.236	.247
	(.950)	(.145)	(.110)	(<.001)	(.001)	(<.001)	(<.001)
Cultural attraction	−.034	−.045	−.083	.175	.096	.241	.252
	(.410)	(.286)	(.046)	(<.001)	(.023)	(<.001)	(<.001)
Highway system	.025	−.047	−.038	.091	.072	.147	.112
	(.560)	(.261)	(.364)	(.034)	(.089)	(<.001)	(.008)
Traffic congestion	−.033	−.025	−.093	.116	.081	.066	.133
	(.442)	(.562)	(.027)	(.007)	(.055)	(.119)	(.002)
Airline schedules	−.042	−.007	−.160	.070	.096	.087	.093
	(.340)	(.866)	(<.001)	(.116)	(.029)	(.047)	(.035)

(Continued)

Table 3. (Continued).

	Age	Education	Information Sources	Attachment 1	Attachment 2	Attachment 3	Attachment 4
Transportation cost	-.032 (.451)	-.026 (.541)	-.080 (.060)	.136 (.002)	.110 (.010)	.130 (.002)	.113 (.008)
Public transport	.055 (.207)	.016 (.713)	-.149 (.001)	.222 (<.001)	.151 (<.001)	.177 (<.001)	.203 (<.001)
Night life	-.046 (.282)	-.005 (.906)	-.181 (<.001)	.048 (.274)	.028 (.517)	.169 (<.001)	.170 (<.001)
Relaxing atmosphere	.046 (.268)	.053 (.203)	-.025 (.545)	.159 (<.001)	.118 (.005)	.182 (<.001)	.180 (<.001)
Local people	-.030 (.472)	-.037 (.381)	-.037 (.374)	.304 (<.001)	.191 (<.001)	.290 (<.001)	.267 (<.001)
Football games	.090 (.069)	-.038 (.441)	-.072 (.144)	.191 (<.001)	.084 (.088)	.106 (.033)	.132 (.007)
Beaches	-.075 (.076)	-.071 (.094)	-.007 (.873)	.269 (<.001)	.184 (<.001)	.205 (<.001)	.217 (<.001)
Weather	-.060 (.149)	-.021 (.617)	-.026 (.531)	.172 (<.001)	.067 (.111)	.162 (<.001)	.163 (<.001)
Green space	-.040 (.336)	-.009 (.835)	-.077 (.064)	.130 (.002)	.068 (.105)	.132 (.002)	.118 (.005)
Squares	-.113 (.007)	.028 (.502)	.012 (.779)	.182 (<.001)	.133 (.002)	.195 (<.001)	.185 (<.001)
Resorts	-.043 (.323)	-.015 (.729)	.048 (.262)	.255 (<.001)	.154 (<.001)	.187 (<.001)	.167 (<.001)
Scenery	.012 (.775)	.069 (.101)	-.011 (.798)	.174 (<.001)	.152 (<.001)	.169 (<.001)	.118 (.005)
Ethnic attractions	-.116 (.007)	-.008 (.854)	-.017 (.695)	.177 (<.001)	.080 (.064)	.178 (<.001)	.143 (.001)

Golf course	−.041	−.027	−.009	.173	.230	.269
	(.423)	(.594)	(.866)	(.001)	(<.001)	(<.001)
Special events	−.110	.002	.040	.047	.058	.089
	(.011)	(.965)	(.356)	(.278)	(.185)	(.041)
Fashion shows	−.114	.010	.087	.098	.186	.155
	(.028)	(.848)	(.094)	(.061)	(<.001)	(.003)
Architecture	−.043	−.071	.002	.203	.177	.172
	(.309)	(.090)	(.963)	(<.001)	(<.001)	(<.001)
Value for money	−.042	.030	−.114	.161	.229	.241
	(.321)	(.470)	(.007)	(<.001)	(<.001)	(<.001)
Hygiene and cleanliness	.028	−.078	−.155	.220	.236	.274
	(.510)	(.061)	(<.001)	(<.001)	(<.001)	(<.001)

Notes. Correlations reported above with probability below in parentheses.

Attachment 1: Visiting Qingdao says a lot about who I am; Attachment 2: I can identify easily with this destination; Attachment 3: I get more satisfaction from visiting Qingdao than from visiting any other destinations; Attachment 4: I enjoy doing the types of activities I do in Qingdao more than at any other destinations.

[a]1 = *extremely arousing*, 2 = *very arousing*, 3 = *neutral*, 4 = *very sleepy*, 5 = *extremely sleepy*.
[b]1 = *very poor*, 2 = *poor*, 3 = *neutral*, 4 = *good*, 5 = *very good*.

When considering the effect of place attachment on visitors' perceived images, the relationships between 4 attachment items and 30 image attributes were computed one by one. The results showed that attachment item 1 (visiting Qingdao says a lot about who I am) was significantly and negatively correlated with 2 affective attributes, that is, arousing–sleepy and relaxing–stressful, and positively correlated with 24 cognitive attributes; for example, seafood and accommodation ($r_s = 0.091$ to .304, $p < .05$). Attachment item 2 (I can identify easily with this destination) was significantly and negatively correlated with 3 affective attributes, that is, arousing–sleepy, pleasant–unpleasant, and relaxing–stressful, and positively correlated with 17 cognitive attributes, for example, seafood and accommodation ($r_s = 0.093$ to .220, $p < .05$). Attachment item 3 (I get more satisfaction from visiting Qingdao than from visiting any other destinations) was significantly and negatively correlated with all 4 affective attributes and positively correlated with 24 cognitive attributes; for example, seafood and accommodation ($r_s = 0.087$ to 0.200, $p < .05$). Attachment item 4 (I enjoy doing the types of activities I do in Qingdao more than at any other destinations) was significantly and negatively correlated with 3 affective attributes, that is, arousing–sleepy, exciting–gloomy, and relaxing–stressful, and positively correlated with all 26 cognitive attributes ($r_s = 0.089$ to 0.294, $p < .05$). The results also showed that almost all the above-identified correlations were weak, with one exception (attachment item 1 and local people, $r_s = 0.304$, $p < .001$), indicating that the greater the attachment to Qingdao, the more favorable the images that are generated.

Influence of Information Sources, Age, Education, and Place Attachment on Resident Images

Spearman's rank correlation was calculated to test for potential correlations between resident images and information sources, age, education, and place attachment (Table 4). The results showed that age was significantly and positively correlated with 7 cognitive attributes ($r_s = 0.129$ to 0.221, $p < .05$) and negatively correlated to 1 affective and 2 cognitive attributes ($r_s = -0.111$ to -0.129, $p < .05$). This indicated that an increase in age level is associated with a more favorable image on the 7 cognitive attributes (e.g., seafood, night life) and a less favorable image on cultural attractions and architecture. Education was identified to be significantly and negatively correlated with 6 cognitive attributes, for example, airline schedules, and beaches ($r_s = -0.111$ to -0.204, $p < .05$) and positively correlated with two affective attributes, that is, pleasant–unpleasant and relaxing–stressful, and two cognitive attributes; that is, night life and special events ($r_s = 0.136$ to 0.192, $p < .05$). This indicated that a higher educational level is associated with a less favorable image of the 6 cognitive attributes (e.g., airline schedules) and the 2 affective attributes (e.g., pleasant–unpleasant) and a more favorable image of night life and special events. Also significantly related were the negative correlations between information sources and 17 cognitive attributes, for example, seafood and shopping ($r_s = -0.110$ to -0.303, $p < .05$), and 1 affective attribute, that is, arousing–sleepy ($r_s = -0.119$, $p < .05$). This indicated that the more information sources used, the less favorable the images of the 17 cognitive attributes were; however, more arousing feeling was generated.

In regard to place attachment, it was found that there were positive correlations between attachment item 1 (I feel that Qingdao is a part of myself, and I am a part of it) and 22 cognitive image attributes, for example, seafood and shopping ($r_s = 0.135$ to .331, $p < .05$); however, this item was significantly and negatively correlated with all

Table 4. Relationships Between Components of Residents' Perceived Images and Age, Education, Information Sources, and Place Attachment.

	Age	Education	Information Sources	Attachment 1	Attachment 2	Attachment 3	Attachment 4	Attachment 5
Affective image[a]								
Arousing–sleepy	-.111	.093	-.119	-.166	-.095	-.118	-.142	-.202
	(.041)	(.090)	(.030)	(.002)	(.080)	(.031)	(.009)	(<.001)
Exciting–gloomy	-.105	.003	-.027	-.178	-.148	-.174	-.138	-.161
	(.055)	(.955)	(.617)	(.001)	(.006)	(.001)	(.011)	(.003)
Pleasant–unpleasant	-.056	.144	-.060	-.176	-.130	-.155	-.200	-.095
	(.308)	(.008)	(.275)	(.001)	(.017)	(.004)	(<.001)	(.084)
Relaxing–stressful	-.002	.111	-.056	-.190	-.111	-.148	-.191	-.235
	(.970)	(.041)	(.306)	(<.001)	(.042)	(.006)	(<.001)	(<.001)
Cognitive image[b]								
Seafood	.130	-.027	-.021	.145	.105	.143	.098	.220
	(.017)	(.624)	(.699)	(.008)	(.053)	(.009)	(.074)	(<.001)
Accommodation	.103	-.013	-.095	.073	.101	.096	-.023	.258
	(.058)	(.810)	(.080)	(.181)	(.064)	(.079)	(.669)	(<.001)
Shopping	.013	.060	-.056	.160	.189	.027	.114	.105
	(.811)	(.269)	(.305)	(.003)	(.001)	(.626)	(.036)	(.058)
Cultural attraction	-.121	-.044	-.028	.175	.199	.129	.167	.038
	(.026)	(.423)	(.612)	(.001)	(<.001)	(.018)	(.002)	(.493)
Highway system	-.015	-.022	-.020	.187	.131	.087	.227	.148
	(.780)	(.684)	(.716)	(.001)	(.016)	(.110)	(.002)	(.007)
Traffic congestion	.085	.060	.084	.095	.165	.093	.207	.121
	(.131)	(.292)	(.137)	(.094)	(.003)	(.100)	(<.001)	(.034)
Airline schedules	-.076	-.129	-.080	.222	.209	.279	.273	.178
	(.178)	(.022)	(.159)	(<.001)	(<.001)	(<.001)	(<.001)	(.002)

(Continued)

Table 4. (Continued).

	Age	Education	Information Sources	Attachment 1	Attachment 2	Attachment 3	Attachment 4	Attachment 5
Transportation cost	.210	-.100	-.121	.237	.229	.256	.180	.283
	(<.001)	(.069)	(.027)	(<.001)	(<.001)	(<.001)	(.001)	(<.001)
Public transport	.129	.033	-.126	.331	.234	.316	.234	.286
	(.019)	(.552)	(.021)	(<.001)	(<.001)	(<.001)	(<.001)	(<.001)
Night life	.221	.136	-.148	.233	.264	.274	.186	.300
	(<.001)	(.016)	(.009)	(<.001)	(<.001)	(<.001)	(.001)	(<.001)
Relaxing atmosphere	-.100	.087	-.255	.250	-.066	.242	.051	.048
	(.066)	(.110)	(<.001)	(<.001)	(.230)	(<.001)	(.346)	(.381)
Local people	.017	-.204	-.110	.136	.059	.065	.132	.140
	(.757)	(<.001)	(.046)	(.013)	(.286)	(.236)	(.016)	(.011)
Football games	-.040	-.156	-.302	.199	.111	.282	.217	.207
	(.481)	(.006)	(<.001)	(<.001)	(.049)	(<.001)	(<.001)	(<.001)
Beaches	.071	-.117	-.184	.272	.106	.289	.153	.236
	(.196)	(.031)	(.001)	(<.001)	(.053)	(<.001)	(.005)	(<.001)
Weather	.014	-.082	-.243	.247	.115	.156	.155	.175
	(.799)	(.134)	(<.001)	(<.001)	(.035)	(.004)	(.004)	(.001)
Green space	.056	-.085	-.227	.071	.055	.026	.102	.020
	(.307)	(.118)	(<.001)	(.192)	(.317)	(.630)	(.062)	(.717)
Squares	.085	-.091	-.211	.067	.154	.096	.153	.084
	(.120)	(.095)	(<.001)	(.219)	(.005)	(.077)	(.005)	(.129)
Resorts	.028	-.163	-.175	.147	.028	.106	.106	.081
	(.609)	(.003)	(.001)	(.007)	(.611)	(.053)	(<.053)	(.143)
Scenery	.183	-.131	-.101	.177	-.002	.194	.152	.266
	(.001)	(.017)	(.067)	(.001)	(.972)	(<.001)	(.005)	(<.001)
Ethnic attractions	.133	.041	-.146	.325	.144	.176	.177	.236

	(.015)	(.461)	(.008)	(<.001)	(.008)	(.001)	(.001)	(<.001)
Golf course	.069 (.252)	.030 (.612)	−.110 (.065)	.300 (<.001)	.136 (.022)	.224 (<.001)	.125 (.037)	.221 (<.001)
Special events	.087 (.119)	.192 (.001)	−.190 (.001)	.258 (<.001)	.046 (.410)	.083 (.135)	.023 (.682)	.287 (<.001)
Fashion shows	−.078 (.171)	.099 (.082)	−.243 (<.001)	.145 (.011)	.053 (.351)	.105 (.066)	.036 (.533)	.257 (<.001)
Architecture	−.129 (.018)	.032 (.555)	−.303 (<.001)	.218 (<.001)	.064 (.242)	.186 (.001)	.113 (.037)	.074 (.183)
Value for money	.194 (<.001)	.076 (.166)	−.128 (.018)	.136 (.012)	.087 (.111)	.023 (.675)	.047 (.388)	.063 (.253)
Hygiene and cleanliness	−.100 (.068)	.017 (.750)	−.240 (<.001)	.174 (.001)	.155 (.004)	.110 (.043)	.102 (.061)	.019 (.743)

Notes. Correlations reported above with probability below in parentheses.

Attachment 1: I feel that Qingdao is a part of myself, and I am a part of it; Attachment 2: I have many relatives and friends in Qingdao; Attachment 3: I will miss Qingdao if I leave Qingdao; Attachment 4: I would like to live in the city; Attachment 5: I do not want to live in other places except Qingdao.

[a] *1 = extremely arousing, 2 = very arousing, 3 = neutral, 4 = very sleepy, 5 = extremely sleepy.*

[b] *1 = very poor, 2 = poor, 3 = neutral, 4 = good, 5 = very good.*

4 affective attributes (r_s = −0.166 to −0.190, $p <$ .05). There were positive correlations between attachment item 2 (I have many relatives and friends in Qingdao) and 14 cognitive attributes, for example, shopping and cultural attractions (r_s = 0.111 to 0.264, $p <$ .05); however, this item was significantly negatively correlated with 3 affective attributes; that is, exciting–gloomy, pleasant–unpleasant, and relaxing–stressful (r_s = −0.111 to −0.148, $p <$ .05). Attachment item 3 (I will miss Qingdao if I leave the city) was positively correlated with 15 cognitive image attributes, for example, seafood and cultural attractions (r_s = 0.110 to 0.316, $p <$ .05), and negatively correlated with all 4 affective attributes (r_s = −0.118 to −0.174, $p <$ .05). Attachment item 4 (I would like to live in Qingdao) was significantly positively correlated with 17 cognitive attributes, for example, shopping and cultural attractions (r_s = 0.113 to 0.273, $p <$ .05), and negatively correlated with all 4 affective attributes (r_s = −0.138 to −0.200, $p <$ .05). Attachment item 5 (I do not want to live in other places except Qingdao) was significantly positively correlated with 17 cognitive attributes, for example, seafood and accommodation (r_s = 0.121 to 0.300, $p <$ .05), and negatively correlated with 3 affective attributes, that is, arousing–sleepy, exciting–gloomy, and relaxing–stressful (r_s = −0.161 to −0.235, $p <$ .05). It can be seen that the 5 attachment items were significantly and positively correlated with the majorities of the cognitive attributes and negatively correlated with most of the affective attributes. This indicated that the more attached respondents were to Qingdao, the more favorable the images of most of the cognitive attributes were and the more positive feelings generated, such as exciting and arousing.

Discussions and Conclusions

Cognitive and affective images often influence the purchase decisions of potential consumers regarding a destination (MacKay & Fesenmaier, 1997). This article investigates the similarities and differences in the cognitive and affective images perceived by visitors and residents associated with Qingdao, China; the results indicate no significant differences in participants' images regarding 18 out of 30 attributes. Additionally, both visitors and residents had relatively positive images associated with these 18 attributes. Given the coherence between the images of visitors and residents and their relatively good images of Qingdao, it can be concluded that Qingdao's image promotion and communication are successful to a certain degree. Marketers in Qingdao could use these image attributes that are preferred by both visitors and residents, especially those that are highly graded, in promoting the city. For example, themes such as relaxing atmosphere can be included in the projected images when promoting a general sense of holiday destination.

The images viewed by visitors and residents were significantly different in 10 cognitive and 2 affective attributes. This could be caused by differences between the two groups in terms of residence, use of the facilities of Qingdao, and levels of attachment to the city. These image differences provide information for marketers to consider in choosing different themes when targeting different consumer groups. For example, themes such as unique scenery and cultural attractions can be used as selling points for tourists, whereas seafood and a clean city may be appropriate for attracting residents to participate in tourism and recreational events.

Factors that influence image formation are considered to be an important aspect of destination marketing (Goodall, 1990). Four factors (information sources, age, education, and place attachment) that have been shown to significantly affect the perceived images in previous studies are examined in this study. Spearman's correlation test revealed that place attachment is positively correlated with most of the image attributes for both visitors and residents, implying that a higher level of participants' attachment to Qingdao leads to a more favorable image of the city in most circumstances. In this regard, marketers could involve themes that help evoke potential consumers' feelings of place identity and themes that emphasize certain tourism products and services when projecting the city. However, because most of the correlations between place attachment items and image attributes were weak, simply focusing on increasing potential consumers' attachment to Qingdao would do little to help inform their image formation.

Age was identified as being weakly correlated with 4 attributes of visitor images and with 10 attributes of resident images. Education was only weakly correlated with 10 attributes of resident images. Because these two sociodemographic characteristics influenced no more than one third of the image attributes (and all these correlations were weak), age and education may not be used to determine Qingdao's market segmentation. The effects of information sources on visitor and resident images indicated that the more information sources were used, the less favourable were the images of 9 attributes generated by visitor participants and 17 cognitive and 1 affective attributes formed by resident participants. This finding suggests that marketers should concentrate on a few media channels when promoting the city's images to both visitors and residents.

This study adds to the literature that place attachment is a predictor of perceived image, although the correlation between these two factors was weak. Because place attachment has been less researched in destination studies, more studies are needed to determine its influence on various destinations. From a practical perspective, this research provides information on the images of potential consumers that can help to evaluate the marketing performance of Qingdao. Additionally, the findings concerning the factors that affect the images of visitors and residents can help marketers with their image construction and marketing initiatives; for example, whether a variety of media channels should be used to facilitate destination marketing.

References

Anand, P., Holbrook, M. B., & Stephens, D. (1988). The formation of affective judgments: The cognitive–affective model versus the independence hypothesis. *Journal of Consumer Research*, *15*, 386–391.

Andreu, L., Bigne, E., & Cooper, C. (2000). Projected and perceived image of Spain as a tourist destination for British travelers. *Journal of Travel & Tourism Marketing*, *9*(4), 47–67.

Baloglu, S. (1997). An empirical investigation of destinations of tourist destination image. *Dissertation Abstracts International*, *57*(11), 4830. (UMI No. 9712726)

Baloglu, S., & Brinberg, D. (1997). Affective images of tourism destinations. *Journal of Travel Research*, *35*(4), 11–15.

Baloglu, S., & McCleary, K. W. (1999). A model of destination image formation. *Annals of Tourism Research*, *26*(4), 868–897.

Beerli, A., & Martin, J. D. (2004). Factors influencing destination image. *Annals of Tourism Research*, *31*(3), 657–681.

Bricker, K. S., & Kerstetter, D. (2000). Level of specialization and place attachment: An exploratory study of whitewater recreationists. *Leisure Sciences*, *22*, 233–257.

Burgess, J. A. (1978). *Image and identity* (Occasional Papers in Geography, 23). Hull, UK: University of Hull Publication.

Carter, J., Dyer, P., & Sharma, B. (2007). Dis-placed voices: Sense of place and place-identity on the sunshine coast. *Social & Cultural Geography, 8*, 755–773.

Castro, C. B., Armario, E. M., & Ruiz, D. M. (2007). The influence of market heterogeneity on the relationship between a destination image and tourists' future behaviour. *Tourism Management, 28*(1), 175–187.

Chen, H. (2006). *A relationship between tourism image and place attachment: An exploratory study in Mei-Nong town, Taiwan* (Unpublished master's thesis). Providence University, Taiwan.

Chen, J. S., & Uysal, M. (2002). Market position analysis: A hybrid approach. *Annals of Tourism Research, 29*(4), 987–1003.

Chon, K. S. (1991). Tourism destination image modification process: Marketing implications. *Tourism Management, 12*(1), 68–72.

Cowley, E., Spurr, R., Robins, P., & Woodside, A. G. (2004). Domestic leisure traveler consumption systems. In G. I. Crouch, R. R. Perdue., H. J. P. Timmermans, & M. Uysal (Eds.), *Consumer psychology of tourism, hospitality, and leisure* (Vol. 3, pp. 75–90). Oxfordshire, UK: CABI Publishing.

Diekhoff, G. (1992). *Statistics for the social and behavioral sciences: Univariate, bivariate, multivariate.* Dubuque, IA: Wm. C. Brown Publishers.

Echtner, C. M., & Ritchie, J. (1991). The meaning and measurement of tourism destination image. *Journal of Tourism Studies, 2*(2), 2–12.

Echtner, C. M., & Ritchie, J. (1993). The measurement of destination image: An empirical assessment. *Journal of Travel Research, 31*(4), 3–13.

Gallarza, M. G., Saura, I. G., & Garcia, H. C. (2002). Destination image towards a conceptual framework. *Annals of Tourism Research, 29*(1), 56–78.

Gartner, W. C. (1993). Image formation process. *Journal of Travel and Tourism Marketing, 2*(3), 191–215.

Goodall, B. (1990). How tourists choose their holidays: An analytical framework. In B. Goodall & G. Ashworth (Eds.), *Marketing in the tourism industry: The promotion of destination regions* (pp. 1–17). London, England: Routledge.

Govers, R., & Go, F. (2004). Cultural identities constructed, imagined and experienced: A 3-gap tourism destination image formation model. *Tourism: An International Interdisciplinary Journal, 52*(2), 165–182.

Govers, R., & Go, F. (2005). Projected destination image online: Website content analysis of pictures and texts. *Information Technology and Tourism, 72*, 73–90.

Gunn, C. (1972). *Vacationscape.* Austin, TX: University of Texas Press.

Gunn, C. (1997). *Vacationscape: Developing tourist areas* (3rd ed.). Washington, DC: Taylor & Francis.

Hailu, G., Boxall, P., & McFarlane, B. (2005). The influence of place attachment on recreation demand. *Journal of Economic Psychology, 26*, 581–598.

Hammitt, W. E., Backlund, E. A., & Bixler, R. D. (2006). Place bonding for recreational places: Conceptual and empirical development. *Leisure Studies, 25* (1), 17–41.

Holbrook, M. B. (1978). Beyond attitude structure: Toward the informational determinants of attribute. *Journal of Marketing Research, 15*, 545–556.

Hosany, S., Ekinci, Y., & Uysal, M. (2006). Destination image and destination personality: An implication of branding theories to tourism places. *Journal of Business Research, 59*(5), 638–642.

Hou, Y. (2007). *An exploratory study of Penghu high school students place attachment toward Centro block in Magong* (Unpublished master's thesis). National Sun Yat-sen University, Taiwan.

Hwang, S. N., Lee, C., & Chen, H. J. (2005). The relationship among tourists' involvement, place attachment and interpretation satisfaction in Taiwan's national parks. *Tourism Management, 26*(2), 143–156.

Kim, S., & Yoon, Y. (2003). The hierarchical effects of affective and cognitive components on tourism destination image. *Journal of Travel & Tourism Marketing, 14*(2), 1–22.

Kneesel, E., Baloglu, S., & Millar, M. (2010). Gaming destination images: Implications for branding. *Journal of Travel Research, 49*(1), 68–78.

Kwek, A., & Lee, Y. (2007). Intra-cultural variance of Chinese tourists in destination image project: Case of Queensland, Australia. *Journal of Hospitality & Leisure Marketing, 16*(1/2), 105–135.

Kyle, G., Graefe, A., Manning, R., & Bacon, J. (2003). An examination of the relationship between leisure activity and place attachment among hikers along the Appalachian Trail. *Journal of Leisure Research, 35*(3), 249–273.

Kyle, G., Graefe, A., Manning, R., & Bacon, J. (2004). Effect of activity involvement and place attachment on recreationists' perceptions of setting density. *Journal of Leisure Research, 36*(2), 209–231.

Lee, T. H. (2009). A structural model to examine how destination image, attitude, and motivation affect the future behavior of tourists. *Leisure Sciences, 31*(3), 215–236.

Li, X., Pan, B., Zhang, L., & Smith, W. W. (2009). The effect of online information search on image development: Insights from a mixed-methods study. *Journal of Travel Research, 48*, 45–57.

Lin, C. H., Morais, D. B., Kerstetter, D. L., & Hou, J. S. (2007). Examining the role of cognitive and affective image in predicting choice across natural, developed and theme-park destinations. *Journal of Travel Research, 46*(2), 183–194.

MacKay, K. J., & Fesenmaier, D. R. (1997). Pictorial element of destination in image formation. *Annals of Tourism Research, 24*, 537–565.

Manstead, S. R. (1996). Attributes and behavior. In G. S. Semin & K. Fiedler (Eds.), *Applied social psychology* (pp. 3–29). London, UK: Sage.

Mi, X. (2003). *Possible gaps between the destination image projected by governments and that perceived by tourists: The case of Dalian, China* (Unpublished master's thesis). University of Waterloo, Ontario, Canada.

Molenaar, C. (1996). *Interactive marketing*. Hampshire, England: Ashgate Publishing.

Molenaar, C. (2002). *The future of marketing: Practical strategies for marketers in the post-Internet Age*. London, England: Pearson Education.

Moore, R. L., & Graefe, A. R. (1994). Attachment to recreation settings: The case of rail-trail users. *Leisure Science, 16*, 17–31.

Naoi, T. (2003). Tourists' evaluation of destinations: The cognitive perspective. *Journal of Travel & Tourism Marketing, 14*(1), 1–20.

Page, S. J., & Connell, J. (2006). *Tourism: A modern synthesis* (2nd ed.). London, England: Thomson Learning.

Pallent, J. (2007). *SPSS survival manual: A step by step guide to data analysis using SPSS for Windows*. Berkshire, UK: Open University Press.

Pike, S., & Ryan, C. (2004). Destination position analysis through a comparison of cognitive, affective, and conative perceptions. *Journal of Travel Research, 42*, 333–342.

Pike, S. D. (2002). Destination image analysis—A review of 142 papers from 1973 to 2000. *Tourism Management, 23*(5), 541–549.

Proshansky, H. M. (1978). The city and self-identity. *Environment and Behavior, 10*, 147–169.

QDSQ. (2008). *A profile of Qingdao*. Retrieved from http://qpinet.qingdao.gov.cn/shizhi.nsf/f4e0fbd36aa4be10482567b3001fc1d0?OpenView&Start=1&Count=60&Expand=36#36

QDTA. (2009a). *Statistics*. Retrieved from http://www.qdta.cn/

QDTA. (2009b). *Tourism development*. Retrieved from http://218.57.137.141/webs/guihua/article.jsp?f policycode=pr0000000001

Ramshaw, G., & Hinch, T. (2006). Place identity and sport tourism: The case of the heritage classic ice hockey event. *Current Issues in Tourism, 9*(4), 399–418.

Rezende-Parker, A. M., Morrison, A. M., & Ismail, J. A. (2003). Dazed and confused? An exploratory study of the image of Brazil as a travel destination. *Journal of Vacation Marketing, 9*(3), 243–259.

Schroeder, T. (1996). The relationship of residents' image of their state as a tourism destination and their support for tourism. *Journal of Travel Research, 34*, 71–73.

Selby, M. (2004). *Understanding urban tourism: Image, culture and experience*. New York, NY: I. B. Tauris & Co. Ltd.

Sinclair, M. T. (1998). Tourism and economic development: A survey. *Journal of Development Studies, 34*(5), 1–51.

Sonmez, S., & Sirakaya, E. (2002). A distorted destination image? The case of Turkey. *Journal of Travel Research, 41*, 185–196.

Stepchenkova, S., & Morrison, A. M. (2008). Russia's destination image among American pleasure travelers: Revisiting Echtner and Ritchie. *Tourism Management, 29*(3), 548–560.

Stern, E., & Krakover, S. (1993). The formation of a composite urban image. *Geographical Analysis, 25*(2), 130–146.

Stokols, D., & Shumaker, S. A. (1981). People in places: A transactional view of settings. In J. Harvey (Ed.), *Cognition, social behavior, and the environment* (pp. 441–488). Hillsdale, NJ: Lawrence Erlbaum.

Tasci, A. D., & Gartner, W. C. (2007). Destination image and its functional relationships. *Journal of Travel Research, 45*(4), 413–425.

Tasci, A. D., Gartner, W. C., & Cavusgil, S. T. (2007). Conceptualization and operationalization of destination image. *Journal of Hospitality and Tourism Research, 31*(2), 194–223.

Um, S. (1993). Pleasure travel destination choice. In M. Khan, M. Olsen, & T. Var. (Eds.), *VNR's encyclopedia of hospitality and tourism* (pp. 811–821). New York, NY: Van Nostrand Reinhold.

Um, S., & Crompton, J. L. (1990). Attribute determinants in tourism destination choice. *Annals of Tourism Research, 17*, 432–448.

Vaske, J. J., & Kobrin, K. (2001). Place attachment and environmentally response behavior. *Journal of Environmental Education, 32*(4), 116–121.

Vogt, C. A., & Andereck, K. L. (2003). Destination perceptions across a vacation. *Journal of Travel Research, 41*, 348–354.

Walmsley, D. J., & Jenkins, J. M. (1993). Appraisive images of tourist areas: Application of personal construct. *Australian Geographer, 24*(2), 1–13.

Walmsley, D. J., & Young, M. (1998). Evaluative images and tourism: The use of personal constructs to describe the structure of destination images. *Journal of Travel Research, 36*, 65–69.

White, D. D., Virden, R. J., & van Ripe, C. J. (2008). Effects of place identity, place dependence, and experience-use history on perceptions of recreation impacts in a natural setting. *Environmental Management, 42*, 647–657.

Williams, D. R., Anderson, B. S., McDonald, C. D., & Patterson, M. E. (1995). Measuring place attachment: More preliminary results. In *Abstracts from the 1995 symposium on leisure research* (p. 78). Arlington, VA: National Recreation and Park Association.

Williams, D. R., Patterson, M. E., Roggenbuck, J. W., & Watson, A. E. (1992). Beyond the commodity metaphor: Examining emotional and symbolic attachment to place. *Leisure Science, 14*, 29–46.

Williams, D. R., & Vaske, J. J. (2003). The measurement of place attachment: Validity and generalizability of a psychometric approach. *Forest Science, 49*(6), 830–840.

Woodside, A. G., & Lysonski, S. (1989). A general model of traveler destination image choice. *Journal of Travel Research, 17*(4), 8–14.

Wu, K. H. (2009). *A study on the relationships among destination image, place attachment and tourist satisfaction—A case of the Sun-Moon Lake National Scenic Area* (Unpublished master's thesis). National Taichuang University, Taiwan.

Zhang, J., Li, Y., & Chen, Y. (2006). Image of landscapes in ancient water towns—Case study on Zhouzhuang and Tongli of Jiangsu Province. *Chinese Geographical Science, 16*(4), 371–377.

Zou, P. (2007). *Image versus position: Canada as a potential destination for Mainland China* (Unpublished master's thesis). University of Waterloo, Ontario, Canada.

Developing a Framework for Assessing Visitors' Responses to Chinese Cities

游客对中国城市反应评估框架的建构

PHILIP L. PEARCE
YONGZHI WU
ARAM SON

Using five dominant themes from the literature on evaluating places, this study builds a framework to assess and present visitors' responses to Chinese cities. The component parts of the framework include views of visitors as wayfinders, image assessors, spenders, users, and performers. Methods to assess and present visitor responses involve survey research, sketch mapping methodology, and the collection of stories and critical incidents. The approach builds a comprehensive view of cities using methods-based triangulation. The procedures and the presentation techniques are illustrated with ongoing work in the city of Xi'an, and the initial evaluation of the framework is described. The wider use of comparative assessments of visitors' responses to Chinese cities is suggested.

本研究参考旅游目的地评估文献的五大主题，建立框架以评估及展示游客对中国城市的反应。框架的组成部分包括作为寻路者、影像评价人、消费者、使用者和表演者的游客对旅游地的意见。评估和展示游客意见的方法包括问卷调查、示意图及收集游客的故事和关键事件，利用方法三角验证整合并得出游客对各城市的综合意见。本文以在西安市进行的研究为例，说明建立框架的过程和展示方法，并对框架的初次评估进行描述。建议未来的研究可以更广泛的比较游客对中国城市的反应。

Introduction

In broad terms, the core aim of this work lies in presenting a new integrative framework for the assessment of visitor responses to cities in China. Further, by considering ongoing studies in one Chinese city, that of Xi'an in western China, the

Philip L. Pearce is Foundation Professor of Tourism of the School of Business at James Cook University, Townsville, Queensland, Australia (E-mail: philip.pearce@jcu.edu.au).

Yongzhi Wu is Associate Professor and Deputy Dean of the School of Tourism at Xi'an International Studies University, Xi'an, Shaanxi Province, China (E-mail: wuyongzhi@xisu.edu.cn).

Aram Son is Lecturer and Researcher of the School of Tourism Management at Zhongshan University, Zhuhai, Guangdong, China (E-mail: sonaram506@msn.com).

study seeks to illustrate some of the key elements of the suggested framework. An assessment of the potential usefulness of the framework will be considered as a third and concluding aim of this research.

This study considers the assessment of visitors' responses to Chinese cities, although the broad ideas have applicability to other countries and different kinds of tourist destinations. The particular value of research attention to Chinese cities lies in appreciating the centrality of such nodes in developing the infrastructure of tourism in China. The numerous large cities spread throughout the country provide the key access points for rail, coach, and air travel, and hence many cities become central linking points for both domestic and international tourists' experiences (Ghimire & Li, 2001; Lew, Yu, Ap, & Zhang, 2003). Additionally, many cities provide an array of attractions in their own right as well as being vital accommodation dormitories for sightseeing in adjacent rural areas (Ap, 2003). In focusing attention on visitor responses to Chinese cities, the study seeks to provide a comprehensive tool for destination managers concerned with monitoring and benefiting from an understanding of the city-based experiences of their visitors (Ritchie, Crouch, & Hudson, 2001). Such information can then be used to develop new and improved promotional tools, and it can guide infrastructure improvements (Orbash & Shaw, 2004). Detailed responses from visitors can also suggest service and personnel training needs (cf. Ritchie, Crouch, & Hudson, 2001).

Literature Review

The construction of a framework for assessing visitor responses to Chinese cities draws on many sources in the existing tourism and environmental assessment literature as well as from multiple practices in research methodology. A key starting point in such an appraisal is to set the conditions and boundaries framing the area of interest with an awareness of the assumptions being made. The proposed framework is concerned with the post-visit appraisal of Chinese cities. This implies that it is not simply about destination image in the way traditionally recognized in the tourism literature, where that term is used to help assess visitors' choice of a destination (Baloglu, 1997; Echtner & Ritchie, 1991, 1993; March & Woodside, 2005; Son & Pearce, 2005). The focus on post-visit responses does not necessarily imply a comparison with pre-visit expectations. Such expectancy-disconfirmation models are just one possibility in the appraisal of tourist satisfaction and post-visit responses and may not be suitable in several settings (Kozak, 2001). In particular, wherever there is ambiguity and uncertainty about what is to be evaluated, researchers need to consider assessment procedures beyond that of the expectancy-disconfirmation paradigm (Pearce, 2005b). Chinese cities represent one kind of tourist destination, where many of those visiting, especially Western tourists, can be deemed to be uncertain as to their character and unsure of what to expect.

Another initial organizing consideration lies in identifying the kind of approach to tourism studies inherent in this work. There are rich debates in the international literature concerning the role of tourism research and its dependence on or independence from the tourism industry (Aramberri, 2001; Dann, 1999; Franklin, 2003; Tribe, 2006). A succinct summary of these multiple arguments is that one body of thought essentially sees tourism analysis and research as a contributor to the well-being of tourism and hospitality businesses, with a focus on applied, useful, relevant, and pragmatic research. Such a view is captured in the very definition of tourism research by Gunn (1994) who asserts:

> Tourism research, while no substitute for superior management practices, provides objective, systematic, logical, and empirical foundations for such management. (1994, p. 2)

In essence, proponents of this view argue that tourism research should be direct and applied, taking on the problems as identified by business interests and doing the job of supporting tourism development. A second view, now somewhat integrated under the title of a "critical turn" in tourism studies, emphasizes that tourism scholars should look at what they are doing in terms of their overall contributions to human well-being. They should be generally aware of the power relations and exploitative tendencies that may follow the consequences of an unquestioning acceptance of the universal good of tourism development (Ateljevic & Doorne, 2004; Tribe, 2006). These perspectives are sometimes referred to as the two styles of tourism research, with T1 referring to the business-oriented studies and T2 summarizing the broader critical and social science interests in tourism's role in society (Tribe, 1997). Such differences may also be cast as a divergence in the immediacy of the relevance of tourism work (Pearce, 2005a). In the deconstruction of relevance, it can be proposed that members of the T1 group emphasize short-term, specific sector relevance, with a strong economic focus, whereas T2 researchers are more concerned with long-term, generic issues driving social, cultural, and environmental sustainability.

The proposed framework for assessing visitor responses to Chinese cities is located more directly within the pragmatic T1 group of studies, although it is beneficial to draw some of the ideas and tools used in the T2 framework into the overall approach. The choice of a more immediate, shorter term, and industry-relevant framework in this study does not negate the importance of longer term discussions and appraisals of the role of tourism in China's development and an associated consideration of the power bases and impacts such developments entail. There is a respect for and a need for such considerations, but, equally, the development of tools to appraise and improve existing tourism has a value that can directly promote tourism research and build some acceptance of more expansive considerations.

The focus on cities in this framework is justifiable in several ways. At this stage in the development of tourism in China there is a strong concentration of hotel development for international tourists in the larger cities (World Tourism Organization [UNWTO], 2006). This has the important implication that the tour routes and the essential experiences of China for many international visitors are arguably built around multiple city locations. Additionally, demographic trends in China over the last 20 years have seen a massive urbanization of the population with the consequence that even many rural families now travel to cities to visit friends and relatives (Ghimire, 2001). This kind of travel is consistent with global domestic tourism trends, emphasizing the importance of family ties for within-country tourism (Pearce & Moscardo, 2006; Rao & Suresh, 2001). These emphases on city tourism do not, of course, constitute the whole of Chinese tourism, with many natural and significant landscapes and rural areas emerging as points of domestic and natural interest. Nevertheless, the large number of Chinese cities with a population of over 1 million people and the intention of many of these cities to benefit from tourism does highlight an opportunity to produce a coherent framework for the appraisal of visitor responses, which could be consistently applied across the country.

Five traditions or waves of thought can be identified throughout the academic literature in the treatment of visitors' responses to places and to cities. These waves of thought co-exist and fluctuate in importance over time. They do not follow a pattern of succession. Instead, it is more useful to think of them as recycling waves varying in intensity. The first of these five traditions is an interest in orientation, where the key issue or defining motif is people finding their way. This kind of work has been to the fore in studies of visitors in tourist towns and cities, as well as in cities and national parks (Lynch, 1960; Melton, 1972; Moscardo, 1999; Pearce, 1977; Pearce & Black, 1984; Thomas, 1996; Walmsley & Jenkins, 1992). Such research has assisted our understanding of the cues and processes individuals use to follow maps and signs and to navigate complex spaces. The studies of orientation have often employed unobtrusive observational techniques and developed their own methodological style of employing sketch maps to elicit people's awareness of spatial relationships.

A second line of inquiry is a concern with the choice of a holiday location, especially the choice of vacation regions and destinations. This kind of work addresses how places are viewed and mentally organized by the observer. The focus here is often on the elements, which constitute the travelers' attitude towards the destination, and the guiding motif is that of people as consumers choosing a product. The tradition has been a dominant one in tourism study and has been powerful in giving rise to quantitative studies appraising destination and city selection (Baloglu, 1997; Downs & Stea, 1977; Echtner & Ritchie, 1991, 1993; Hunt, 1975; March & Woodside, 2005; Um & Crompton, 1990; Woodside & Lysonki, 1989; Yau & Chan, 1990). The style of work has often been to have respondents rate a number of destination attributes for their importance and apply these ratings to destinations presumed to vary in these characteristics. In these studies, respondents have sometimes been to the destinations but most often they have not. The images being rated and assessed are frequently built entirely on public and marketing information.

A third tradition is also concerned with consumption, but on this occasion it is not the tourists' choice of the destination that features most strongly in the guiding motif, but rather it is that of people as spenders at the destination. The emphasis on what people purchase, which is usually assessed in terms of daily expenditure, represents a tradition in tourism microeconomics where places are considered in terms of their earning power (Dwyer, Forsyth, & Spur, 2004; Suh & Gartner, 2004; Wanhill, 1994). Efforts to measure regional economic expenditure and the impact of new attractions or the value of specific attractions all fit into this economic analysis (Ryan, 2002; Stoeckl, Smith, Newsome, & Lee, 2005). An interest in how people spend their money in locations such as cities and the distribution of that expenditure involves some measurement challenges. Since different types of tourists in different seasons will vary in their expenditure patterns, adequate samples of all types of visitors are needed if researchers are to avoid false inferences. An additional complexity is that there is a distinction between direct and indirect expenditure, with the latter term considering how the tourist spending drives economic activity in other supportive industries and services. Again, careful segmentation of the visitor data is called for since different tourist activities and travel styles generate diverse linkages to other sectors.

There is a fourth area of concern, which can be labeled functionality. This body of work considers the servicescapes and the micro-environments that make places fit for their human users. It is a tradition that has a strong deterministic emphasis, with the view that setting characteristics strongly shape people's experiences. An appropriate organizing label for this body of work is people as place users. Some formative studies in this tradition include the post-occupancy evaluation of offices and buildings as well as the assessment of visitor displays and museum exhibits (Miles, Alt, Gosling, Lewis, & Tout, 1982; Zube, 1980). The appraisal of micro-climates and setting features such as music and vegetation forms an additional dimension to this functional tradition (Bitgood, 1987; Bitner, 1992; Pearce & Vogt, 2005). This kind of work is consistent with the satisfaction literature in national parks and recreation research emphasizing the functional rather than the expressive components of the experience (Noe, 1999). In this kind of tradition, there are appraisals of the suitability of places for various kinds of recreation, leisure, and tourism purposes. These considerations give rise to zoning and planning models, and the evaluations may be used to justify the use of space in economic or environmental terms (Gunn & Var, 2002; Sax, 1980). The classification of natural environments and parts of cities as world heritage areas is built on these kinds of approaches to the assessment of places. Often experts and specialists are involved in the assessment rather than users. Some concerns with the topics of authenticity and heritage are a part of this tradition of considering the fit between places and their users (Kaplan & Kaplan, 1982; MacCannell, 1976, 1989).

A final and less deterministic view is offered in what can be labeled a performative approaches style. This relatively recent tradition places importance on issues of power and gender and considers how people re-interpret and control their experience of places, partly through language and telling their stories of environmental settings, but also through their own choice of roles and activities. The guiding motif for this last grouping of studies and approaches is people involved as performers. This kind of emphasis places attention on the detail of what people do in the places they visit, what it means to them, and how it is connected to or extends their life overall (Baerenholdt, Haldrup, Larsen, & Urry, 2004; Coleman & Crang, 2002; Crang, 1997; Crouch, 2005; Lew & Wong, 2005). The contribution of this emphasis to the overall development of place and city research is to remind analysts that tourism is linked to leisure and all the complexities of modern existence and not an isolated phenomenon that researchers should be content merely to describe rather than explain and interconnect with related phenomenon and developments.

The core constructs used to build a comprehensive framework for the assessment of visitor responses to Chinese cities are built upon a considered integration of the key ideas deriving from these five traditions. In brief, the existing literature suggests that an approach to studying post-visit responses to Chinese cities can develop ideas where travelers are seen as wayfinders, image assessors, spenders, users, and performers. The additional contribution of the present study lies in searching out methods appropriate to each of these perspectives and then using the tradition of methodological triangulation to seek the commonalities amongst the obtained responses, thus forming a holistic and balanced view of the destination (cf. Veal, 2005).

Study Aims

As stated in the introduction, the first aim of this study seeks to both propose and justify a framework for the assessment of visitor responses to Chinese cities. A second major aim is the illustration of the main features of the framework, with both original data collected in the city of Xi'an and with information supplied by visitors to that city. This aim is linked to the approach of methodological triangulation to search for commonalities in the visitors' responses. The third and final aim lies in a succinct consideration of the adequacy of the framework based on the illustrative material and the themes identified in the relevant literature. Necessarily, a new framework requires evaluation and analysis by many researchers, so the consideration of the usefulness of the proposed structure can only be at a preliminary level.

A Visitor-Based City Assessment Framework

The different perspectives on visitor response to cities can be used to build the framework. These perspectives can be assessed in different ways, although there is some overlap in the methodologies that can be used. The presentation and reporting of the results are also described as a part of a comprehensive framework. Attention to this issue is important if the assessment activities are to be used by other researchers and practitioners. A summary of this approach is provided in Figure 1.

The first row in Figure 1 uses the five themes identified in the previous literature on visitor responses to cities. Some wider considerations are valuable in interpreting the focus of the framework and the comprehensiveness of these five views. The intention of this presentation of views of visitors is to provide a thorough treatment of perspectives on those who visit cities, but it is an emphasis on how they respond to the cities rather than what impacts and effects they have. While visitors' economic impacts are considered in the five thematic areas (the visitors as spenders motif), other dimensions of the impact of visitors such as in the socio-cultural and environmental spheres are not included (cf. Elkington, 1997). The contemporary and increasingly powerful concern with sustainability in tourism studies justifies persistent attention to these concerns, but they are not easily or adequately assessed in analyses of visitors alone (Bramwell & Lane, 2005). Instead, a full sustainability assessment of tourism in Chinese cities requires multiple environmental audits and community studies of attitudes and cultural change, all of which are beyond the specific visitor appraisal system being developed here.

It might be argued that there are other labels that could be used to characterize the approaches to visitor studies. Some analysts, for example, might partition the performance category into two different kinds of respondents–those who are self-directed and independent travelers and those who are on group tours. This kind of demographic or tripographic (trip characteristics) distinction is not unimportant but fails to adequately capture the meaning of the performance metaphor, which is directing attention to the mentally active, selective filtering of experience by the tourist rather than their physical activity choices (Hu & Morrison, 2002).

Similarly, some tourism researchers and analysts might want to separate the people as users category into distinct sub–motifs, with the long tradition on

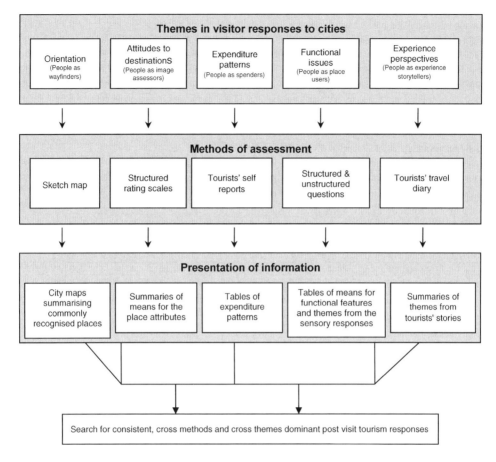

Figure 1. A Framework for Considering Tourists' Responses to Cities

authenticity potentially being seen as distinct from the more instrumental approaches inherent in the servicescape literature (Franklin, 2003). There is, however, an important counter to this view–as long as the main perspectives and considerations pertaining to the visitor response to cities are included, then the internal divisions within the motifs or perspectives are a matter of emphasis. The true test of the adequacy of the framework is whether or not some major additional perspectives need to be included rather than the issues of the realignment of the perspectives already included. Nevertheless, this kind of thinking raises the important question of what kinds of demographic, psychographic, and tripographic information should be collected in a visitor response framework. This topic is a well-worn path in survey research generally and is usually answered by adopting the view that researchers should only include those questions and variables that are central to their hypotheses or descriptive goals. For tourists' responses to city visits, the minimum characteristics to be included are visitors' origin, age, length of stay, tour type–independent or group travel, motivational profile, and previous experience (cf. Oppenheim, 1966; Pearce, 2005b; Ryan, 1995).

The second row in Figure 1 proposes a number of different methods for collecting information on visitor responses. Each of these methods has its own history of use in tourism and environmental research. Further, each technique is a contributor to or closely associated with the suggested styles of reporting described in column three. The dominant technique, which carries the major role in assessing visitors' responses to the cities they experience, is that of the comprehensive survey. As outlined in Figure 1, this approach serves three of the principle interest areas in city appraisal; specifically, the areas of image assessment, visitor appraisal of specific instrumental issues, and visitor expenditure. The survey material needs to include the core demographic, psychographic, and trip characteristics information cited earlier in order that any required segmentation of visitors or modeling to more rudimentary but broader scale national and regional visitor statistics can be made. There are several key requirements to be met to create a quality visitor survey instrument serving these needs. In addition to the generally accepted good practices in survey design (cf. Gomm, 2004; Oppenheim, 1966), specific requirements in surveying visitors include ensuring that there is a full range of items to be assessed in the image characteristics as well as in the city micro-environment and instrumental attributes. This same issue of requiring visitor survey research to reflect a comprehensive array of items can also be applied to the psychographic profile material, especially the assessment of motivation (Pearce, 2005b; Ryan, 1995, 2002). Further recommendations for good practice in this area include employing 7-point Likert response scales, which facilitate quantitative analyses of responses. Some examples of these practices are demonstrated in the case of the Xi'an visitor survey to be reported in a later section.

One of the two subsidiary techniques that can add to a rounded assessment of visitors' responses to cities is the use of the sketch map methodology (cf. Lynch, 1960; Oliver, 2001; Son & Pearce, 2003). These approaches ask visitors to draw a rough sketch in the form of a map of the layout of the city or destination area noting its chief points of interest. These maps can be drawn without any guidelines or scale, but some researchers have chosen to provide examples of maps from other settings or to use a baseline grid with two to three reference points (Falco-Mammone, 2006). The appeal of employing the sketch map technique is that the cognitive schema that comprise human memory are being accessed in a different way. That is, accessing spatially organized images may supplement the recall elicited by verbal and text-based styles used in survey work (Pearce & Black, 1996; Pearce & Fagence, 1996). It is important to allow respondents enough time to complete these sorts of tasks, usually at least 15 minutes, so that the map details are sufficiently numerous to permit aggregation and hence the production of group or summary image maps. The technique is equally applicable to domestic and international visitors, but for those with extensive experience of a city, more time to complete the task is required (cf. Francescato & Mebane, 1973).

A third technique for summarizing visitor responses to cities is to access the stories visitors tell about their travels (Woodside, Cruickshank, & Dehuang, 2007). This family of techniques is linked to the performance motif for visitor responses where visitors are seen as selecting, recording, and communicating their travel incidents and episodes to others. It is recognized that there are biases in the kinds of stories people are prepared to tell to others (Kozinets, 2002; Pearce, 1991), but there is a significant body of work emphasizing the centrality of stories in summarizing human activities and being core to the formation and maintenance of memories (Holt, 2003; Schank, 1990; Weick, 1995). Visitor stories can be accessed from the increasingly popular web-based travel stories (blogs). They can also be obtained by asking respondents to identify their best and worst experiences in a critical incident approach or by discussing travel experiences in detailed interviews (Phillimore & Goodson, 2004; Pritchard & Havitz, 2006; Woodside et al., 2007).

The third row in Figure 1 considers the presentation of the data or resources obtained from these different techniques. While there are many forms of presentation that can serve to provide an overview of visitors' responses to the cities they experience, it is an expressed aim of the present work that the presentation is readily accessible for destination managers. This requirement directs the styles of presentation to user friendly benchmarking information, permitting managers and researchers to make comparative judgments to guide action. An analogy and model for this kind of communication comes from the work on comparing visitor responses to national parks in the United States, where the theme of useable knowledge guides the reporting process (Machlis, 1996). The case for benchmarking tourist responses to the settings they visit is particularly strong. There is considerable evidence that tourist satisfaction data are positively skewed: a situation where visitors repeatedly express relatively high satisfaction scores (Noe, 1999). There are arguments that such high scores reflect ego protection, in that tourists do not want to admit having made a mistake in spending discretionary income poorly (Hanan & Karp, 1989; Hazelrigg & Hardy, 2000). By providing longitudinal data (the ratings of the same city over time) or cross sectional data (the ratings of multiple cities), the benchmarking approach improves the readers' interpretation of any set of scores because, while the results may be persistently high, they can be placed in a context of similar responses. It is, for example, easier to assess the value of a score of 3.6 on a 5-point rating scale for the cleanliness of a city in the year 2007, if one already has a score for that city from 2004 and 2003 or, alternatively, scores from three other cities in 2007. Until such comparative data sets are widely available, a more immediate internal benchmarking approach can be employed (Fuchs, 2002). This kind of comparative analysis seeks to subdivide the sample into different groups to compare their scores. Careful attention must be paid in this kind of work to the scales used, with a larger range in the scales assisting in the provision of more fine grained discriminations. Additionally, a precision in additional question asking can yield some further rewards. For example, asking respondents to describe the actual performance of the city or more simply what they thought of a characteristic of it can be contrasted with what they think is acceptable for a Chinese city. The contrast between acceptable performance and actual performance may then be used to direct and stimulate change. As with much attitudinal work, a separate assessment of how important or significant this characteristic is to the visitor may also be needed if this idea is not implicit in the rating-scale wording being used. These additional questions represent a way of using the benchmarking approach to serve not just a comparative goal but to register simultaneously the performance against a desired standard, with the significance of the characteristic also being assessed.

The results from sketch maps drawn by city visitors can also be presented in summary form. In these composite maps, a frequency of inclusion criterion is set, which amounts to a decision that a certain percentage of respondents have to include the item on a sketch map before it appears as an entry in the composite map. Earlier studies of city images and regional stereotypes have tended to use figures such as 15% or 20% (Berry, 1969; Downs & Stea, 1977; Pearce, Innes, O'Driscoll, & Morse, 1981). Other researchers have been interested in the common errors in the maps, which may be used to indicate difficulties of orientation and infrastructure provision (Pearce, 1981; Young, 1998). A coding scheme originally developed by Lynch (1960) remains at the heart of the analysis of sketch maps. This scheme, which subsequent authors have used in either its original or a slightly modified form, draws attention to landmarks, paths, districts, edges, and nodes in summarizing the elements of the city. Other researchers have recorded errors, distance measures, social comments, and texture or density of information as supplementary coding elements (Walmsley & Jenkins, 1992). The use of these schemes has done much to bring an order and a clarity to the contents and structure of the maps and has facilitated their use for planning and research purposes (Oliver, 2001; Pearce & Fagence, 1996).

The communication of stories or critical incidents through some kind of summary mechanism represents an inherent difficulty in transferring information because stories themselves are a fundamental way in which people store, retrieve, and relate their experiences to others (Schank, 1990). Nevertheless, a systematic attempt to summarize stories as a part of a broad and comprehensive picture on responding to cities is seen by a number of researchers as providing creative clues about the management and marketing of the destination (McKee, 2003; Woodside et al., 2007), extending this enthusiasm for the value of considering tourists' stories by suggesting that they contain an early warning system for detecting problems as well as clues to better position city developments that meet visitor experiences and needs. Buoyed by the potential value of examining the travelers' tales, there have been some recent attempts in the consumer and tourist behavior literature to map the main elements of stories by subdividing them into constituent elements (Woodside & Chebat, 2001). The elements used may include persons, places, acts, and outcomes with beliefs and emotions being used to link the steps or components of any story. Woodside and Chebat follow the ideas of Heider (1958) and balance theory to suggest that there are forces pushing people to have an integrated view of their consumer experiences. A criticism of this approach, however, is that some stories may be of interest or worth telling simply because they are about the contradictions and puzzles generated by the incongruent elements encountered while traveling. In this view, searching for a neat set of balance relationships may not be the key to unlocking the deeper implications of the story. Balance theory is, however, only one way to examine the stories, and McKee (1997) recommends a simpler procedure of searching for the controlling idea. In his view, a controlling idea may be expressed in a single sentence and describes how and why life or the event shows change from one state to another during the story development. In this view, stories are about the creation and then at least the partial resolution of that tension, so a simple listing of places visited might be a travel itinerary but it is not yet a story. A common researcher procedure here is for researchers to work independently on the analysis of the stories and then meet to negotiate their explanations as a way of validating the interpretations of the controlling ideas (De Crop, 2004).

The concluding section of Figure 1 portrays an important integrating element in the framework. This force can be described as the search for commonalities and is underpinned by the procedure known as methodological triangulation (Veal, 2005). In this approach, the skilled researcher uses the insights generated from each technique to organize a succinct summary of the views of the city being studied. In effect, this is a qualitative synthesis of the research that can guide the actions of summary informed by managers and operators.

Xi'an-Data Sources

This section describes elements of ongoing work in the city of Xi'an to illustrate some of the reporting parts of the framework. It is not a complete or comprehensive appraisal of a Chinese city as implied by the full details of Figure 1, but instead is presented as indicating some of the possibilities of the core ideas of benchmarking, sketch map presentation, and storytelling analysis.

The data and resources which serve as the foundation for these presentations come from three sources. The first data source is a Xi'an Holiday survey conducted during October 2005. One thousand visitors to the city were approached either at key attractions or at the city's main airport, and an overall return rate of 78.9% was obtained. Five hundred questionnaires were supplied in Mandarin and 500 in English, with 433 respondents being Chinese and 356 Western visitors constituting the effective sample. Information was collected on the respondents' demographics (gender, age, and origin), trip characteristics (travel companions, length of trip, and type of accommodation), psychographic profile (visitor motivation–10 items drawn from a larger motivation instrument), and expenditure patterns, including the kinds of items purchased and overall money spent. Additionally, satisfaction with some key instrumental or use features of the destination were obtained, and the more expressive and performative elements were approached with a critical incident technique asking travelers to describe their best and worst experiences in the location. There was no attempt to assess detailed destination images of Xi'an or to seek sketch maps and spatial information in the Xi'an Holiday survey.

Additional resources were obtained by asking 10 Australian travelers who had been to the city of Xi'an to draw sketch maps of the city. The instructions followed those in other studies, and an example map of Sydney, Australia, was used as a guide to alleviate any anxiety the respondents may have felt about their cartographic skills. No grid or locational cues were supplied to the respondents. The 10 visitors to China were students, staff, or their friends who had been involved in university links to China (five respondents) or who had been on a tour or business trip of that city (five respondents). All of these visitors had spent less than 3 days in the city. All of these respondents were international visitors.

A third and final source of information followed the procedure for accessing stories recommended by Woodside et al. (2007). Following the suggestions of Kozinets (2002) on conducting ethnography in cyberspace–a process Kozinets defines as netnography– the search for informant reports focused on finding visitors who had included Xi'an in their travels. Google searches using the city name of "Xi'an" plus "blog" plus the term "positive" and then the term "negative" were employed. Several thousand Web sites were generated by this procedure and, since the purpose of this procedure was to access material for illustrative purposes, 10 sites were selected by choosing one Web site and Xi'an story from each of the first 10 pages of the blogs identified.

Reporting Visitor Responses

The data collected in the Xi'an Holiday survey permits some integration of psychographic and demographic information as an initial organizer to describe the respondents. Using the international versus domestic tourist dichotomy as the basis for exploring relationships with other descriptive variables, some clear differences emerged. Domestic tourists stayed longer, traveled more with family members, and stayed much more often in the homes of family or friends. Additionally, international visitors were motivated by items concerned with learning about and experiencing the novelty and excitement of Chinese culture. They were less motivated by strengthening relationships and developing oneself. These differences are summarized in Table 1. It is notable in Table 1, however, that the Chinese respondents do have a high score for enjoying and improving their knowledge of Chinese culture. International and domestic tourists also differed in terms of some of the main themes about visitor perspectives described in the framework presented in Figure 1 – notably, in terms of expenditure and shopping items purchased, and also with the satisfaction levels with service and infrastructure elements in Xi'an. These differences are presented in Table 2.

It can be readily established that there is some immediate value in having comparative information in the accompanying tables, even though they provide only a very limited version of the full benchmarking approach advocated in Figure 1 and the associated discussion. Following Fuchs (2002), the challenge for interpreting this kind of data is to recognize that "what counts is not so much a measure of the absolute but the relative satisfaction level" (p. 154). For example, there are substantially different expenditure patterns on jade and pottery products (purchased much more by domestic tourists) and on silk products and information items (purchased much more by international tourists). The domestic Chinese visitors are only relatively pleased with the local food (3.44 on a 5-point scale), but the international tourists seem more satisfied with this attribute (3.80), but substantially less satisfied with toilets (2.52 compared to 3.23 for domestic visitors). The core argument here is that the construction of a cumulative data base for this city and for more Chinese cities would substantially increase the interpretation that can be placed on these numbers. Hanan and Karp (1989) and Noe (1999), reporting on satisfaction studies in North American parks, report that a wide array of scores help managers to set standards for excellent service provision. In particular, by having an array of data to assess the meaning of respondents' satisfaction scores, Hanan and Karp suggest that visitors are only very satisfied if more than 85% of them are providing scores on the top two levels of the rating scale being employed. Interpolating from this admittedly different scenario would imply that a mean satisfaction score beneath 3.5 on these Xi'an city ratings is not very high, and a preferred benchmark would be 4.0 or more (see also Pearce, 2006).

The presentation of sketch map information can be achieved with a combination of tabulated data and the construction of a composite sketch map. The 10 respondents who provided the sketch maps for this illustrative component of the research traveled independently to Xi'an and were recalling their images and experiences for one- to three-day visits up to two years after the visit. This delay undoubtedly reduced the detail in the mapping products. The main features recalled are presented in Table 3 and illustrated in Figure 2.

The summary maps and responses provide a broad indication of the commonly-reported city highlights, albeit in a very small sample to illustrate the kind of data that can be collected. The uncertainty and diversity in the maps is not well represented in the aggregate map. The accuracy in the directions and relative positions of the attractions is somewhat misleading in Figure 1, as at least three out of the 10 maps were much more of a jumble of places centered around the defining features of the Bell Tower, the visitors' hotels, and the Terracotta warriors site. The

Table 1. Select Relationships Among Respondents' Origins and Demographic Characteristics for Visitors to Xi'an

Respondents' Origin and Length of Trip		
	Frequency, %	
	International (*n*=349)	Domestic (*n*=423)
One night	57	42
	16.3%	9.9%
Two nights	141	76
	40.4%	18.0%
Three nights	75	112
	21.5%	26.5%
Four nights	44	80
	12.6%	18.9%
Five nights or longer	32	113
	9.2%	26.7%

$\chi^2(4)=78.39$, $p=.000$.

Respondents' Origin and Travel Companions		
	Frequency, %	
	International (*n*=353)	Domestic (*n*=430)
Alone	37	47
	10.5%	10.9%
Package tour	176	46
	49.9%	10.7%
Family	56	224
	15.9%	52.1%
Friends	84	113
	23.8%	26.3%

$\chi^2(3)=176.52$, $p=.000$.

Respondents' Origin and Type of Accommodation		
	Frequency, %	
	International (*n*=353)	Domestic (*n*=431)
Hotel	235	175
	66.6%	40.6%
Motel	7	105
	2.0%	24.4%
Youth hostel	104	16
	29.5%	3.7%
Home of relative	5	17
	1.4%	3.9%
Home of friend	2	118
	0.6%	27.4%

$\chi^2(4)=272.68$, $p=.000$.

Table 1. Continued

Respondents' Origin and Travel Motivation Items				
	Mean[1]			
	International (n=320)	Domestic (n=388)	T value	Prob. Value
To do and experience things that I can't do in home country	4.38	2.82	16.43	0.00*
To spend time with family/close friend(s)	2.14	3.92	16.93	0.00*
To enjoy/improve knowledge of Chinese culture	4.28	4.11	2.15	0.32
To challenge myself	3.04	2.47	5.22	0.00*
To develop my skills and abilities	2.71	2.16	5.27	0.00*
To meet people with similar values	2.74	2.35	3.76	0.01
To understand myself more	2.58	2.78	−1.79	0.74
To have a break from work and my daily routine	3.72	3.23	4.63	0.00*
To seek excitement/ adventure	3.94	2.26	17.38	0.00*
To experience a well-publicized new travel destination	3.67	2.89	7.00	0.00*

*Significant at the 0.01 level. [1]Five-point scale: (1=not important, 5=very important).

textual comments and remarks written on the maps are not reported in Table 3, but two of the common ones– specifically, wide streets and much traffic– were included in the aggregate map. A diversity of other remarks identifies further issues defining the mapping images and included such comments as modern stores, street hawkers around here, and cheap eating areas. The power of this approach, for example, if the same number of visitors provided maps as they did survey forms, could be considerable with the greater detail allowing more information to be extracted on the commonalities and the problems reported.

The reporting of the blog information or, more accurately, a very small randomized sample of 10 blogs from all of those available is provided in Table 4. The table records the Web site and follows McKee (2003) by using the notion of a controlling idea to summarize the parts of the recorded information. The controlling ideas were checked by two academic colleagues who read the blogs and were asked to agree with, disagree with, or modify the way the idea was expressed. There was minimal disagreement using this approach, and only one idea was slightly reworded. The approach adopted in Table 4 is somewhat wasteful of data in that each

Table 2. The Relationships Among Respondents' Origins, Expenditure, Type of Expenditure, and Select Attributes of Xi'an's Tourism Infrastructure

Respondents' Origin and Expenditure on the Previous Day		
	Frequency, %	
	International ($n=287$)	Domestic ($n=343$)
999 yuan or less	215	189
	74.9%	55.1%
1000–2500 yuan	43	96
	15.0%	28.0%
2501–5000 yuan	13	39
	4.5%	11.4%
5000–7500 yuan	3	7
	1.0%	2.0%
7501 yuan or more	13	12
	4.5%	3.5%

$\chi^2(4)=31.79$, $p=.000$.

Respondents' Origin and Type of Expenditure		
	Frequency, %	
	International ($n=353$)	Domestic ($n=430$)
Local food	142	270
$\chi^2(1)=33.291$, $p=.000$	44.4%	66.2%
Pottery crafts	66	98
$\chi^2(1)=1.181$, $p=.277$	20.6%	24.0%
Jade products	57	107
$\chi^2(1)=7.210$, $p=.007$	17.8%	26.2%
Silk products	57	24
$\chi^2(1)=25.264$, $p=.000$	17.8%	5.9%
Clothes	66	88
$\chi^2(1)=112$, $p=.738$	20.6%	21.6%
Calligraphy/paintings	53	47
$\chi^2(1)=3.737$, $p=.053$	16.6%	11.5%
Others (postcards, CDs, books)	96	70
$\chi^2(1)=16.89$, $p=.000$<tb>	30.0%	17.7%

Table 2. Continued

Respondents' Origin and Travel Satisfaction				
	Mean[1]			
	International (n=339)	Domestic (n=378)	T value	Prob. Value
Facilities at the tourist attractions	3.75	3.88	−1.82	0.06
Quality of food	3.80	3.44	4.81	0.00*
Restaurant hygiene	3.57	3.35	2.75	0.00*
Facilities of accommodation	3.84	3.45	5.05	0.00*
Shopping experience and bargaining	3.31	2.86	5.09	0.00*
Public transportation	3.30	3.23	0.57	0.56
General service of your tour guide	4.16	3.25	9.83	0.00*
Information service (signs on site, pamphlets, etc.)	3.37	3.45	−0.86	0.38
Toilets in general	2.52	3.23	−7.41	0.00*

*Significant at the 0.01 level. [1]Five-point scale: (1=not satisfied, 5=very satisfied).

individual blog contains several stories or incidents, but only one from each traveler has been extracted for this illustrative exercise. There is also an important limitation noted by previous researchers in using the blog material. A rudimentary examination of the sites identified by the Google procedure revealed that a very large number of the sites are written by younger travelers on extended holidays. There is, therefore, an obvious omission in the available data from older travelers, those on very short visits, and/or those who are less comfortable or adept at using the Web technology. Importantly, the Web sites in Mandarin or languages other than English were also not assessed in the process described. As is the case with the mapping information, the power of the technique briefly illustrated here grows with the number of cases analyzed, and, although this may still represent a defined market segment, the ready availability of the material and the summaries achieved by looking at the controlling ideas offer the promise of insights into the city responses of many visitors.

The Value of the Framework

The efforts to illustrate the proposed framework by considering ongoing studies in one Chinese city highlight several points of achievement and some points for further development. The multiple approaches used to assess visitors' response provide some valuable points of triangulation. Guided by the elements of Figure 1, the illustrative research on the city of Xi'an can be seen as producing data that can be summarized by some consistent themes. The summary of the visitors' responses to Xi'an can be articulated as follows. Despite an overwhelming positive appraisal of the grand sights of Xi'an and their ready identification in the travelers' sketch maps and stories, there is an undercurrent of common criticism of the city. These less than positive appraisals appear most clearly in the low or modest mean scores for some

Table 3. Principal Features Used by Visitors to Xi'an to Construct Their Sketch Maps

Paths*	Landmarks	Nodes	Edges	Districts
Unnamed grid System of roads	Bell Tower Drum Tower	South Gate	City Walls River	Muslim area
Route to airport	Big Goose Pagoda Little Goose Pagoda			Market areas Hotel/restaurant district
	Shaanxi History Museum			
Route to Terracotta Warriors Site	Hua Shan Mountain Mosque			

*Items recorded by 5 or more of the 10 respondents.

items in the visitor survey. There are concerns, for example, with some basic visitor needs, including the adequacy of toilets as well as the management of crowding and minor street crime. These points are also raised in the blogs and identified in a few of the maps, thus providing the triangulation to indicate items of significance for managerial and operator attention. Such points of negativity may exist in almost any

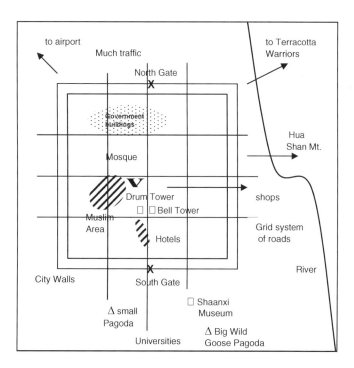

Figure 2. Summary Sketch Map of Visitor Recall (International Visitors) with 1- to 3-Day Visits to Xi'an

Table 4. Examples of Controlling Ideas in Web Site Logs (Blogs) Featuring Xi'an*

http://blogs.warwick.ac.uk/odonnelle/entry/xian_stuff
  Xi'an stuff written September 17, 2006.
  Story/paragraph title: Almost got robbed.
  Controlling idea: Small children may be thieves rather than innocent.
http://thelifeoreilly.blogspot.com/2006/01/xian-china-warrior-country.html
  Xi'an Xi'an, China Warrior Country, January 20, 2006.
  Story/paragraph title: Guidebook more than a couple of years old.
  Controlling idea: Massive city redevelopment makes guidebooks obsolete.
http://realtravel.com/xian-reviews-a1479253.html
  Review of Terracotta Warriors, June 6, 2006.
  Story/paragraph title: People warned me–I wasn't disappointed.
  Controlling idea: Seeing the Warriors site will affect tourists differently.
http://blog.lib.umn.edu/hiscockj/chinatrip
  Xi'an, May 2006.
  Story/paragraph title: A dancing square.
  Controlling idea: Capturing the opportunity to join local dancing–fun and
    energetic.
http://eyeseast.blogspot.com/search/label/XI%27an
  A walking tour of Xi'an, September 5, 2006.
  Story/paragraph title: I think I walked every street.
  Controlling idea: Gleaming new wealth lives next door to staggering old poverty.
http://www.shanghaidiaries.com/archives/2004/08/17/chewing_the_fat_in_xian/index.php
  Chewing the fat in Xi'an, August 2004.
  Story/paragraph title: You can never meditate for long.
  Controlling idea: Congestion and crowding can make touring tedious work.
http://myradaly.blogspot.com/2006/04/xian.html
  April 20, 2006.
  Story/paragraph title: Checking out the local parks.
  Controlling idea: Participating in local activities for atmosphere and entertainment.
http://realtravel.com/xian_journals_jl749872.html
  "The foreigner is coming," July 1, 2006.
  Story/paragraph title: A seedy walk to the Muslim quarter.
  Controlling idea: Delicious food in the midst of very commercial tourism.
http://jolou.blogspot.com/2004_07_01_joulou_archive.html
  Xi'an, July 30, 2004.
  Story/paragraph title: Tandem biking along the city wall.
  Controlling idea: Participating in a new activity gives new feelings and rewarding
    outcomes.
http://aperifle.cinosplice.com/archives/2004/07/28/travel_journal_%E8%A5%BF%E5%
    AE%89_xian/
  Travel journal Xi'an, July 28, 2004.
  Story/paragraph title: Like most things in China.
  Controlling idea: Close examination reveals problems beneath the city's grand scale.

*All accessed December 6, 2006.

contemporary city, but the first steps to managing such problems are to confirm their localized existence and further assess the importance placed on these issues by tourists. The full benefits of the blogs and the sketch maps need to be developed with much larger samples of visitors, and then the contributions of these approaches to visitor assessment could be even more powerful. In terms of the visitor survey material, the example of Xi'an can also be seen as demonstrating the value of moving toward even more benchmarking approaches. If comparative information from other locations were available, the substantive meaning of the Xi'an ratings would be enhanced. The comparative study of visitors' responses to Chinese cities represents an important opportunity that can be facilitated by the kind of framework being proposed. Additionally, when issues are rated by visitors, it is apparent that the importance or significance of the issue should also be assessed. The travelers' stories and even some of the comments on the sketch maps address in a spontaneous way some dimensions of importance, but a systematic inclusion of importance and performance for the lists of satisfaction items is an area for development.

There are other ways to access and develop some of the central visitor motifs identified in the first column of the framework. The blogs are one pathway to understanding visitor stories, but detailed interviews may also be used, and agreement with or recognition of commonalities in provided stories may be a further tactic. The sketch map methodology can be enhanced by providing a grid or framework and key landmarks, but again a more recognition-based approach rather than recall-based approach could be an innovative way to explore city imagery. In this kind of work, visitors can be shown key landmarks, districts, and streets and, if they recognize them, be asked to locate them on a base map or give directions to get to them. This kind of work can explore the accessibility of the city and provide its own suite of managerial directions and cues.

While innovations and development of the methods suggested may assist future studies, it can be argued that the basic framework outlined in this research holds the promise of providing a wide and useful perspective on how visitors perceive Chinese cities. Not all studies will be able to use all techniques at once, but recognition of the diversity of ways in which tourists' responses can be collected and presented is hopefully a useful contribution to tourism management in the world's most populous country.

References

Ap, J. (2003). An assessment of theme park development in China. In A. A. Lew, L. Yu, J. Ap, & G. Zhang (Eds.), *Tourism in China* (pp. 195–216). New York: Haworth Hospitality Press.

Aramberri, J. (2001). The host should get lost. Paradigms in the tourism theory. *Annals of Tourism Research, 28*(3), 738–761.

Ateljevic, I., & Doorne, S. (2004). Theoretical encounters: A review of the backpacker literature. In G. Richards & J. Wilson (Eds.), *The global nomad: Backpacker travel in theory and practice* (pp. 60–76). Clevedon, Avon, UK: Channel View.

Baerenholdt, J., Haldrup, M., Larsen, J., & Urry, J. (2004). *Performing tourist places*. Aldershot, Hants, UK: Ashgate.

Baloglu, S. (1997). The relationship between destination images and sociodemographic and trip characteristics of international travelers. *Journal of Vacation Marketing, 3*(3), 221–233.

Berry, J. (1969). The stereotypes of Australian states. *Australian Journal of Psychology, 21*, 227–233.

Bitgood, S. (1987). When is a zoo like a city? *Visitor Behavior, 1*(4), 5.

Bitner, M. J. (1992). Servicescapes: The impact of physical surroundings on customers and employees. *Journal of Marketing, 56*(2), 57–71.

Bramwell, B., & Lane, B. (2005). From niche to general relevance? Sustainable tourism, research, and the role of tourism journals. *The Journal of Tourism Studies, 16*(2), 52–62.

Coleman, S., & Crang, M. (Eds.). (2002) *Tourism: Between place and performance*. Oxford: Beryhahn Books.

Crang, P. (1997). Performing the tourist product. In C. Rojek & J. Urry (Eds.), *Touring cultures: Transformations of travel and theory* (pp. 137–154). London: Routledge.

Crouch, D. (2005). Flirting with space: Tourism geographies as sensuous/expressive practice. In C. Cartier & A. A. Lew (Eds.), *Seductions of place: Geographical perspectives on globalization and touristed landscapes* (pp. 23–35). London: Routledge.

Dann, G. (1999). Theoretical issues for tourism's future development: Identifying the agenda. In D. Pearce & R. Butler (Eds.), *Contemporary issues in tourism development* (pp. 13–30). London: Routledge.

De Crop, A. (2004). Trustworthiness in qualitative tourism research. In J. Phillimore & L. Goodson (Eds.), *Qualitative research in tourism: Ontologies, epistemologies and methodologies* (pp. 156–169). London: Routledge.

Downs, R., & Stea, D. (1977). *Maps in minds*. New York: Harper & Row.

Dwyer, L., Forsyth, P., & Spur, R. (2004). Evaluating tourism's economic effects: New and old approaches. *Tourism Management, 26*(2), 307–317.

Echtner, C. M., & Ritchie, J. R. B. (1991). The meaning and measurement of destination image. *Journal of Tourism Studies, 2*(2), 2–12.

Echtner, C. M., & Ritchie, J. R. B. (1993). The measurement of destination image: An empirical assessment. *Journal of Travel Research, 31*(4), 3–13.

Elkington, J. (1997). *Cannibals with forks: The triple bottom line of 21st century business*. Oxford: Capstone.

Falco-Mammone, F. (2006). *Beach images: Meaning, measurement, and management*. Unpublished doctoral dissertation, James Cook University, Townsville, Queensland, Australia.

Francescato, D., & Mebane, W. (1973). How citizens view two great cities: Milan and Rome. In R. M. Downs & D. Stea (Eds.), *Image and environment: Cognitive mapping and spatial behaviour* (pp. 131–147). London: Edward Arnold.

Franklin, A. (2003). *Tourism: An introduction*. London: Sage.

Fuchs, M. (2002). Benchmarking indicator systems and their potential for tracking guest satisfaction. *Tourism, 50*(2), 141–155.

Ghimire, K. B. (2001). *The native tourist: Mass tourism with developing countries*. London: Earthscan.

Ghimire, K. B., & Li, Z. (2001). The economic role of national tourism in China. In K. B. Ghimire (Ed.), *The native tourist: Mass tourism within developing countries* (pp. 86–108). London: Earthscan.

Gomm, R. (2004). *Social research methodology: A critical introduction*. Basingstoke, Hampshire, UK: Palgrove MacMillan.

Gunn, C. (1994). A perspective on the purpose and nature of tourism research methods. In J. R. B. Ritchie & C. R. Goeldner (Eds.), *Travel, tourism, and hospitality research* (2nd ed., pp. 3–11). New York: John Wiley & Sons.

Gunn, C. A., & Var, T. (2002). *Tourism Planning: Basics, concepts, cases*. (4th ed.). New York: Taylor and Francis.

Hanan, M., & Karp, P. (1989). *Customer satisfaction*. New York: Amacom.

Hazelrigg, L. E., & Hardy, M. A. (2000). Scaling the semantics of satisfaction. *Social Indicators Research, 49*(2), 147–180.

Heider, F. (1958). *The psychology of interpersonal relations*. New York: Wiley.

Holt, D. B. (2003). What becomes an icon most? *Harvard Business Review, 81*(3), 43–49.

Hu, B., & Morrison, A. (2002). Tripography: Can destination use patterns enhance understanding of the VFR market? *Journal of Vacation Marketing, 8*(3), 201–220.

Hunt, J. D. (1975). Image as a factor in tourism development. *Journal of Travel Research, 13* (3), 1–7.

Kaplan, S., & Kaplan, R. (1982). *Cognition and environment: Functioning in an uncertain world*. New York: Praeger.

Kozac, M. (2001). A critical review of approaches to measure satisfaction with tourist destinations. In J. A. Mazanec, G. Crouch, J. R. B. Ritchie, & A. Woodside (Eds.), *Consumer psychology of tourism hospitality and leisure* (Vol. 2, pp. 303–320). Wallingford, Oxon, UK: CABI.

Kozinets, R. V. (2002). The field behind the screen: Using netnography for marketing research in online communities. *Journal of Marketing Research, 39*(1), 61–72.

Lew, A. A., & Wong, A. (2005). Existential tourism and the homeland: The overseas Chinese experience. In C. L. Cartier & A. A. Lew (Eds.), *Seductions of place: Geographical perspectives on globalization and touristed landscapes* (pp. 23–35). Abingdon, Oxon, UK: Routledge.

Lew, A. A., Yu, L., Ap, J., & Zhang, G. (Eds.). (2003). *Tourism in China*. New York: Haworth Hospitality Press.

Lynch, K. (1960). *The image of the city*. Boston: MIT Press.

MacCannell, D. (1976). *The tourist: A new theory of the leisure class*. New York: Schocken Books.

MacCannell, D. (1989). *The tourist: A new theory of the leisure class*. (2nd ed.). New York: Random House.

Machlis, G. E. (1996). *Usable knowledge: A plan for furthering social science and the national parks*. Washington, DC: United States Department of the Interior, National Park Service.

March, R., & Woodside, A. (2005). *Tourism behaviour: Travellers' decisions and actions*. Wallingford, Oxon, UK: CABI International.

McKee, R. (2003). Storytelling that moves people. *Harvard Business Review, 81*(6), 51–55.

Melton, A. W. (1972). Visitor behavior in museums: Some early research in environmental design. *Human Factors, 14*(5), 393–403.

Miles, R. S., Alt, M. B., Gosling, D. C., Lewis, B. N., & Tout, A. F. (1982). *The design of educational exhibits*. London: George, Allen, & Unwin.

Moscardo, G. (1999). *Making visitors mindful: Principles for creating quality sustainable visitor experiences through effective communication*. Champaign, IL: Sagamore.

Noe, F. P. (1999). *Tourism service satisfaction*. Champaign, IL: Sagamore.

Oliver, T. (2001). The consumption of tour routes in cultural landscapes. In J. A. Mazanec, G. I. Crouch, J. R. B. Ritchie & A. G. Woodside (Eds.), *Consumer psychology of tourism, hospitality, and leisure* (Vol. 2, pp. 273–284). Wallingford, Oxon, UK: CABI.

Oppenheim, A. N. (1966). *Questionnaire design and attitude measurement*. London: Heinemann.

Orbash, A., & Shaw, S. (2004). Transport and visitors in historic cities. In L. Lumsdon & S. J. Page (Eds.), *Tourism and transport: Issues and agenda for the new millennium* (pp. 93–104). Amsterdam: Elsevier.

Pearce, P. L. (1977). Mental souvenirs: A study of tourists and their city maps. *Australian Journal of Psychology, 29*(3), 203–210.

Pearce, P. L. (1981). Route maps: A study of travelers' perception of a section of countryside. *Journal of Environmental Psychology, 1*, 141–155.

Pearce, P. L. (1991). Travel stories: An analysis of self-disclosure in terms of story structure, valence, and audience characteristics. *Australian Psychologist, 26*(3), 172–174.

Pearce, P. L. (2005a). Professing tourism: Tourism academics as educators, researchers, and change leaders. *Journal of Tourism Studies, 16*(2), 21–33.

Pearce, P. L. (2005b). *Tourist behaviour: Themes and conceptual schemes*. Clevedon, Avon, UK: Channel View.

Pearce, P. L. (2006). The value of a benchmarking approach for assessing service quality satisfaction in environmental tourism. In B. Prideaux, G. Moscardo & E. Laws (Eds.), *Managing tourism and hospitality services* (pp. 282–299). London: CABI.

Pearce, P. L., & Black, N. (1984). Dimensions of national park maps: A psychological evaluation. *Cartography, 13*(3), 189–203.

Pearce, P. L., & Black, N. (1996). *The simulation of tourist environments: Methodological perspectives for enhancing tourism research*. Paper presented at the Australian Tourism Research Conference, Coffs Harbour, NSW.

Pearce, P. L., & Fagence, M. (1996). The legacy of Kevin Lynch: Research implications. *Annals of Tourism Research, 23*(3), 576–598.

Pearce, P. L., Innes, J. M., O'Driscoll, P., & Morse, S. J. (1981). Stereotyped images of Australian cities. *Australian Journal of Psychology, 33*(1), 29–39.

Pearce, P. L., & Moscardo, G. M. (2006). Domestic and visiting friends and relatives tourism. In D. Buhalis & C. Costa (Eds.), *Tourism business frontiers: Consumers, products, and industry* (pp. 48–55). Oxford: Elsevier.

Pearce, P. L., & Vogt, H. (2005). Warriors, emperors and tourists: Environmental setting factors and visitor comfort at two Chinese tourist attractions. *China Tourism Research, 1* (2/3), 161–177.

Phillimore, J., & Goodson, L. (Eds.). (2004). *Qualitative research in tourism*. London: Routledge.

Pritchard, M. P., & Havitz, M. E. (2006). Destination appraisal: An analysis of critical incidents. *Annals of Tourism Research, 33*(1), 25–46.

Rao, N., & Suresh, K. T. (2001). Domestic tourism in India. In K. Ghimire (Ed.), *The native tourist: Mass tourism within developing countries* (pp. 198–228). London: Earthscan.

Ritchie, J. R. B., Crouch, G. I., & Hudson, S. (2001). Developing operational measures for the components of a destination competitiveness/sustainability model: Consumer versus managerial perspectives. In: J. A. Mazanec, G. I. Crouch, J. R. B. Ritchie & A. G. Woodside (Eds.), *Consumer psychology of tourism, hospitality, and leisure* (Vol. 2, pp. 1–18). Wallingford, Oxon, UK: CABI.

Ryan, C. (1995). *Researching tourist satisfaction: Issues, concepts, problems*. London: Routledge.

Ryan, C. (Ed.). (2002). *The tourist experience*. London: Continuum.

Sax, J. L. (1980). *Mountains without handrails: Reflections on the nation parks*. Ann Arbor: The University of Michigan Press.

Schank, R. C. (1990). *Tell me a story: A new look at real and artificial memory*. New York: Charles Scribner's Sons.

Son, A., & Pearce, P. L. (2003). Overseas students' image of Australian cities: Applying a sketch map methodology. In J.-K. Jun (Ed.), *Second Asia Pacific forum for Graduate Students Research in Tourism* (pp. 154–169). Busan, Korea: Dong-A University.

Son, A., & Pearce, P. L. (2005). Multi-faceted image assessment: International students' views of Australia as a tourist destination. *Journal of Travel & Tourism Marketing, 18*(4), 21–35.

Stoeckl, N., Smith, A., Newsome, D., & Lee, D. (2005). Regional economic dependence on iconic wildlife tourism: Case studies of Monkey Mia and Hervey Bay. *The Journal of Tourism Studies, 16*(1), 69–81.

Suh, Y. K., & Gartner, W. C. (2004). Preferences and trip expenditures–A conjoint analysis of visitors to Seoul, Korea. *Tourism Management, 25*(1), 127–137.

Thomas, M. (1996). *Tourism and small towns*. Unpublished doctoral dissertation, James Cook University, Townsville, Queensland, Australia.

Tribe, J. S. (1997). The indiscipline of tourism. *Annals of Tourism Research, 24*(3), 638–657.

Tribe, J. (2006). The truth about tourism. *Annals of Tourism Research, 33*(2), 360–381.

Um, S., & Crompton, J. L. (1990). Attitude determinants in tourism destination choice. *Annals of Tourism Research, 17*(3), 432–448.

Veal, A. J. (2005). *Business research methods: A managerial approach.* (2nd ed.). Frenchs Forest NSW, Australia: Addison Wesley.

Walmsley, D. J., & Jenkins, J. M. (1992). Tourism cognitive mapping of unfamiliar environments. *Annals of Tourism Research, 19*(2), 268–286.

Wanhill, S. (1994). The measurement of tourist income multipliers. *Tourism Management, 15*(4), 281–283.

Weick, K. E. (1995). Sensemaking in organizations. Thousand Oaks, CA: Sage.

Woodside, A. G., & Chebat, J. C. (2001). Updating Heider's balance theory in consumer behavior. *Psychology & Marketing, 18*(5), 475–496.

Woodside, A. G., & Lysonski, S. (1989). A general model of traveler destination choice. *Journal of Travel Research, 27*(4), 8–14.

Woodside, A. G., Cruickshank, B. F., & Dehuang, N. (2007). Stories visitors tell about Italian cities as destination icons. *Tourism Management, 28*(1), 162–174.

World Tourism Organization (2006). *Global tourism statistics.* Madrid: Author.

Yau, O. H. M., & Chan, C. F. (1990). Hong Kong as a travel destination in Southeast Asia: A multidimensional approach. *Tourism Management, 11*(2), 123–132.

Young, M. (1998). The Daintree region. Unpublished doctoral dissertation, James Cook University, Townsville, Queensland, Australia.

Zube, E. H. (1980). *Environmental evaluation.* Monterey, CA: Brooks/Cole.

Index

www.routledge.com/9780415697538

Related titles from Routledge

Contemporary Perspectives on China Tourism

Edited by Honggen Xiao

Contemporary Perspectives on China Tourism is an innovative and engaging collection which presents unique approaches and critical insights into the policy, development and management practices of tourism and hospitality in modern China.

This volume consists of nine independent research reports overarching the consequences of tourism from economic, sociocultural, community, and humanistic perspectives. The book addresses generic issues such as tourism demand, mega events, leisure, tourist experience, cultural representation, community development, and quality of life through tourism, as well as strategies and techniques specific to the tourism and hospitality industries.

Seven of the nine chapters in this book were originally published in a special issue on 'Methodological Innovations in China Tourism Research' in the *Journal of China Tourism Research*.

December 2011: 246 x 174: 224pp
Hb: 978-0-415-69753-8
£80 / $125

For more information and to order a copy visit
www.routledge.com/97804156975385

Available from all good bookshops